Carsten Niebuhr

Travels Through Arabia and Other Countries in the East

Carsten Niebuhr

Travels Through Arabia and Other Countries in the East

ISBN/EAN: 9783744796224

Printed in Europe, USA, Canada, Australia, Japan

Cover: Foto ©Andreas Hilbeck / pixelio.de

More available books at **www.hansebooks.com**

TRAVELS

THROUGH

ARABIA,

AND OTHER

COUNTRIES IN THE EAST.

PERFORMED BY

M. NIEBUHR,

NOW A CAPTAIN OF ENGINEERS IN THE SERVICE OF
THE KING OF DENMARK.

TRANSLATED INTO ENGLISH
BY
ROBERT HERON.

WITH NOTES BY THE TRANSLATOR;

AND

ILLUSTRATED WITH ENGRAVINGS AND MAPS.

IN TWO VOLUMES.

VOL. II.

EDINBURGH:
PRINTED FOR R. MORISON AND SON, BOOKSELLERS, PERTH;
G. MUDIE, EDINBURGH; AND T. VERNOR,
BIRCHIN LANE, LONDON.
1792.

CONTENTS.

SECTION XVI.

Of Arabia in general.

	Page
Chap. I.—Concerning the Defcription of Arabia.	1
Chap. II.—Of the Extent and the Divifions of Arabia.	5
Chap. III.—Of the Revolutions of Arabia.	10
Chap. IV.—Of the Government of the Arabs.	16

SECTION XVII.

Of the Province of Hedjas.

Chap. I.—Of the general Appearance of this Province, and fome of the Towns in it.	23
Chap. II.—Of the Power of the Turks in Hedjas.	25
Chap. III.- Of the Sheriffe of Mecca.	28
Chap. IV.—Of the City of Mecca.	32
Chap. V.—Of the Pilgrimage of the Muffulmans.	36

Chap.

	Page
Chap. VI.—Of the City of Medina.	39
Chap. VII.—Of the Independent Schiechs, Arab and Jewifh.	41

SECTION XVIII.

Of Yemen in General.

Chap. I.—Of the Boundaries and Subdivifions of Yemen.	45
Chap. II.—Of the Principality of Aden.	48
Chap. III.—Of the Principality of Kaukeban.	49
Chap. IV.—Of the Allied Princes of Hafchid-u-Bekil.	50
Chap. V.—Of the Principality of Abu Arifch, and the Neighbouring Bedouins.	53
Chap. VI.—Of the Territories of Saham and Khaulan.	57
Chap. VII.—Of the Principalities of Nedsjeran and Cachtan.	59
Chap. VIII.—Of the Principalities of Nehhm and Khaulan.	62
Chap. IX.—Of the Country of Dsjof.	63
Chap. X.—Of the Country of Jafa.	68

SECTION XIX.

Of the Dominions of the Imam of Sana.

Chap. I.—Of the Extent and Divifions of the Imam's Dominions.	69
Chap. II.—Origin and Hiftory of the Imams.	71
Chap. III.—Of El Mahadi, the reigning Imam.	75

Chap.

	Page
Chap. IV.—Hiftory of Schiech Ab Urrah.	78
Chap. V.—Of the Conftitution and Government of the Dominions of Sana.	82
Chap. VI.—Of the Revenues of the Imam.	87
Chap. VII.—Of the Military Force of Sana.	89
Chap. VIII.—Of the Arts and Commerce of Yemen.	92
Chap. IX.—Of the Principal Towns in the Imam's Dominions.	94
Chap. X.—Of the Princes and Schiechs within the Dominions of the Imam.	98

SECTION XX.

Of the Province of Hadramaut.

Chap. I.—Of the General Character, and of the Commerce of this Province.	104
Chap. II.—Of the Principal Towns in Hadramaut.	107
Chap. III.—Of the Sovereign Princes in Hadramaut.	111

SECTION XXI.

Of the Province of Oman.

Chap. I.—Of Oman in general.	113
Chap. II.—Of the Territories of the Imam of Oman, or Mafkat.	114
Chap. III.—Of the Revolutions of Oman.	117
Chap. IV.—Of the Reigning Imam.	120
Chap. V.—Of the Principality of Seer.	123

SECTION XXII.

Of the Provinces of Lachfa and Nedsjed.

                                                  Page
Chap. I.—Of Lachfa, in particular.   -   125
Chap. II.—Of the Province of Nedsjed.   -   128
Chap. III.—Of the new Religion of a Part of Nedsjed.   - - -   130

SECTION XXIII.

Of the Independent Arabian States upon the Sea-coaſt of Perſia.

Chap. I.—Of the Arabs inhabiting around the Perſian Gulph.   - -   137
Chap. II.—Of Places ſubject to the Dominion of Perſia.   - - -   140
Chap. III.—Of the Territories of the Tribe of Houle.   - - -   143
Chap. IV.—Of the Principalities of Abu Schæhhr and Bender Rigk.   - -   145
Chap. V.—Of the Tribe of Kiab, and their Schiech Soliman.   - - -   149
Chap. VI.—Of ſome other Independent States.   151
Chap. VII.—Of the Iſle of Karek.   -   154

SECTION XXIV.

Of the Bedouins, or Wandering Arabs.

                                                  Page

Chap. I.—Peculiarities in the Manners of the Bedouins. - - - 158
Chap. II.—Of the Political Constitution of the Wandering Arabs. - - 163
Chap. III.—Of the Bedouins on the Confines of the Desart. - - - 168
Chap. IV.—Of the Bedouins of Mesopotamia. 172
Chap. V.—Of the Bedouins of Syria. - 176
Chap. VI.—Of the Bedouins of Arabia Petræa, and Palestine. - - 180

SECTION XXV.

Of the Religion and Character of the Arabs.

Chap. I.—Of the different Sects of Mahometans in Arabia. - - - 184
Chap. II.—Of the other Religions tolerated in Arabia. - - - 191
Chap. III.—Of the Character of the Arabs. 194
Chap. IV.—Of the Vengeance of the Arabs. 197
Chap. V.—Of the Arabian Nobility. - 203

SECTION XXVI.

Of the Manners and Ufages of the Arabians.

Page

Chap. I.—Of Marriage among the Arabians. 212
Chap. II.—Of the Domeſtic Life of the Arabs. 220
Chap. III.—Of the Food of the Arabians, and their Manner of Eating. - - 226
Chap. IV.—Of the Drefs and Faſhions of the Arabians. - - - 233
Chap. V.—Arabian Politenefs - - 240
Chap. VI.—Of ſome Peculiar Cuſtoms. - 248

SECTION XXVII.

Of the Language and Sciences of the Arabians.

Chap. I.—Of the Language and Writing of the Arabians. - - - 253
Chap. II.—Of the Education and Schools of the Arabians. - - - 262
Chap. III.—Of Arabian Poetry and Eloquence. 264
Chap. IV.—Of the Aſtronomy of the Arabians. 268
Chap. V.—Of the Difeaſes and Medicine of the Arabians. - - - 273
Chap. VI.—Of the Ocult Sciences of the Arabians. 280

SEC-

SECTION XXVIII.

Agriculture of the Arabians.

	Page
Chap. I.—Fertility of the Soil.	289
Chap. II.—Of the Modes of Plowing and Sowing.	294
Chap. III.—Of the Harveſt.	298
Chap. IV.—Of the Domeſtic Animals.	300

SECTION XXIX.

Natural Hiſtory of Arabia.

Chap. I.—General Reflections on the Natural Hiſtory of Arabia.	307
Chap. II.—Climate and Salt of Arabia.	315
Chap. III.—Arabian Quadrupeds.	323
Chap. IV.—Of the Birds of Arabia.	327
Chap. V.—Of Amphibious Animals and Fiſhes.	332
Chap. VI.—Inſects and Shells.	334
Chap. VII.—The Common and Rare Plants.	341
Chap. VIII.—Of Trees and Shrubs.	350
Chap. IX.—The Minerals of Arabia.	363

SECTION XXX.

Voyage from Mokha to Bombay.

Chap. I.—Departure from Mokha.	368
Chap. II.—Of the Iſle and the city of Bombay.	374

Chap.

	Page
Chap. III.—Of the Inhabitants of Bombay.	377
Chap. IV.—Of the Government and Power of the Englifh and the Coaft of Malabar.	380
Chap. V.—Of the Trade of Bombay.	387
Chap. VI.—Antiquities of the Ifle of Elephanta.	391

SECTION XXXI.

Voyage to Surat.

Chap. I.—Occafion of this Voyage, and Departure from Bombay.	400
Chap. II.—Of the City of Surat, and its Environs.	403
Chap. III.—Of the Inhabitants of Surat, and fome Peculiar Cuftoms.	407
Chap. IV.—Of the Government of Surat, and the Revolutions it has undergone.	412
Chap. V.—Trade of Surat.	417
Chap. VI.—Manners of the Hindoos.	420
Chap. VII.—Of the Religion of the Hindoos.	426
Chap. VIII.—Of the Perfees.	429
NOTES.	433

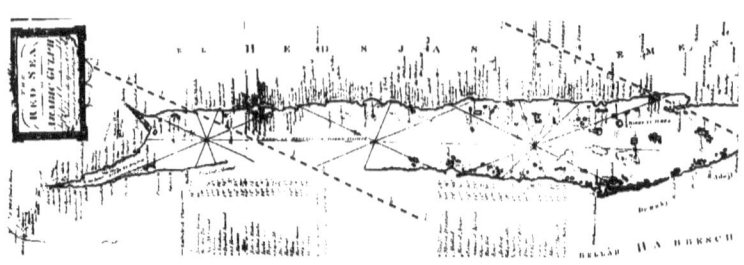

VOYAGE TO ARABIA,

AND

TRAVELS

IN THAT COUNTRY, &c.

SECTION XVI.

OF ARABIA IN GENERAL.

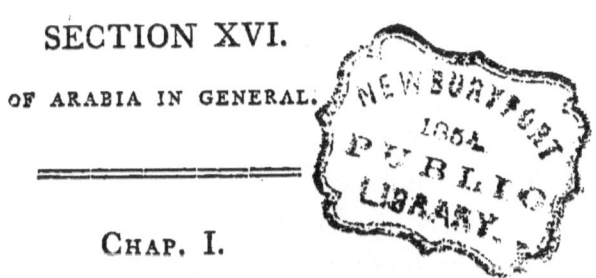

Chap. I.

Concerning the Description of Arabia.

MAN, even in society, where civilization has been carried perhaps to excess, where art extinguishes or disguises the sentiments of nature, never forgets his original destination. He is still fond even of the very shadow of that liberty, independence, and simplicity, which he has lost by refinement, although they are so congenial to his existence. He is charmed to meet with these again, even in the illusions of pastoral poetry.

We are no lefs fond of tracing thefe native features of the human mind, where they are to be difcovered in the records of remote ages, in which the natural manners of mankind appear undifguifed by affectation, and not yet altered by the progrefs of arts or policy. Even without adverting to the caufes of the pleafure which we feel, we are always pleafed to find fome faint traces even, of our natural and primary rights, and of the happinefs to which we were originally deftined.

If any people in the world afford in their hiftory an inftance of high antiquity, and of great fimplicity of manners, the Arabs furely do. Coming among them, one can hardly help fancying one's felf fuddenly carried backwards to the ages which fucceeded immediately after the flood. We are here tempted to imagine ourfelves among the old patriarchs, with whofe adventures we have been fo much amufed in our infant days. The language, which has been fpoken for time immemorial, and which fo nearly refembles that which we have been accuftomed to regard as of the moft diftant antiquity, completes the illufion which the analogy of manners began.

The country in which this nation inhabit, affords many objects of curiofity, no lefs fingular and interefting. Interfected by fandy defarts,

and

and vaft ranges of mountains, it prefents on one fide nothing but defolation in its moft frightful form, while the other is adorned with all the beauties of the moft fertile regions. Such is its pofition, that it enjoys, at once, all the advantages of hot and of temperate climates. The peculiar productions of regions, the moft diftant from one another, are produced here in equal perfection. Having never been conquered, Arabia has fcarcely known any changes, but thofe produced by the hand of nature; it bears none of the impreffions of human fury, which appear in fo many other places.

With all thefe circumftances, fo naturally calculated to engage curiofity, Arabia has been hitherto but very little known. The ancients, who made their difcoveries of countries, by conquering them, remained ignorant of the ftate and hiftory of a region, into which their arms could never penetrate. What Greek and Latin authors mention concerning Arabia, proves, by its obfcurity, their ignorance of almoft every thing refpecting the Arabs. Prejudices relative to the inconveniencies and dangers of travelling in Arabia, have hitherto kept the moderns in equal ignorance. I fhall have occafion to remark, that our beft books of Geography abound with capital errors upon this head; as, for inftance, stance, concerning the subjection of the Arabs to the Turks and Persians.

For these reasons, I have resolved to give a more minute and circumstantial description of a country, and a people, which deserve to be better known than they are at present. In the course of the former part of my travels, I have mentioned in part what I saw myself. But, as during so short a stay in Arabia, I had time to travel over only a few of the provinces of that widely extended country, I sought information concerning the rest, from different honest and intelligent Arabs. This information I was most successful in obtaining among the men of letters and the merchants; persons in public offices were more entirely engrossed with their own affairs, and generally of a more reserved character.

This mode of obtaining my information appeared to carry with it several peculiar advantages; and it will be of no less utility, that I distinguish in this manner between what I observed myself, and what I was informed of by others. The reader will thus be enabled to discern between what I mention barely upon the authority of my own observation, and what I relate upon the concurrent evidence of many of the most enlightened persons in the nation. I shall find many more favourable opportunities

of

of introducing certain particulars which I could not otherwife have inferted in the account of my travels, without interrupting too frequently the progrefs of the narrative. The reader will alfo be better entertained, when prefented with a fketch, exhibiting the features no lefs of the country, than of the people inhabiting it.

I fhould have wifhed to add a brief compend of the hiftory of this fingular nation. But this I found impoffible. In the Eaft there are no libraries, and no men of deep erudition, refources which a traveller might find with great facility in Europe. Yet there are ancient Arabic hiftorians; but the copies of their works are very rare, as I learned at Kahira and Mokha. It would be of confequence, however, to examine thofe authors, who are ftill unknown in Europe. The fearch, I am perfuaded, could hardly prove fruitlefs. Thofe works would throw new light on feveral epochs in the hiftory of ancient nations (A).

Chap. II.

Of the Extent and the Divifions of Arabia.

ARABIA, properly fo called, is that great peninfula formed by the Arabic Gulph, the Indian Ocean, and the Perfian Gulph. The ancients appear

appear to have comprehended under the name of Arabia, the whole tract lying between thofe feas, and a line drawn from the point of the Perfian to that of the Arabic Gulph. This line, however, was not the real boundary of the country, but merely fancied fuch by ignorance.

Whatever may be thought of the limits affigned to this country by the ancients, a much wider extent muft, at any rate, be allowed to prefent Arabia. In confequence of the conquefts and fettlements of the Arabs in Syria and Paleftine, the defarts of thefe countries are now to be regarded as part of Arabia, which may thus be confidered as being bounded on one fide by the river Euphrates, and on the other by the ifthmus of Suez.

Yet, we are not to confider all thofe countries in which this people have ever made conquefts, or eftablifhed colonies, as forming a part of Arabia. Of all nations, the Arabs have fpread fartheft over the world, and in all their wanderings, they have, better than any other nation, preferved their language, manners, and peculiar cuftoms. From eaft to weft, from the banks of the Senegal to the Indus, are colonies of Arabs to be met with; and between north and fouth, they are fcattered from Euphrates to the ifland of Madagafcar. The Tartar hordes have not occupied fo wide an extent of the globe.

The

The Senegal in Africa is known to feparate the negroes from thofe people who are only diſtinguiſhed by a dark complexion. On its bank are fome tribes of wandering Arabs, who live in tents. The mountainous parts of Morocco, and the republics of Barbary, contain many other tribes of the fame nation, who, it ſhould feem, ſpread through Africa in the progreſs of the conqueſts of the Caliphs. Thofe tribes are all governed by chiefs of their own; they fpeak Arabic, and in their manners refemble the reſt of the Arabian nation. They are to be regarded rather as allies than ſubjects of the governments of the different countries in which they have eſtabliſhed themſelves.

On the eaſtern coaſt of Africa, the Arabs have ſpread themſelves as far as to Mofambique. At leaſt, the fovereigns of feveral kingdoms upon that coaſt were anciently Arabs. The fame nation made themfelves likewife maſters of the iſles of *Comorra*, and of a part of the iſle of *Madagaſcar*, in which Arab colonies ſtill remain.

As I could learn nothing very particular concerning the Arab tribes, difperfed through Africa, I ſhall not pretend to fpeak of them (B); nor do I need to fay any thing more of the Egyptian Arabs, after what I have already mentioned concerning them, in the account of my travels in that country.

I

I shall likewise pass on, without noticing the pretended Arabian colonies in Habbesch, or examining the opinion, which represents the Abyssinians as originally sprung from the inhabitants of Arabia. This notion, which has been advanced by some learned men, depends on probabilities so slender, and so uncertain, that, to enter into a particular discussion of them, would be taking more pains about them, than they are worth (c).

But I cannot pass, in equal silence, over the more considerable colonies, which, although they are also settled without the limits of Arabia, are, however, nearer to it. I mean the Arabs upon the southern coast of Persia, who are commonly in alliance with, and sometimes subject to the neighbouring Schiechs. A variety of circumstances concur to indicate, that these tribes were settled along the Persian Gulph, before the conquests of the Caliphs, and have ever preserved their independence. It is ridiculous in our Geographers, to represent a part of Arabia, as subject to the Kings of Persia; when, so far from this, the Persian monarchs have never been masters of the sea-coast of their own dominions, but have patiently suffered it to remain in the possession of the Arabians.

In order to proceed upon the most natural plan, in the geographical delineation of this country,

country, I shall follow that division of Arabia which is in use among the inhabitants. They divide their country into six great provinces; HEDJAS, lying along the Arabic Gulph, between Mount Sinai and Yemen, and extending inland so far back as to the confines of Nedsjed; YEMEN, a province stretching from the border of Hedjas, along the Arabic Gulph and the Indian Ocean, to Hadramaut, and bounded on the north by Nedsjed; HADRAMAUT, on the Indian Ocean, conterminous with Yemen on one side, and with *Oman* on the other, bounded northwards by *Nedsjed;* OMAN, lying also on the shore of the Indian Ocean, and encompassed by the provinces of *Hadramaut, Lachsa,* and *Nedsjed;* LACHSA, or HADSJAR, extending along the Persian Gulph, and having *Nedsjed* for its interior boundary; NEDSJED, comprehending all the interior country, and bounded by the other five provinces; its northern limits are the territories occupied by the Arabs in the desert of Syria. These territories may indeed be reckoned a seventh province; and to them may also be added the description of the Arabian establishments on the southern coast of Persia.

The two provinces of Yemen and Hadramaut, were formerly known by the name of *Arabia the Happy*. But, as no such name is used among

mong the Arabs, I have not thought of attending to this arbitrary divifion of the country.

Chap. III.

Of the Revolutions of Arabia.

ALL that is known concerning the earlieft period of the hiftory of this country, is, that it was governed in thofe days by potent monarchs, called *Tobba*. This is thought to have been a title common to all thofe Princes, as the name of *Pharaoh* was to the 'ancient Sovereigns of Egypt.

There exifts, however, a pretty diftinct tradition among the learned Arabs, with refpect to thofe ancient Kings, which deferves to be taken notice of. They pretend to know, from ancient monuments, that *Tobba* was the family name of thofe Sovereigns, that they came from the neighbourhood of Samarcand, were worfhippers of fire, and conquered and civilized Arabia. This tradition accords with the plaufible hypothefis of an ingenious writer, who derives the knowledge and civilization of the people of the fouth, from a nation who once flourifhed in that part of Tartary in which Samarcand is fituate (D).

One

One thing I had occafion to obferve myfelf, wh ch feems to me to ma..e in favour of the fame hypothefis. A Dutch renegado, who had travelled feveral times over Arabia, fhowed me, at Mokha, a copy of an infcription, in ftrange and unknown characters, which he had found in a province remote from the fea coaft. I was then in ill health and ne lected to copy it. But the uncommon form of the characters, which confifted entirely of ftraight lines, made fuch an impreffion upon my memory, that, on my return, I diftinguifhed he infcriptions at Perfepolis to be in he ame alphabe (r). A tradition prevails through Perfia, that the conqueror who founded Perfepolis, was originally from the vicinity of Samarcand ; fo that both the Arabians and the Perfians would appear to have had Sovereigns from the fame nation, who fpoke the fame language, or at leaft employed the fame characters in writing.

Whatever may have been the origin of thofe conquerors, many circumftances concur to prove that, in remote times, the Arabians acted an important part on the theatre of human affairs ; although the memory of the revolutions which took place among them has not been handed down to pofterity. There can be no doubt of their having conquered Egypt at a time previous to the commencement of Grecian hiftory.

What

What Greek hiſtorians ſay of the ſhepherd-kings of Egypt, can be referred to none but the Arabs. The famous republic of robbers muſt undoubtedly have been a tribe of this nation, who, after the expulſion of their countrymen, maintained themſelves for ſeveral ages in a diſtrict in lower Egypt.

It is certain that moſt of the nations ſo frequently mentioned in the hiſtory of the Jews, muſt have been Arab tribes, who went often to war with thoſe turbulent neighbours, and ſometimes ſubdued them. It may even be conjectured, that the Jews themſelves were originally Arabs, deſcended from ſome branch of theſe far ſpread tribes (F).

Thoſe events, in the fate of this nation, which took place in the time of the Perſians, Greeks, Romans, and Parthians, are all unknown to us; except ſome faint and unſucceſsful attempts which theſe conquerors made to reduce the Arabians under ſubjection. They ſucceeded only againſt a few tribes, ſettled in the cities on the Arabic Gulph, or in the vicinity of Syria, and even here their power was extremely tranſient.

Arabia ſeems to have been a rich and powerful country in the time of the ancient Egyptians. The averſion of theſe laſt for the ſea, left to the Arabs the whole commerce with India, by the

Arabic

Arabic Gulph. That trade, when once brought within this channel, continued to flow through it, under the Ptolemies, the Romans, the Greek Emperors, and the Caliphs of Egypt. But the difcovery of a new line of communication with India, deprived Arabia of the advantages of this traffic, and produced the rapid decline of many flourifhing cities (g).

It muft have been during the more fplendid ages of the exiftence of this nation, that the *Hamjare* Kings reigned over a great part of Arabia. The hiftory of thofe Princes is fo involved in obfcurity, that we are ignorant even of their origin, and know not to what nation they properly belonged. But, they were probably indigenous.

Neither do we know in what period to place the Abyffinian invafion, of which fome authors fpeak. That people muft have attacked the Arabs, of purpofe to convert them to Chriftianity. It is even pretended that, after fubduing a part of Arabia, they accomplifhed the purpofe of their enterprife, and a great part of the Arabs became Chriftians. But the circumftances of this event are fo vague, and have fo fabulous an air, that we will be in the right to doubt if it ever took place; or at leaft, if it was produced by the caufes to which it has been afcribed (h).

A

A revolution, of the reality of which we are more certain, and which involved in it more important confequences, was that which Mahomet effected in the religion, and the political ftate of his country. This fortunate ufurper, with the arms of his countrymen, fpread his conquefts over diftant regions. His fucceffors, for a while, profecuted the career of conqueft with the fame fuccefs. But neither he, nor the Caliphs, could ever entirely fubdue their own nation. Many chiefs in the interior parts of the country, ftill maintained their independence, without refpecting the Caliph in any other light than as the head of their religion. The authority of the Caliphs was merely fpiritual, except in their dominions over a part of the coaft, where they were acknowledged as Sovereigns (I).

After the ruin of the power of the Caliphate by the Turks, Arabia fhook off the yoke to which it had been in part fubjected, and came to be governed, as formerly, by a number of chiefs, more or lefs powerful, defcended from different indigenous families.

No neighbouring power ever attempted to fubdue this country, till the Portuguefe penetrated to India, and made their appearance in the Red Sea. Then, in the beginning of the fixteenth century, Sultan EL GURY, defirous to rid

rid himself of those new comers, whom he viewed as dangerous, fitted out a fleet to expel the Portuguese. That fleet, availing themselves of the opportunity, seized almost all the sea-port towns of Arabia. But, when the dynasty of the Mammalukes was terminated by the Turks, these cities fell again into the hands of their natural Sovereigns.

The Turks continued the war with the Portuguese, in order to secure Egypt, their new conquest. Soliman Pacha, at the head of a powerful fleet, after the example of the last Sultan of the Mammalukes, seized all the towns upon the Arabic Gulph. His successors pushed their conquests still farther, and subdued great part of Yemen, penetrating backwards to the Highlands; so that Arabia became almost entirely a province of the Sultan of Constantinople, and was governed by Pachas, like the other provinces of the Ottoman empire.

In the interior parts, however, there still were independent Princes and Schiechs, who had never been subdued, but continued to harass the Turks, and to drive them towards the coasts. After various reiterated efforts, a Prince of the family now reigning at Sana, at length succeeded, about the middle of the last century, and obliged the Turkish nation to evacuate all the places upon the Arabian coast, which they
had

had occupied for more than a century. The Turks now poffefs nothing in this country, but a precarious authority in the city of Jidda: And it is therefore abfurd to reckon Arabia among the Ottoman provinces, fince it is properly to be confidered as independent of all foreign Powers.

A people who, like the Arabs, have fo long detached themfelves from the reft of the world, cannot undergo any very important revolutions, that may deferve to be commemorated in hiftory. The events which take place among them, are only petty wars and trifling conquefts, worthy of their poor chiefs, and narrow divifions of territory. I fhall not notice them, therefore, unlefs when in the defcription of any province, fome event comes into view, that is remarkable either for its fingularity, or for its influence upon the affairs of other nations.

CHAP. IV.

Of the Government of the Arabs.

THE moft natural authority is that of a father over his family, as obedience is here founded upon the opinion of benevolence in the ruler. When the mournful furvivors of the human race

race settled themselves anew, after the awful revolution by which the globe was, for a time, divested of its beauty, and depopulated; every family submitted readily to the guidance and direction of him to whom they owed their existence.

As those families multiplied, the younger branches still retained some respect for the eldest branch. Of all the progeny, it was esteemed the nearest to the parent stem. And, altho' the subdivisions became more and more numerous, they still regarded themselves as composing but one body, in remembrance of their common origin. Such an assemblage of families, all sprung from the same stock, forms what we call a tribe. It was, in this manner, easy for the representative of the eldest branch to retain somewhat of the primary paternal authority over the whole tribe to which he belonged.

Sometimes, when a family became too numerous, it divided from the rest with which it was connected, and formed a new tribe. Upon other occasions, when several tribes found themselves separately too weak to resist a common enemy, they would combine, and acknowledge one common chief. And sometimes it would happen, that a numerous tribe might force some others that were weaker, to unite themselves to, and become dependent upon it; but feldom has this dependence degenerated into flavifh fubjection.

This primitive form of government, which has ever fubfifted without alteration among the Arabs, proves the antiquity of this people, and renders their prefent ftate more interefting than it would otherwife be. Among the Bedouins it is preferved in all its purity. In other parts of Arabia, it has fuffered fome changes, but yet is not materially altered. I fhall have occafion to take notice of thefe, fuch as they are, when I come to defcribe each particular province by itfelf. For the prefent, I fhall content myfelf with making fome general reflections upon the fpirit of the Arabian government.

The Bedouins, or paftoral Arabs, who live in tents, have many Schiechs, each of whom governs his family with power almoft abfolute. All the Schiechs, however, who belong to the fame tribe, acknowledge a common chief, who is called *Schech es Scheuch*, Schiech of Schiechs, or *Schech el Kbir*, and whofe authority is limited by cuftom. The dignity of Grand Schiech is hereditary in a certain family; but the inferior Schiechs, upon the death of a Grand Schiech, choofe the fucceffor out of his family, without regard to age or lineal fucceffion, or any other confideration, except fuperiority of abilities,

abilities. This right of election, with their other privileges, obliges the Grand Schiech to treat the inferior Schiechs rather as affociates than as fubjects, sharing with them his fovereign authority. The fpirit of liberty, with which this warlike nation are animated, renders them incapable of fervitude.

This fpirit is lefs fenfibly felt among thofe who live in towns, or are employed in hufbandry. It was eafier to reduce them under fubjection. In the fertile diftricts of this country, there have always been monarchies, more or lefs extenfive, formed, either by conqueft, or by religious prejudices. Such are the prefent dominions of the *Sherriffe of Mecca*, of the *Imams* of *Sana* and *Mafkat*, and of fome princes in the province of *Hadramaut*. However, as thefe countries are interfected by large ranges of mountains, the mountains are occupied by independent Shiechs.

But, although fo many independent chieftains have their domains interfperfed through the territories of thofe feveral fovereigns, yet nothing of the feudal form of government appears here. The Schiechs poffefs no fiefs; they have only a fort of property in the perfons of the people of their feveral tribes. Even thofe who feem to be tributary fubjects to the princes within whofe dominions they dwell, are not actually

tually fo. They remain independent; and the tribute which they pay is nothing but a tithe for the ufe of the land of which they are in fome fort farmers. Such are the Schiechs fettled in Syria, Egypt, and over all Mount Atlas (J).

A nation of this character cannot readily fink into a fervile fubjection to arbitrary power. Defpotifm would never have been known, even in the flighteft degree, in Arabia, had it not been for theocracy, the ufual fource of it. The Imams being reputed fucceffors of Mahomet, and his defcendants, and being acknowledged both as temporal and fpiritual heads within their dominions, have thus found means to abufe the fimplicity of their fubjects, and to enlarge their authority. Neverthelefs, the genius of the people, their cuftoms, and even their religion, are all inimical to the progrefs of defpotifm, and concur to check the Imams in the exercife of their power.

The idea of forming republican governments feems never to have occurred to the Arabians. This form is not a neceffary confequence of the primitive condition of mankind. It muft have originated among people whofe patience was exhaufted by the outrages of arbitrary power; or fometimes, perhaps, from the fortuitous concourfe of perfons not connected by the ties of family-relation. The united ftates of Hafchidu

Bekil

Bekil are not fo much a federative republic, as an affociation of feveral petty princes, for the purpofe of mutual defence againft their common enemies. Their government refembles that of the German empire, not the States of Switzerland, or the United Provinces. Concerning the pretended Republic of Brava, upon the eaftern coaft of Africa, little certain is known. There is ground for thinking that it likewife is merely a confederation among the Arabian Schiechs in that country.

The colony of Jews, who occupy a diftrict in the province of Hedjas, are governed by a hereditary independent Schiech. Having been for ages divided from their countrymen, they have adopted that form of government which they faw prevalent among their immediate neighbours.

This multiplicity of petty fovereigns occafions feveral inconveniencies to the people in general. Wars cannot but frequently arife among ftates whofe territories are fo intermingled together, and whofe fovereigns have fuch a variety of jarring interefts to manage. But, happily, thefe quarrels are fcarcely ever productive of very fatal confequences. An army of a thoufand Arabs will take to flight, and think themfelves routed, if they lofe but feven or eight of their number.

Thus

Thus are thefe contefts terminated as eafily as excited.

No doubt, fuch a multitude of nobles and petty princes, whofe numbers are continually increafed by polygamy, muft have an unfavourable influence upon the general happinefs of the people. It ftrikes one with furprife, to fee the Arabs, in a country fo rich and fertile, uncomfortably lodged, indifferently fed, ill clothed, and deftitute of almoft all the conveniencies of life. But the caufes fully account for the effects.

The poverty of the wandering Arabs is plainly voluntary. They prefer liberty to wealth, paftoral fimplicity to a life of conftraint and toil, which might procure them a greater variety of gratifications. Thofe living in cities, or employed in the cultivation of the land, are kept in poverty, by the exorbitancy of the taxes exacted from them. The whole fubftance of the people is confumed in the fupport of their numerous princes and priefts. The inftance of the territory of Zebid, which I adduced in my account of that city, fhews that the hufbandman cannot bear fuch exceffive impofts without being reduced to mifery.

One general caufe of the impoverifhment of Arabia is, no doubt, its having ceafed to be the channel of the trade with India, fince the difcovery of the paffage by the Cape of Good Hope. Yet,

Yet, if the lands were better cultivated, this country might, without the aid of foreign trade, afford sufficient resources to supply all its inhabitants with abundance of the neceffaries and common conveniencies of life.

SECTION XVII.

OF THE PROVINCE OF HEDJAS.

CHAP. I.

Of the general Appearance of this Province, and of some of the Towns in it.

HEDJAS is bounded on the eaſt ſide by Nejed; on the north by the defart of Sinai; on the ſouth by Yemen; and on the weſt by the Arabic Gulph. Its interior limits I cannot pretend to know diſtinctly, having ſeen only the ſea-coaſt: Whatever I may mention concerning the other parts is entirely from hearſay.

By what I have heard, this diſtrict bears an entire refemblance to Yemen. From the ſea-ſhore, a plain, varying in breadth, ſtretches backwards to the bottom of a chain of mountains, running in a direction parallel to the Red Sea. This plain, like Tehama, is entirely fandy and barren, with the exception only of the openings of the vallies, which may be watered by torrents from the mountains.

The highlands of Hedjas produce abundance of fruits, and other commodities of various kinds: Yet I have not heard coffee mentioned among their productions. Balm of Mecca comes from thofe lofty regions, and chiefly from the extenfive mountain of *Safra*, which is a three days journey diftant from the Arabic Gulph.

This barren plain cannot be populous. I have mentioned already, that I could fee no towns or villages in my paffage from Suez to Loheya. I have defcribed *Jambo*, *Jidda*, and *Ghunfude*, the only towns or harbours on all this extenfive coaft. The other villages, that may be thinly fcattered here and there, are too few and too paltry to merit notice.

In the interior parts of this country, I could difcover no confiderable city, except *Taaif*, fituate upon a lofty mountain, in fo agreeable a country, that the Arabs compare its environs to thofe of Damafcus and Sana. This city fupplies Jidda and Mecca with excellent fruits, particularly raifins, and carries on a confiderable trade in almonds, which grow in great plenty in its territories.

There

There are fome towns, of no great confequence, belonging to the Schiech of the tribe of *Harb*. I was alfo told of a charming valley, called *Wadi Fatima*, between Mecca and Medina, which Mahomet gave for dowry to his favourite daughter Fatima, and which is prefently poffeffed by the *Dani Barkad*, a younger branch of the reigning family of Mecca, and confequently defcendants from that princefs.

The curiofities of Mecca and Medina, the two capitals of Hedjas, are fo numerous, that each of thefe cities muft be confidered in a chapter by itfelf.

CHAP. II.

Of the Power of the Turks in Hedjas.

THE Grand Signior ftiles himfelf Sovereign of Hedjas; and our geographers, upon the faith of that empty title, reprefent this part of Arabia as a province of the Turkifh empire. But, the authority of the Sultan is here nothing but a mere fhadow, which the Arabs would long fince have annihilated, if they had not found their intereft in preferving it.

Nothwithftanding the lofty pretenfions of the Grand Signior, his power in Arabia confifts folely in a few flender prerogatives. He fends yearly

yearly caravans to Mecca, with troops to protect them, that are often obliged to make their way by force of arms. Like any other powerful Sovereign, when he chooses to opprefs a weak neighbour, he can depofe the reigning Sherriffe, and exalt another, while his caravan lords it at Mecca. He fends a Pacha to Jidda, who fhares the government of this city with the Sherriffe, but who dares neither go to the feat of his government, nor return from it, unlefs when he can be protected by the great caravan. Laftly, the Arabs fuffer the Turkifh Sovereign to maintain, for the fecurity of the pilgrims, and in order to guard the wells, a few janizaries, cooped up in fome wretched towers.

The revenues which he draws from this pretended province are proportionate to his power in it. The Sultan divides with the Sherriffe the duties paid at the cuftom-houfe of Jidda. But, the revenue thus obtained, is not fufficient to defray the expences of the Pacha's houfehold. A Turk, therefore, thinks himfelf difgraced when nominated to this fine government, and is unhappy till he be recalled.

If the Arabs did not receive, every year, large fums of money, and other advantages of all forts from the Sultan, they would long fince have expelled this handful of Turks from their country. The Sultan allows large penfions to all the

Sher-

Sherriffes, and to the principal nobility of Hedjas, as guardians of the facred family. With thefe penfions, and the freight of four or five large veffels, which he fends every year to Jidda, laden with provifions, he fupports almoft all the inhabitants of Mecca and Medina. During the whole time, while the pilgrims remain in the city of Mecca, as much water as two thoufand camels can bear is daily diftributed gratis; not to fpeak of the vaft number of prefents with which he adorns the *Kaba*, and gratifies the defcendants of Mahomet.

The principal Arabs likewife gain by the many pious foundations eftablifhed by the Sultans, or by opulent private perfons among the Turks, at different holy places. Through all the cities of the Ottoman empire are *kans*, baths, and houfes belonging to the *Kaba*. Some perfons, to fecure their property, after their deceafe, from the rapacity of defpotifm, bequeath it, failing their own family, to the mofque at Mecca. The revenues of this mofque, and of the *kaba*, are fhared between the Sherriffe and the chief nobility of Hedjas. Thefe Arabs would therefore endanger their income, if they offered to break off an apparent dependence, which flatters the Sultan's vanity, without affecting their liberty.

The Sultan no longer commands refpect upon the Arabic Gulph. Poffeffing only a precarious authority

authority over Egypt, and having but a poor navy, he cannot hinder the Arabs from plundering Turkish ships, whenever these approach so near to the shores as to fall into their hands, nor yet punish such acts of insolent piracy.

CHAP. III.

Of the Sherriffe of Mecca.

SHERRIFFE, as I have already had occasion to remark, is the title of the descendants of Mahomet by *Haffan ibn Ali.* Although this branch of the posterity of Mahomet have never attained to the dignities of Caliph or Imam, they, however, appear to have always enjoyed the sovereignty over most of the cities in Hedjas.

The descendants of *Haffan ibn Ali* are now divided into several branches, of which the family of *Ali Bunemi*, consisting at least of three hundred individuals, enjoy the sole right to the throne of Mecca. The *Ali Bunemi* are, again, subdivided into two subordinate branches, *Darii Sajid*, and *Darii Barkad;* of whom sometimes the one, sometimes the other, have given sovereigns to Mecca and Medina, when these were separate states.

Not only is the Turkish Sultan indifferent about the order of succession in this family, but

but he seems even to foment the diffentions which arife among them, and favours the ftrongeft, merely that he may weaken them all. As the order of fucceffion is not determinately fixed, and the Sherriffes may all afpire alike to the fovereign power, this uncertainty of right, aided by the intrigues of the Turkifh officers, occafions frequent revolutions. The Grand Sherriffe is feldom able to maintain himfelf on the throne; and it ftill feldomer happens that his reign is not difturbed by the revolt of his neareft relations. There have been inftances of a nephew fucceeding his uncle, an uncle fucceeding his nephew; and fometimes of a perfon, from a remote branch, coming in the room of the reigning prince of the ancient houfe.

When I was in Arabia, in 1763, the reigning Sherriffe *Mefad* had fitten fourteen years on the throne, and, during all that period, had been continually at war with the neighbouring Arabs, and with his own neareft relations fometimes. A few years before, the Pacha of Syria had depofed him, and raifed his younger brother to the fovereign dignity in his ftead. But, after the departure of the caravan, *Jafar*, the new Sherriffe, not being able to maintain himfelf on the throne, was obliged to refign the fovereignty

vereignty again to *Mefad*. *Achmet*, the fecond brother of the Sherriffe, who was much beloved by the Arabs, threatened to attack Mecca while we were at Jidda. We were foon after informed of the termination of the quarrel, and of Achmet's return to Mecca, where he continued to live peaceably in a private character.

Thefe examples fhew, that the Muffulmans obferve not the law which forbids them to bear arms againft their holy places. An Egyptian Bey even prefumed, a few years fince, to plant fome fmall cannons within the compafs of the Kaba, upon a fmall tower, from which he fired over that facred manfion, upon the palace of Sherriffe Mefad, with whom he was at variance.

The dominions of the Sherriffe comprehend the cities of Mecca, Medina, Jambo, Taaif, Sadie, Ghunfude, Hali, and thirteen others lefs confiderable, all fituate in Hedjas. Near Taaif is the lofty mountain of *Gazvan*, which, according to Arabian authors, is covered with fnow and froft in the midft of fummer. As thefe dominions are neither opulent nor extenfive, the revenue of their Sovereign cannot be confiderable.

He finds a rich refource, however, in the impofts levied on pilgrims, and in the gratuities offered him by Muffulman monarchs. Every pilgrim pays a tax of from ten to an hundred crowns,

crowns, in proportion to his ability. The Great Mogul remits annually fixty thoufand roupees to the Sherriffe, by an affignment upon the government of Surat. Indeed, fince the Englifh made themfelves mafters of this city, and the territory belonging to it, the Nabob of Surat has no longer been able to pay the fum. The Sherriffe once demanded it of the Englifh, as the poffeffors of Surat; and, till they fhould fatisfy him, forbade their captains to leave the port of Jidda. But the Englifh difregarding this prohibition, the Sherriffe complained to the Ottoman Porte, and they communicated his complaints to the Englifh ambaffador. He at the fame time opened a negociation with the nominal Nabob, who refides in Surat. But thefe fteps proved all fruitlefs: And the Sovereign of Mecca feems not likely to be ever more benefited by the contribution from India.

The power of the Sherriffe extends not to fpiritual matters. Thefe are entirely managed by the heads of the clergy, of different fects, who are refident at Mecca. Rigid Muffulmans, fuch as the Turks, are not very favourable in their fentiments of the Sherriffes, but fufpect their orthodoxy, and look upon them as fecretly attached to the tolerant fect of the *Zeidi.*

CHAP.

CHAP. IV.

Of the City of Mecca.

This city is situate in a dry and barren tract of country; a full day's journey from Jidda. A few leagues beyond it, nearer the highlands, however, abundance of excellent fruits is to be found. In the summer months, the heat is excessive at Mecca; and, to avoid and moderate it as much as possible, the inhabitants carefully shut their windows and water the streets. There have been instances of persons suffocated in the middle of the streets by the burning wind called *Samoum* or *Samiel*.

As a great part of the first nobility in Hedjas live at Mecca, the buildings are better here than in any other city in Arabia. Among its elegant edifices, the most remarkable is the famous *Kaba*, or house of God, which was held in high veneration by the Arabians, even before the days of Mahomet.

My curiosity would have led me to see this sacred and singular structure; but no Christian dares enter Mecca. Not that there is any such express prohibition in the laws of Mahomet, or that liberal-minded Mahometans could be offended; but the prejudices of the people in general,

neral, with respect to the sanctity of the place, make them think that it would be profaned by the feet of infidel Christians. They even persuade themselves, that Christians are restrained from approaching it by a supernatural power. They tell of an infidel, who audaciously advanced within sight of Mecca, but was there attacked by all the dogs of the city, and was so struck with the miracle, and with the august aspect of the Kaba, that he immediately became Mussulman.

There is therefore ground for the presumption, that all the Christians of Europe, who describe Mecca as eye-witnesses, have been renegadoes who have escaped from Turkey. A recent example confirms this suspicion. Upon a promise of being suffered to adhere to his religion, a French surgeon was prevailed with to attend the Emir Hadgi to Mecca, in the quality of his physician. But he had not proceeded far, when he was forced to submit to circumcision, and then suffered to continue his journey.

Although the Mahometans permit not Europeans to visit Mecca, they make no difficulty of describing the Kaba to them. I even obtained at Kahira a drawing of that holy place, which I had afterwards an opportunity of correcting, from another draught by a Turkish painter. This painter gained his livelihood by making such draughts of the Kaba, and selling them to pilgrims.

To judge from those designs, and from the relations of many Mussulmans of sufficient veracity, the Kaba must be an aukward shapeless building; a sort of square tower it is, covered on the top with a piece of black gold-embroidered silk stuff. This stuff is wrought at Kahira, and changed every year at the expence of the Turkish Sultan. The gutters upon this building are of pure gold.

What seems to be most magnificent about this sacred edifice, is the arcades around the square in which the Kaba stands. They speak, in terms of high admiration, of a vast number of lamps and candlesticks of gold and silver with which those arcades are illuminated. However, even by these accounts, in which the truth is apparently exaggerated, the riches of the Kaba are far from equal in value to what is displayed in some Catholic churches in Europe.

In the Kaba is particularly one singular relic, which is regarded with extreme veneration. This is the famous black stone, said to have been brought by the angel Gabriel in order to the construction of that edifice. The stone, according to the account of the clergy, was, at first, of a bright white colour, so as even to dazzle the eyes at the distance of four days journey;

journey; but it wept fo long, and fo abundantly for the fins of mankind, that it became at length opaque, and at laft abfolutely black. This ftone, of fo compaffionate a character, every Muffulman muft kifs, or at leaft touch, every time he goes round the Kaba. Neither the ftone of Abraham, nor that of Ifmael, receives the fame honours; pilgrims are not obliged either to vifit or to kifs them.

The Arabs venerate the Kaba, as having been built by Abraham, and having been his houfe of prayer. Within the fame inclofure is the well of *Zemzem*, valued for the excellence of its water, and no lefs for its miraculous origin. Hagar, when banifhed by her mafter, fet little Ifmael down here, while fhe fhould find fome water to quench his thirft. Returning, after an unfuccefsful fearch, fhe was furprifed to fee a fpring burfting up from the ground between the child's legs. That fpring is the prefent well of Zemzem.

Another ornament of the Kaba, is a row of metal pillars furrounding it. Thefe pillars are joined by chains, on which hang a vaft number of filver lamps. The porticos or arcades above mentioned are defigned to protect the pilgrims from the torrid heat of the day. They anfwer likewife another purpofe; for the merchants, of

whom

whom great numbers accompany the caravans, expofe their wares for fale under thofe arcades.

The Mahometans have fuch high ideas of the fanctity of Mecca, that they fuppofe it to extend even to the environs of the city. Its territory is reputed facred to a certain diftance round, which is indicated by marks fet for this purpofe. Every caravan find one of thofe marks on their way, which warns the pilgrims to put on the modeft garb which it becomes them to wear on that facred ground.

CHAP. V.

Of the Pilgrimage of the Muffulmans.

EVERY Muffulman, it is well known, is obliged, once in his life, to vifit Mecca, and perform acts of devotion in the facred places. If this law were ftrictly obferved, the concourfe of pilgrims would be immenfe; nor could the city contain fuch crowds from every country in which the Mahometan religion has been introduced. It may be prefumed, therefore, that none but fuch as are more than ordinarily devout difcharge this duty.

Thofe indeed, whofe circumftances do not admit of their undertaking fo diftant a journey, are allowed to hire a perfon to perform it for them.

them. But a pilgrim, in this character, can act for no more than one perſon at the ſame time; and, to prevent impoſture, he muſt bring back a formal atteſtation from an Imam in Mecca, bearing, that he has actually performed the appointed devotional exerciſes in the holy places, in the name of ſuch a perſon, living or dead; for, even after the death of a man, who, during his life, neglected the fulfilling of this point of the law, the duty may ſtill be diſcharged in his name, and for his benefit. I have ſometimes met with pilgrims by profeſſion, who had been ill paid by their employers, and were obliged to aſk alms.

Few as the caravans are, in proportion to the numbers of the Muſſulmans, even thoſe few are compoſed, in great part, of perſons who go upon other motives than devotion; ſuch as merchants, who think this the ſafeſt opportunity for the conveyance of their goods, and the moſt favourable for the ſale of them;---purveyors of all ſorts, who furniſh the pilgrims with neceſſaries; and ſoldiers, paid by the caravan for eſcorting them. From this it happens, that many perſons have ſeen Mecca ſeveral times, without ever viſiting it upon any but views of intereſt.

The moſt conſiderable of theſe caravans is that of Syria, commanded by the Pacha of Damaſcus. At a certain diſtance from Mecca, it joins that from Egypt, which is the ſecond in numbers,

bers, and is conducted by a Bey, who takes the title of Emir Hadgi. A third comes from Yemen; and a fourth, ſtill ſmaller in numbers, from the country of Lachſca. A *few* pilgrims come by the Red Sea, and from the Arabian ſettlements on the coaſt of Africa. The Perſians join that which is from Bagdad, and is conducted by the Pacha. *His* poſt is lucrative; for he ſqueezes large ſums from the Perſian heretics.

When giving an account of what I ſaw on board our veſſel, in the paſſage between Suez and Jidda, I had occaſion to ſpeak of the Ihhram, and of the place where pilgrims are obliged to aſſume that garb of humility. I may add, that they muſt proceed without delay to Mecca, as ſoon as they arrive on the border of the ſacred territory. A Greek renegadoe, who had come in our company from Suez, was difpoſed to reſt for ſome time at Jidda; but the reproaches which he found thrown out upon him, for ſuch an inſtance of indifference about the object of his journey, obliged him to ſet off for Mecca ſooner than was favourable to the ſtate of his buſineſs in Jidda.

Beſides, it is truly advantageous to a pilgrim to haſte forward to the holy places. If he has not been preſent from the commencement, at the celebration of all the ceremonies, and performed every appointed act of devotion, he cannot

not obtain the title of *Hadgi;* an honour much coveted by the Turks, becaufe it confers fubftantial privileges, and commands refpect to thofe who bear it. The rarity of this title, in Mahometan countries, is a proof how negligently the law enjoining pilgrimage is obferved.

A fimilar cuftom prevails among the Chriftians in the eaft, who alfo make much ado about the title of *Hadgi* or *Mokdafi*, which they gave to pilgrims of their communion. In order to acquire this title, it is not enough for a perfon to go in pilgrimage to Jerufalem; he muft fpend the feafon of the paffover in that city, and affift at all the ceremonies in the holy weeks (κ).

CHAP. VI.

Of the City of Medina.

About a day's journey diftant from the port of Jambo ftands Medina, a city of moderate extent, furrounded with *indifferent* walls, and fituate in a fandy plain. It belongs to the Sherriffe of Mecca, but has of late been governed by a Sovereign of its own, of the family of *Darii Barkad*. At this prefent time, the Sherriffe rules it by a Vizir, who muft be of the royal family.

Before

Before the days of Mahomet, this city was called *Jathreb*. But it was called *Medinet en Nebbi*, the City of the Prophet; from the period at which Mahomet, upon his expulfion out of Mecca by the Koreifchites, took refuge here, and continued to make it the place of his refidence for the reft of his life.

The tomb of Mahomet at Medina is held in refpect by the Muffulmans; but they are not obliged to vifit it in order to the performance of any devotional exercifes; only, as the caravans from Syria neceffarily pafs near by Medina, in their return from Mecca, they turn afide to behold the Prophet's tomb.

I alfo obtained from a Turk a drawing of the mofque in which the tomb ftands. It is fituate in a corner of the great fquare; whereas the Kaba is in the middle of the fquare at Mecca. For fear that the people might fuperftitioufly offer worfhip to the afhes of the Prophet, the tomb is inclofed within iron rails, and is only to be feen by looking through thefe. It is of plain mafon-work, in the form of a cheft; and this is all the monument. I could never learn the origin of the ridiculous ftory, which has been circulated in Europe, concerning vaft magnets faid to fupport the coffin of Mahomet in the air.

This tomb is placed between two other tombs, in which reft the afhes of the two firft Caliphs.

Al-

Although not more magnificent than the tombs of the founders of moſt other moſques, the building that covers it, is hung with a piece of ſilk ſtuff embroidered with gold, which is renewed every ſeven years by the Pacha of Damaſcus.

This building is guarded by forty eunuchs, chiefly for the ſecurity of the treaſure which is ſaid to be kept in it. This treaſure conſiſts chiefly of precious ſtones, the offerings of rich Muſſulmans. But there was evidently ſuch a mixture of fable in the account I received of it, that I knew not what to think. Several reſpectable Mahometans ſeriouſly aſſured me, that the philoſopher's ſtone, or a large quantity of powder for converting other metals into fine gold, was one of the moſt valuable articles of that treaſure. An eminent Arabian merchant informed me, that the guard was poſted for no other purpoſe but to keep off the populace, who had begun to throw dirt upon the tomb, which they afterwards ſcraped off, and preſerved as a ſort of relic.

CHAP. VII.

Of the independent Schiechs, Arab and Jewiſh.

THE highlands of Hedjas are poſſeſſed by a number of independent Sovereign Schiechs. The moſt

moſt powerful of theſe is the Schiech of the tribe of *Harb*, who can bring two thouſand men into the field. He reſides in the city of *Makſchous;* and his domains contain ſeveral cities, and a number of villages.

During the months favourable for paſturage, the moſt diſtinguiſhed perſons of this tribe live in tents; in the reſt of the year, they inhabit the towns and villages. The lower claſs live, commonly through the whole year, in huts thatched with graſs. This principality is ſituate upon the mountains between Mecca and Medina.

I could not learn either the names or the ſituation of the territories of the other independent Schiechs in this province. What I know is, that they all live with their ſubjects in towns and villages, thro' the whole year, and have for their places of defence ſome caſtles built upon precipitous rocks. They ſometimes join their neighbours to attack the Turkiſh caravans; but theſe never paſs thro' *their* dominions.

The chief of the tribe of *Harb* is the perſon who chiefly harraſſes the caravans, and lays them under contribution. Unleſs the Syrians and Egyptians pay the tribute he demands, for permiſſion to paſs through his territories, he muſters up an army of his own ſubjects and his

neigh-

neighbours, all of whom are very willing to pillage a caravan.

The moft remarkable, and the leaft known of thofe highland communities, is that which the Jews have formed upon the mountains lying to the north-eaft of Medina. That tract of country is called *Khiebar;* and the Jews inhabiting it are known in Arabia by the name of *Beni Khiebar.* They have independent Schiechs of their own, and are divided into three tribes; *Beni Miffead, Beni Schahan, Beni Anaeffe.* So odious are they to the Mahometans, who accufe them of pillaging the caravans, that, in Syria, the greateft affront which can be offered a man is to call him *Beni Kheibar.* Thofe robberies feem, however, to be unjuftly imputed to them. Some Mahometans, whom I could credit, affured me, that the Jews indeed furnifhed auxiliaries to the Arab army, which had lately pillaged the caravan from Damafcus; but, that the authors of that enterprife were, the Schiech of the tribe of *Harb* in Hedjas, and he of the tribe of *Anaeffe* in *Nejed.*

It does not appear that the Jews of Kheibar keep up any intercourfe with their brethren who are difperfed over Afia. When I afked the Jews in Syria concerning them, they told me, that thofe falfe brethren durft not claim their fellowfhip, for that they did not obferve the law. The Beni Kheibar muft therefore be of the feet

of

of the *Karaites*, who are not numerous, and are much difperfed; and, by the other Jews, who are in general attached to the fect of the Pharifees, are ftill more detefted than the Chriftians or Mahometans.

The name of *Anaeffe* is not unlike *Hanaffi*, the name of a tribe of whom Benjamin de Tudela fpeaks as being his countrymen. It alfo has a confiderable refemblance to *Baruc Anzab*, a race of Jews who gave much trouble to Mahomet and the firft Caliphs. It fhould feem, therefore, that this branch of the Jews muft have fubfifted here for more than twelve centuries. *Barthema* was the firft modern that made mention of this little ftate of independent Jews, in the neighbourhood of Medina.

The circumftances of this fettlement have, perhaps, given rife to the fable of the *Sabbatical River*. Thefe Jews cannot accompany a caravan, becaufe their religion permits them not to travel on the Sabbath. Yet the country which they inhabit is furrounded by fuch vaft and fandy defarts, that, unlefs with a caravan, fo fequeftered a tract cannot be fafely either entered or left.

SECTION XVIII.

OF YEMEN IN GENERAL.

CHAP. I.

Of the Boundaries and Subdivisions of Yemen.

This great province, comprehending the finest and most fertile part of Arabia, is surrounded by the Arabic Gulph, and by the provinces of Hadramaut, Nejed, and Hedjas.

Yemen is naturally divided into two parts, differing greatly in soil and climate. That bordering on the Arabic Gulph is a dry and sandy plain, nearly two days journey in breadth, and is scorched by the most torrid heats. The other, extending immediately beyond this, is a highlying country, full of precipitous, yet fertile hills, and enjoying a much more temperate air. But, these circumstances will fall properly within the natural history of Arabia; and I am here speaking only of its political divisions.

Yemen is, like the rest of Arabia, parcelled out among a number of different sovereigns in unequal portions. Some of them are princes of considerable power; but many are petty Schiechs, who are, however, perfectly independent.

The moſt confiderable of thofe princes is the Imam, who refides at Sana. Having travelled through a part of his dominions, and by confequence acquired particular knowledge of them, I ſhall defcribe them in a feparate article, and the rather, as they extend through the greater part of Yemen. At prefent, I proceed to give an abſtract of what I could learn concerning the reſt of this province.

The independent ſtates of Yemen, befide the dominions of the Imam, are, as I learned from perfons who were the moſt likely to be accurately informed,

1. The territory of *Aden*, which has been for fome time governed by a particular prince;

2. The principality of *Kaukeban*, poffeffed by a *Sejid;*

3. *Kobail*, or *Hafchid-u-Bekil*, in which are many Schiechs, united in a fort of confederation;

4. The principality of *Abu-Arifch*, belonging to a Sherriffe;

5. A large diſtrict between *Abu-Arifch* and Hedjas, inhabited by free Bedouins;

6. The territory of *Khaulan*, under the dominion of its own Schiech;

7. The

7. The territory of *Sahan*, comprehending the principality of *Saade*, which belongs to a *Sejid*, with the domains of some independent Schiechs;

8. *Nedsjeran;*

9. *Kachtan;*

10. *Nehhm ;*

11. East *Khaulan*, consisting of four small sovereignties, under the government of as many independent Schiechs;

12. The vast country of *Dsjof* or *Mareb*, governed by a Sherriffe, and some independent Schiechs;

13. The territory of *Jafa*, in which are at least three independent Schiechs.

There are possibly several other sovereign states in Yemen, which might be too small to come to my knowledge. A traveller, who should only stop a short time on his way, could not readily learn the names of all the petty German baronies. What I know certainly, however, as having witnessed striking enough instances of it, is, that those endless subdivisions of territory, among such a multitude of petty sovereigns, are, in a great measure, the cause of the state of decline in which Arabia at present appears: Such a collection of jarring interests is naturally fatal to trade and industry.

CHAP.

CHAP. II.

Of the Principality of Aden.

This fmall ftate is bounded on the fouth by the Indian Ocean; on the weft and north by the dominions of the Imam; and on the eaft by the country of *Jafa*. It formerly belonged to the Imam; but, in 1730, the inhabitants expelled the Imam's governor, and elected a Schiech, who is perfectly independent.

Aden, an ancient and celebrated city, gives its name to this principality. It has ftill a good harbour, although much declined from what it once was. Its trade is now trifling; for the Sovereign is never at peace with his neighbours. Coffee from Jafa is the only article for export which this city affords.

Among a number of cities, and a good many caftles of no great ftrength, belonging to this fmall ftate, the only place that is ftill in any degree confiderable, is *Lahadsje*, the feat of the prefent Schiech *Abd ul Kerim el Foddeli*. This town was befieged by the famous *Abd Urrab*, from whom it fuffered confiderably. *Foddeli* is a narrow diftrict, containing a city and feveral villages, known from its having been the original feat of the reigning family.

CHAP.

CHAP. III.

Of the Principality of Kaukeban.

THE country bearing this name, is furrounded almoft on all hands by the dominions of the I-mam of Sana; only, on one fide, meeting the territory of the confederated Schiechs of Hafchid-u-Bekil. The reigning family are defcendants from Mahomet, by *Hadi*, Imam of *Saade*. They, for feveral ages, poffeffed confiderable dominions in Yemen; and retained the title of I-mam even during the ufurpation of the Turks. But, when this nation was driven out of Yemen by *Khaffem el Kebir*, that illuftrious family were obliged to yield up their title of Imam to the new Arabian conqueror, and to content them-felves with that of *Sidi* or *Sejid*. However, they ftill retain fovereign authority over a con-fiderable territory.

A feries of thofe fovereigns was communicated to me; but I could not find means to fatis-fy myfelf of its authenticity. The reigning prince, in 1763, was *Sejid Achmet*. He had feveral fons and brothers, and a good many nephews.

He refides at Kaukeban, a fmall unfortified town, but fituate on the fummit of an almoft in-acceffible mountain. The aunt of the reigning prince has made a caufeway be formed, by which loaded camels can now advance up to the city.

In the different diftricts into which this country is divided, are a good many towns and villages, moft of which have caftles or citadels upon adjoining hills. Thefe are not unneceffary precautions for the defence of thofe petty princes, againft fo powerful a neighbour as the Imam of Sana.

Wadi Laa is a valley fertile in coffee, which belongs to *Sejid Ibrahim*, brother to the reigning Imam. In its neighbourhood are fome hot mineral fprings.

CHAP. IV.

Of the allied Princes of Hafchid-u-Bekil.

THE extenfive country of Hafchid-u-Bekil, poffeffed by a number of confederated Schiechs, is properly named *Bellad el Kobail*, the Country of the Highlanders: But the other, expreffive of the confederacy, is the name by which it is more commonly known. It extends northward as far as to the Defart of *Amafia;* on the fouth and the eaft, it is bounded by the dominions of the Imam, and the principality of Kaukeban; weftward, it meets the fovereign ftate of Abu A-rifch.

rifch. The republican fpirit prevails fo little through Afia, that thefe ftates may be regarded as a fingular political phenomenon in the eaft.

This highland country contains many Schiechs, defcended from very ancient noble families, each of whom rules within his own domains as a fovereign prince. Thefe Schiechs, finding themfelves unable to make feparately any fuccefsful refiftance to a powerful neighbour, have combined, in order to defend themfelves by the common force.

It is not eafy, even in Europe, to obtain a thorough knowledge of the principles of any political conftitution; but, among the miftruftful, fufpicious inhabitants of the eaft, fuch a thing is almoft impoffible. I could not learn upon what laws and conditions the confederation of Hafcid-u-Bekil is maintained. All I know is, that they choofe a certain number of chiefs, and, in war, fo many generals, to command their united forces.

Thefe allied princes, and their fubjects, are much better foldiers, and more inclined to war, than the reft of the Arabians. The Imam of Sana, and the Sherriffe of Mecca, entertain each feveral regiments of thofe highlanders, and pay them better than their other troops. They muft have officers of their own nation; and the Schiechs ufually both raife the regiments, and
nominate

nominate the officers. For this reafon, the Imam fears to quarrel with the confederates. When they go to war with the Sovereign of Sana, their countrymen in his fervice defert and join them.

A tradition which fubfifts concerning their common origin, may have been the caufe which firft gave rife to the confederation among thofe Schiechs, and which has difpofed them to maintain it hitherto. Hafchid and Bekil, whofe names the confederates have affumed, were, by this tradition, brothers, fons of one *Babrofcham*, by a princefs called *Nedsjema*. Babrofcham, who was born of honourable parents in Natolia, after fome romantic adventures, carried off that princefs, who was daughter to the king of Bithynia, and fought refuge upon thefe mountains of Yemen; where, through his fons, Hafchid and Bekil, he became the anceftor of all the Schiechs of *Bellad el Kobail;* and they accordingly look all up to him as their common parent.

It is certain, however, that in this country are Schiechs, whofe families can be traced farther back than the date of this tale. In the diftrict of *Kheivan*, and in the city of *Beit il Toba*, refides the chief of the family of *Toba*, a defcendant from the ancient Arabian monarchs of this name,

I

I was told of fifty of thefe independent Schiechs, fome of whom poffefs domains in the midft of the Imam's territories. It is needlefs to put down their names.

The country inhabited by thefe confederates is of various degrees of fertility. Some vallies, which produce fruits in great abundance, are interfperfed among the hills; and even the higher grounds are cultivated and fertile.

A number of caftles are fcattered upon the heights; but few confiderable villages are to be feen. The town of Kheivan, in the diftrict of the fame name, is remarkable for having been the feat, firft of the Hamjare Monarchs, and afterwards of the Imams. Ruins of a very ancient palace are ftill to be feen there.

In fome other fmall villages are feveral monuments, from which it appears, that, before the Turkifh conqueft, a great part of *Bellad el Kobail* was under the dominion of the ancient Imams.

CHAP. V.

Of the Principality of Abu Arifch, and the neighbouring Bedouins.

THE principality of Abu Arifch, which is alfo named after its capital, is properly a part of Tehama.

hama. It ſtretches along the Arabic Gulph, northward from Loheya, for the ſpace of two degrees. Like the reſt of the Tehama, it is every where dry and barren, except only where watered by the rivers from the mountainous parts of Yemen.

This country was, not long ſince, within the Imam's dominions. The Sovereigns of Sana uſually intruſt the government of their provinces to none but perſons of mean birth; often to ſlaves, who may be leſs likely than the Arab nobles to aſpire at independence. But a late Imam imprudently appointed a Sherriffe, named Achmed, to the government of Abu Ariſch. The conſequence was, that this Sherriffe revolted againſt his Sovereign: Thus juſtifying the ſaying among the Arabs, that the poſterity of Mahomet have all a thirſt for ſovereign power.

His ſon Mahommed, the reigning Sherriffe of Abu Ariſch, has hitherto withſtood all the efforts of the Imam to reduce him to his obedience. The confederates of Haſchid-u-Bekil have been repeatedly excited, by preſents from the Imam, to attack the Sherriffe; but their attacks have been made without any regular concerted plan of conqueſt. Schiech *Mecrami* of Nedsjeran likewiſe penetrated into this country, with a ſmall army, in two ſucceſſive winters. To expel this enemy, the Sherriffe levied ſix hundred men

men in the country of Hafchid-u-Bekil, and gave him battle in January 1763. The Sherriffe was defeated, with the lofs of fix or feven men, upon which he fhut himfelf up, in defpair, in his palace. But Schiech Mecrami did not avail himfelf of his victory; for, learning that the Schiech of Kachtan had entered Nedsjeran in his abfence, he haftened home to the defence of his own dominions.

The remarkable places in the principality of Abu Arifch, are the capital, known by the fame name, which is encompaffed with walls, and is the feat of the Sherriffe; and the town and harbour of *Gezan*, a day's journey from Abu Arifch. This province of Gezan, fituate upon the Arabic Gulph, and in a fertile country, carries on a confiderable trade in fenna; great plenty of which grows in the circumjacent territory; and in coffee, which is brought hither from the mountains of Hafchid-u-Bekil. It has a trade likewife with the ports on the oppofite fide of the Arabic Gulph; but has no intercourfe with the fubjects of the Imam. A few towns, and feveral large villages, form the reft of this principality.

The plain extended along the Arabic Gulph, for the fpace of a degree, from the borders of Abu Arifch to Hedjas, is occupied by a tribe of free Arabs, called *Beni Halal*. Thefe Bedouins live

live in tents, under the government of Schiechs. They are poor, and addicted to robbery, as I have already obferved in the account of our journey from Jidda to Loheya. But they value themfelves on their courage, and glory in bearing pain without fhrinking.

Thefe Bedouins, when afked what religion they are of, call themfelves Muffulmans. But their neighbours, not crediting this account, call them infidels, and accufe them of profeffing a peculiar religion, the followers of which are called *Mafaliks*. It appears indeed, that they depart widely, in feveral points, from pure Mahometifm; their circumcifion at leaft is totally different. It may be thought, that thefe wandering Arabs, having never been fubdued, by either Mahomet or his fucceffors, have retained fome part of their ancient religion. The Muffulmans confider the Bedouins, in general, as fcarcely orthodox, and reproach them as not being true believers.

Thefe Arabs of Beni Halal inhabit a barren territory. They are poor, and live upon the fcanty produce of their flocks.

CHAP.

CHAP. VI.

Of the Territories of Saham and Khaulan.

THE Arabs call the mountainous tract between Hafchid-u-Bekil and Hedjas, Sahan. This tract of country is of confiderable extent, and produces abundance of excellent fruits of all kinds, but efpecially grapes. Iron mines have alfo been difcovered in it, but for want of wood have not been wrought. From this circumftance, the iron in Yemen is both dear and bad.

The inhabitants of this country, efpecially the highlanders, who have little intercourfe with ftrangers, are faid to fpeak the beft Arabic, correfponding more entirely than that fpoken any where elfe with the language of the Alcoran; although, at the fame time, they are almoft abfolutely ftrangers to the book.

Thefe people differ effentially in their manners from the Arabs in the cities of Yemen. They feldom take more than one wife each. Their women are not permitted to marry till they have completed their fifteenth year; whereas, in the dominions of the Imam, girls are married at the age of nine or ten. They live upon meat, honey, milk, and fome vegetables. Their country affords plenty of thefe articles. By this

this simple mode of living, they commonly attain to a very advanced age, retaining the perfect use of their sight to the last. They are very hospitable, and yet rob with no less rapacity, when they meet with travellers not embodied in a caravan, than the Bedouins of the desart.

In this country are many independent lordships. The principal of these is *Saade*, in the possession of Prince *Khassem*, a descendant from Imam *Hadi*, of the same stock as the present royal families of Kaukeban and Sana. This Prince takes also the title of Imam; but his principality is so small, that he can hardly defend himself against the Schiechs of the neighbouring mountains.

At Saade, his capital, and the place of his residence, is a custom-house, which brings him a considerable revenue. All goods from the dominions of the Imam must pass this way to Nedsjeran, Kachtan, or Mecca; and high duties are exacted. In the neighbourhood of this city is a high hill, famous as being the post upon which a prince of this state sustained a seven years siege by the Turks.

A part of the great desart of Amasia lies between Saade and Hafchid-u-Bekil. In the middle of that desart is *Birket Soidan*, the only place where travellers can halt for refreshment.

The

The small district of Khaulan, which comes to be here taken notice of, and which is to be carefully distinguished from that of the same name near Sana, lies among the mountains westward from Saade, upon the road from Sana to Mecca, four days journey from Hali, the extreme city upon that side of the Sherriffe's territory. It has likewise an independent Schiech. This is all that I could learn concerning it.

CHAP. VII.

Of the Principalities of Nedsjeran and Cachtan.

NEDSJERAN is situate in a pleasant and well watered country, three days journey north-east from Saade. This narrow territory is fertile in corn and fruits, especially in dates. It affords excellent pasturage; and its horses and camels are in high request through all Arabia.

Its present Schiech, whose name is Mecrami, has gained a very high reputation. He is said not to be of the stock of the ancient nobility. In his youth, he travelled through all Arabia, Persia, and India. After his return, the Imam of Saade intrusted him with the government of the province of Nedsjeran. But, scarce had Mecrami been invested in this office, when he threw off his allegiance.

The

The new Schiech of Nedsjeran has made himſelf formidable by his genius and valour, not merely to his neighbours, but even to diſtant princes. Not long ſince, he introduced his troops, by ſmall detachments, into the territory of Hafchid-u-Bekil; penetrated into the dominions of the Imam; and made himſelf maſter of the province of *Safan*. In January 1763, as has already been mentioned, he defeated the Sherriffe of Abu Arifch. In the end of the fame year, he had traverſed all Arabia with his army, and entered the province of *Lachſa*. In Europe, it would be impoſſible to conduct an army, in ſo ſhort a time, through ſuch an extent of ſtrange and defart countries. But an army of Arabs are not incumbered with artillery, tents, or ammunition. The ſcanty proviſions which they need are borne by camels; and the ſoldiers, being light-armed, and almoſt naked, fear no fatigue.

Schiech Mecrami enjoys through Arabia the reputation, no leſs of a profound theologian, than of a valiant warrior. His religious opinions differ eſſentially from thoſe of the ſtanding ſects among the Muſſulmans. He honours Mahomet as the Prophet of God, but looks with little reſpect on his fucceſſors and commentators. Some of the more fenſible Arabs ſay, that this Schiech has found means to avail himſelf of heaven, even in this life; for, to uſe their expreſſion, fion, he fells paradife by the yard; and afligns more or lefs honourable places in that manfion according to the fums paid him. Simple, fuperftitious perfons actually purchafe affignments upon heaven, from him and his procurators, and hope to profit by them. A Perfian, of the province of *Kirman* too, has lately begun to iffue fimilar bills upon heaven, and has gained confiderably by the traffic. The people of the Eaft appear to approach daily nearer to the ingenious invention of the Europeans in thefe matters.

The knowledge of many fecrets, and, among others, of one for obtaining rain when he pleafes, is likewife afcribed to this Schiech. When the country fuffers by drought, he appoints a faft, and after it a public proceffion, in which all muft affift, with an air of humility, without their turbans, and in a garb fuitably mean. Some Arabs of diftinction affured me, that this never fails to procure an immediate fall of rain.

The capital of this fmall kingdom is Nedsjeran, an ancient city, famous in Arabian hiftory. The other towns in it are places of little confequence.

The fmall diftrict of Kachtan lies among the mountains, three days journey northward from Nedsjeran. At Loheya, I faw a perfon of diftinction

tinction from that country, who had been at Sana with horses for the Imam. He became suspicious of my intentions, when I put some questions to him respecting his country, and would give me no information. All that I could learn concerning Kachtan, was, that it is governed by a peculiar Schiech.

CHAP. VIII.

Of the Principalities of Nehhm and Khaulan.

NEHHM is a small district between Dsjof and Hafchid-u-Bekil. The present Schiech, who is of a warlike character, and often troublesome to the Imam, is an independent prince. He possesses a few small inconsiderable towns, with a fertile mountain, on which are many villages. The inhabitants of *Deiban* are free; but they always join the Schiech of Nehhm in his wars with the Imam.

The small district of Khaulan, which is different from that of the same name of which some account has already been given, lies a few leagues south-east from Sana. It is governed by an independent Schiech, the representative of a very ancient family. Schiech *Rajech Khaulani*, who reigned in 1763, dwelled at Sana, being general of the Imam's troops. His ordinary place

place of residence is at *Beit Rodsje*, a small town in his own dominions.

In this principality is the small city of *Tanaeim*, famous among the Jews of Arabia, who had anciently their chief seat, with many spacious synagogues, in it. At present it is almost desolate; and few Jews are among its inhabitants. *Beit el Kibsi* is a village inhabited solely by Sherriffes, one of whom must always be at the head of the caravan which goes annually from Sana to Mecca. This caravan consists of about three thousand persons, and is forty-five days upon the road, although the whole length of the journey be not more than an hundred German miles, at least if it could be travelled in a straight line.

Several places, which once pertained to the prince of Khaulan, have been, by degrees, annexed to the dominions of the Imam.

CHAP. IX.

Of the Country of Dsjof.

This great province of Yemen extends southward from Nedsjeran to Hadramaut, and eastward from Hafchid-u-Bekil to the Desart, by which Yemen is separated from Oman. It is full of sandy and desart plains. In several places,

ces, however, the inhabitants want neither cheefe, nor durra, nor any other of the neceffaries of life. The horfes and camels of Dsjof are greatly in requeft in the Imam's dominions.

The country of Dsjof is divided into *Bellad el Bedoui*, that diftrict which is occupied by wandering Arabs; *Bellad es Saladin*, the highland diftrict, governed by independent chiefs, who take the title of *Sultan;* and *Bellad es Scheraf*, the diftrict in which the fupreme power is poffeffed by Sherriffes.

The wandering Arabs in this country are of a martial character. In their military expeditions they ride upon horfes or camels. Their arms are a lance, a fabre, and fometimes a match-firelock. Sometimes they put on coats of mail, a piece of defenfive armour which the other Arabs have ceafed to wear. They are not a little troublefome to their neighbours, who are fettled in villages,----plundering them, and often carrying off their young women. But neither thefe, nor any other of the Bedouins, are ferocioufly cruel; they only rob ftrangers, but never kill them. Thefe Bedouins of Dsjof are faid to have uncommon talents for poetry, and to excel all the other Arabs in this elegant art.

In the diftrict of Bellad es Saladin are many petty fovereigns. Of thefe, none was named to me me but the Sultan of *Baham*. The title of Sultan is no where ufed in Arabia, except in Dsjof and Jafa. It feems to be applied to diftinguifh the Schiechs of the Highlanders from thofe of the Bedouins.

The moft confiderable princes in the diftrict of Bellad es Scheraf, are the three Sherriffes of *Mareb*, *Harib*, and *Rachvan*. But the firft, although chief of the defcendants of Mahomet in this country, poffeffes only the town of Mareb, with fome adjacent villages.

Mareb, though confifting only of about three hundred poor houfes, is the capital of the province. It is fituate fixteen leagues north-eaft from Sana. It was known to the ancients as the capital of the Sabeans, by the name of *Mariaba*. It is not certain whether it was ever called *Saba*. In its neighbourhood are fome ruins, which are pretended to be the remains of the palace of Queen *Balkis*. But there is no infcription to confirm or refute this affertion.

The Sabeans had a refervoir or bafon for water, which was anciently famous, and which I often heard talked of in Arabia; but nobody could give me an exact defcription of it, except one man of rank, who had been born at Mareb, and had always lived there. He told me, that the famous refervoir, called by the Arabs *Sitte Mareb*, was a narrow valley between two ranges of hills,

hills, and a day's journey in length. Six or feven fmall rivers meet in that valley, holding their courfe fouth and fouth-weft, and advancing from the territories of the Imam. Some of thefe rivers contain fifhes, and their waters flow through the whole year; others are dry, except in the rainy feafon. The two ranges of hills which confine this valley, approach fo near to each other upon the eaftern end, that the intermediate fpace may be croffed in five or fix minutes. To confine the waters in the rainy feafon, the entrance into the valley was here fhut up by a high and thick wall; and, as outlets, through which the water thus collected, might be conveyed, in the feafon of drought, to water the neighbouring fields,----three large flood-gates were formed in the wall, one above another. The wall was fifty feet high, and built of large hewn ftones. Its ruins are ftill to be feen. But the waters, which it ufed formerly to confine, are now loft among the fands, after running only a fhort way.

Thus was there nothing incredibly wonderful in the true account of the Sabæan refervoir. Similar, although much fmaller refervoirs, are formed at the roots of the mountains in many places through Yemen. Near Conftantinople is a vale, the entrance into which is likewife fhut up by a wall to confine the water, which is conveyed

veyed thence in aqueducts into the capital of the Ottoman empire.

The tradition, that the city of Mareb was deftroyed by a deluge, occafioned by the fudden burfting of the wall, has entirely the air of a popular fable. It feems more probable, that the wall, being neglected, fell gradually into difrepair, when the kingdom of the Sabæans declined. But the ruin of the wall proved fatal to the city in a different way. The neighbouring fields, when no longer watered from the refervoir, became wafte and barren; and the city was thus left without means of fubfiftence. Befides, Mareb is not fo fituate that it could fuffer an inundation in confequence of the demolition of the wall. It ftands upon a fmall eminence, at a league's diftance from it, upon the water fide.

The fertility of the diftrict might be renewed by the reparation of this work. But, fuch undertakings can be executed only by opulent fovereigns. *Mariaba* was the feat of a powerful prince, who reigned over Yemen and Hadramaut. *Mareb* is but the abode of a poor Sherriffe, who can fcarcely withftand the encroachments of feeble neighbours.

The only other place in the country of Dsjof, that I heard of as remarkable, is *Kaffer el Nat*, a citadel which ſtands upon a lofty hill, and was built by the Hamjare princes.

CHAP. X.

Of the Country of Jafa.

This territory is ſurrounded by Aden, ſome part of the Imam's dominions, and the extenſive province of Hadramaut. It is fertile, and a-bounds particularly in coffee and cattle.

It was formerly under the dominion of the I-mam; but, in the end of the laſt century, the inhabitants revolted, and made themſelves independent. They are governed at preſent by three ſovereign princes, who have conquered alſo a part of the province of Hadramaut. Thoſe princes are, 1. The Sultan of *Reſſes*, who re-ſides at *Medsjeba;* 2. The Sultan of *Moſaka*, who takes his title from the place of his reſi-dence; 3. The Sultan of *Kara*, who reſides in a caſtle upon the mountain of Kara.

One of theſe Sultans of Jafa likewiſe poſſeſſes *Schæhhr*, a ſea-port town, from which incenſe, but inferior in quality to that of India, is exported. Nobody could inform me concerning the interior parts of this diſtrict of *Schæhhr*.

Bellad Schafel, and *Ed Dahla*, are the domi-nions of two petty Schiechs. *Medina el Aſfal*,

is

is a city famous for the tombs of various faints. The inhabitants are confequently Sunnites.

SECTION XIX.

OF THE DOMINIONS OF THE IMAM OF SANA.

CHAP. I.

Of the Extent and Divifions of the Imam's Dominions.

Speaking of Yemen in general, I unavoidably gave fome account of that part of this province which is fubject to the Imam. The fame intermixture of fertile and barren territory, and the fame productions, appear every where through the whole province. The Imam, however, feems to be mafter of the richeft, the moft agreeable, and the moft interefting part of this tract of country.

It would not be eafy to explain diftinctly the extent and limits of this fovereign's territories, as they are fo interfected by the domains of a number of petty princes. On the north fide, they

they meet the territory of Hafchid-u-Bekil; weftward they are bounded by the principality of Abu-Arifch and the Arabic Gulph; to the fouth by the principality of Aden; and on the eaft by the territories of Dsjof and Jafa.

The general divifion of Yemen into *Tehama*, the Lowlands, and *Djebal*, the Highlands, obtains in the Imam's dominions, as well as elfewhere. Upon this grand divifion depends the fubdivifion of the kingdom of Sana into thirty governments or counties. Tehama contains fix of thefe governments, and the highland country twenty-four.

Thefe fmall governments are not all alike populous or remarkable. It would be a tedious and fuperfluous labour, therefore, to enumerate the names of all the towns and villages contained in them. I fhall content myfelf with taking notice of the principal of thofe, after I have given fome general account of the Sovereign of thefe dominions, and of the nature of his government.

As there are, in the territory of the Imam, many Schiechs difperfed among the mountains, who acknowledge not his authority, and are but in a very flight degree dependent upon him, I fhall be more careful to take notice of thefe independent Lords, than of the petty towns and villages. The reader will be more entertained by an account of the

the political conftitution under which this fingular people are united, than he could poffibly be by a lift of Arabic names.

CHAP. II.

Origin and Hiftory of the Imams.

In the abftract of the revolutions of Arabia, I have briefly mentioned that by which the expulfion of the Turks was accomplifhed. This event took place in 1630; and, from this period, are we to date the elevation of the prefent royal family of Sana. Their great anceftor is *Khaffem Abu Mahomed*, who was the chief author of that revolution.

Khaffem was defcended from Mahomet by Imam *Hadi*, who is buried at Saade, where his pofterity ftill reign. From him are fprung both the Imams of Saade, and the princes of Kaukeban, whom the Turks could never fubdue. Khaffem lived as a private perfon, upon the revenue of an eftate which had been left him by his anceftors, upon the mountain of *Schaehara*, northeaft from Loheya. Although but a private individual, he enjoyed the friendfhip of the independent Schiechs in the Highlands; and, feeing the Turks to be odious to his countrymen, he, with the aid of thofe Schiechs, attacked the Pachas, and,

and, by degrees, expelled them out of all the cities of Yemen. Thus attaining the dignity of a Sovereign Prince, and affuming the title of Sejid Khaffem, he ftill continued, however, to refide upon the mountains of Schaehara, and died there, after a reign of nine years. The gratitude of the nation honoured him with the epithet *Great;* and he has accordingly been denominated *Khaffem el Kbir*, or Khaffem the Great.

After this revolution, the ancient royal family of Kaukeban, being obliged to yield its prerogatives to the family of Khaffem, the eldeft fon of Khaffem affumed the title of *Imam*, and the name of *Metwokkel Allah*. The Imam is properly the clerygman who fays public prayers in the mofques. The royal fucceffors of Mahomet have continued the practice of performing thefe religous fervices, in proof that they enjoy fpiritual, no lefs than temporal power. Various Arabian Princes, who dare not affume the title of Caliph, content themfelves with that of Imam, or *Emir el Mumenim*, Prince of the Faithful. All thofe Sovereigns, thus invefted with fpiritual authority, whether Caliphs or Imams, obferve the ancient cuftom of changing their name, like the Popes in Chriftendom, when they mount the throne. This change feems to indicate, that the whole character of the man is entirely altered,

upon

upon his being invefted with an employment, which impreffes a degree of fanctity upon the character.

Imam Metwokkel Allah proceeded to deliver his country from the Turks, who do not appear to have made any very vigorous efforts to maintain themfelves in fo remote a conqueft, by which they were rather lofers than gainers. The Arabs honour that Imam as a faint: To fpare the public revenue, he, like many other Mahometan Monarchs, earned his livelihood by his labour, employing himfelf in making caps. He had only one wife, and fhe contented herfelf with one houfehold fervant. Metwokkel Allah refided at *Doran*, and reigned thirty years.

His fon *Mejid Billah* fucceeded him; was no lefs fcrupulous than his father with refpect to the revenues of the ftate; and reigned feven years.

His fucceffor was his coufin *Mahadi Achmet*, who, after reigning likewife feven years, and, notwithftanding his devout turn of mind, extending by his conquefts the limits of the kingdom, was fucceeded by

His nephew *Mejid Billah*. He was proclaimed Imam by the name of *Mahadi Hadi*. This prince had reigned only two years, when *Mahadi Mahomed*, fon of Imam Mahadi Achmed, dethroned him, and affumed his place.

This Imam Mahadi Mahomed refided at *Mou-ahheb*, and reigned thirty years. The French vifited his court in 1707: An account of the circumftances of which vifit has been publifhed by *La Roque*. Hamilton fpeaks alfo of this prince, and fays, that he was eighty years of age in the year 1714. Mahadi Mahomed was continually at war with the confederates of Hafchid-u-Bekil. In the beginning of this conteft, he put his nephew Khaffem at the head of his army, and he proved victorious; but the Imam ungratefully fhut up the fuccefsful general in the citadel of Damar. At a fubfequent period, the Imam's fon being defeated by the confederates, that prince was obliged to releafe Khaffem, and intruft him again with the command of his forces. Khaffem was again victorious; but, before he could return to his uncle's court, another perfon, of the fame family, from Schæhhara, had poffeffed himfelf of the throne, affuming the name of *El Nafer*. However, the ufurper had fcarcely enjoyed the fupreme power two years, when Khaffem expelled him, and afcended the throne under the name of El Metwokkel.

Imam El Metwokkel chofe Sana for the place of his refidence, and there reigned in tranquility for ten years.

After his death, *El Manfor* his fon afcended the throne. But, hardly was he feated upon it,

when

when a nephew of Mahadi Mahomed, with the affiftance of the prince of Kaukeban, made himfelf mafter of all the country except Sana. El Manfor, however, found means to feize the perfons of the ufurper and his protector; and caft them both into confinement. He, with the fame good fortune, repreffed the rebellion of another of his coufins, and of one of his brothers; and fhut thefe alfo up for the reft of life. He reigned one and twenty years.

CHAP. III.

Of El Mahadi, the reigning Imam.

IMAM EL MANSOR left feveral fons, the eldeft of whom, *Ali*, had naturally the beft right to fucceed him. His mother was the firft wife that his father had married, and daughter to the prince of Kaukeban : Confequently he was lineally defcended from Mahomet both by father and mother. But, the princefs, who was living at Sana in 1763, had not influence or addrefs enough to fecure the fucceffion to her fon, although it was the general wifh of the country that he fhould be fovereign.

A fon, who was named Abbas, had been born to El Manfor by a negrefs flave. This woman artfully concealed her mafter's death, till the *Ka-*

di Jachja, one of El Manfor's principal minifters, had time to fecure the troops, and the governors of the provinces, in the intereft of her fon Abbas, whom fhe then made to be proclaimed Imam, by the name of El Mahadi. Prince Ali was thrown into confinement, in which he died in the year 1759.

In the beginning of El Mahadi's reign, the prince of Kaukeban repeatedly difputed with him the title of Imam. But, being twice defeated, and his beard being burnt in the fecond engagement by the accidental explofion of his magazine of powder, he renounced his pretenfions to the character of Imam, and made peace with the Monarch of Sana.

In the year 1750, an army of three thoufand Arabs from Nehhm and Deiban advanced nearly to Sana: But they were routed and difperfed by the Imam. Seven years after, the confederates of Hafchid-u-Bekil attacked the Imam, and routed his forces. But, in the year following, 1758, the Imam's general furprifed and routed the allies.

Imam El Mahadi Abbas was five and forty years of age, and had reigned feventeen years, in 1763. He was of a dark complexion, like his anceftors by the mother's fide, and did not at all refemble the other defcendants of Mahomet. Had it not been for fome negro traits, his coun-

tenance

tenance might have been thought a good one. He had twenty brothers, of whom fome that I faw were black as ebony, flat-nofed, and thick-lipped, like the Caffres of the South of Africa. He had married the daughter of a relation, one of the pretenders to the crown of *Taaes;* and, befide her, feveral other free women; but he kept fewer female flaves than his father had. El Manfor had more than two hundred of thefe in his haram.

The reigning Imam had a number of fons; but only four of them were fo much grown up as to be permitted to appear in public. His relations, who are numerous, live all at Sana; and fome of them are very well provided for. He has feveral uncles; but he leaves all his relations in private ftations, employing none of them in any public office.

On his acceffion to the throne, he continued Kadi Jachja, to whom he owed his advancement, for fome time in the poft of Prime Minifter. But, finding that his fubjects were difcontented with the adminiftration of *Jachja,* and ftill regretted Ali, who, before his death, had written an affecting letter to his brother; the Imam facrificed his minifter to the public hatred, depofing him, confifcating his effects, and throwing himfelf and his confidential fervant into prifon. The degraded minifter was reftored to liberty

foon

foon after our arrival at Sana. But, inftead of reftoring his effects, the Imam only allowed him a fmall penfion, which was fcarcely enough to make him live.

CHAP. IV.

Hiftory of Schiech Abd Urrab.

OF the enemies with whom Imam El Mahadi had to contend, the moft formidable, both by genius and courage, was Schiech Abd Urrab of *Hodsjerie*. When fpeaking of the fiege of *Taaes*, I mentioned by the way fomething of the adventures of this Schiech, who is regarded as a hero among his countrymen. I found his hiftory interefting, and fhall now enter into it more at length, becaufe it involves feveral particulars illuftrative of the principles of the Imam's government, and of the general manners of the Arabs.

Abd Urrab, fon to a *Nakib* or General, who was governor of a fmall province, fucceeded his father in the government. The Imam, pleafed with his fervices, conferred on him the government of *Kataba*, which was more confiderable; and at the fame time intrufted him with a commiffion to demolifh the caftles of fome neighbouring lords. The zeal with which he carried this

this order into execution, raifed him many enemies among the nobility; the moft bitter of whom was a Nakib, of the ancient family of *Wadei*, who, among others, had loft his caftle.

This Nakib prepoffeffed the Imam againft Abd Urrab, by accufing him of rebellion; and obtained three thoufand men to reduce him to obedience. With this army, he befieged the pretended rebel for eleven months in Kataba, the capital of the diftrict under his government. When Abd Urrab could no longer hold out, he fallied forth with fix hundred men, made his way through the midft of the enemy, and retired to the diftrict of Hodsjerie, where his friends opened to him the gates of their fortreffes, and acknowledged him their Schiech. Another army, fent by the Imam to befiege him here, was as unfuccefsful as the firft.

As yet, the new Schiech had only ftood upon the defenfive; but, beginning now to feel his ftrength, he attacked the dominions of the Imam, made himfelf mafter of various places, and levied heavy contributions. The Imam, unable to reduce him to obedience, entered into an alliance againft him with the prince of *Aden*. Abd Urrab upon this entered Aden, befieged the fovereign in his capital, and forced a large fum of money from him. The Imam,

mam on this occasion entirely abandoned his ally.

In the account of the siege of *Taaes*, I have a' y lated in what manner the Imam concl. a peace with the Schiech, and how the lat..r took that city. The conditions, I may here add, were, that the Imam should treat the Schiech as a friend, acknowledge him Shiech of Hodsjerie, and renounce all his own pretensions to the sovereignty of that province. This engagement the Imam not only confirmed with seven oaths; but, according to a prevalent custom in the East, sent to the Schiech the copy of the Koran upon which he had sworn, and the rosary which he used at prayers, as pledges of his sincerity. Moreover, his two generals, *El Mas*, and *Achmed el Hamer*, also bound themselves that the Imam should abide by his promise.

Trusting to so many oaths, to those pledges of faith, and to the assurances of the two generals, Abd Urrab yielded to the pressing invitations of the Imam, and repaired to his court. By the way he was treated with the highest marks of respect. The inhabitants of Sana went out to meet, and gaze upon him, as a hero. His valour, his address, his noble exploits, were generally talked of with passionate admiration.

It is not known whether the Imam had any previous intention of destroying him, or became

jealous

jealous of those praises, and began to fear that a party might be formed, even in his own capital, in behalf of the rebel. However it might be, the Schiech, soon after his arrival, was seized, bedaubed on the face and hands with red paint, and, in this condition, placed on a camel, with his face to the tail, and conducted through the streets. His sister, who was at this time in Sana, seeing her brother thus maltreated, sprang from the roof of a house, and fell dead at his feet. After being led about in this plight, and still farther abused with blows, the Schiech was thrown upon a dunghill, and, at the end of three days, beheaded.

This perfidious act of the Imam moved the indignation of his subjects. The two generals, who had pledged themselves for the safety of Abd Urrab, were particularly enraged. The first, Nakib *El Mas*, was commander of the national troops; the other, Nakib *Achmed El Hamer*, commanded the mercenaries from Haschid-u-bekil, and his brother Khassem was general of the confederates. These two considerate persons thought that it became them to shew their resentment.

El Hamer, therefore, reproached the Imam for his perfidious cruelty, but was immediately cast into prison. El Mas, now more enraged than ever, formed a party to dethrone the Imam;

but the prince preventing him, made coffee to be given him, upon a friendly vifit; by the effects of which the Nakib died before he could leave the palace.

As foon as Khaffem received notice of the imprifonment of his brother El Hamer, he attacked the Imam's dominions with the forces of the confederates; but happening to lofe his fon in a fkirmifh, he retreated home. The Imam, fearing new movements on the part of the allies of Hafchid-u-bekil, fet Nakib El Hamer at liberty, by beheading him in prifon. Since that time, the allies have never ceafed avenging his death, by inroads upon the dominions of the Imam; in which they burnt feveral cities, foon after our arrival in Arabia.

The conduct of the Imam, in refpect to this unfortunate Schiech of Hodsjerie, has rendered him odious to his neighbours and fubjects, and may probably occafion his depofition from the throne, and premature death.

CHAP. V.

Of the Conflitution and Government of the Dominions of Sana.

THE throne of Yemen is hereditary. If generally approved of by the fubjects, the eldeft legitimate fon of an Imam is his rightful fucceffor. But

But, the revolutions which I have briefly narrated, shew, that this order of succession is often violated. In the despotic governments of the East, indeed, no order can be closely observed, because there are no fundamental laws. The practice of polygamy has also a tendency to confound the order of succession in Asia, as it often happens, that brothers, by different mothers, found their pretensions to succeed their father upon grounds equally false, or equally specious. The blind preference of a father, sunk into dotage, or the intrigues of a favourite, in such cases, determine the difference.

The Imam is an absolute prince, and the more so for uniting in his own person supreme authority, both spiritual and temporal, over his subjects. His jurisdiction in ecclesiastical matters, however, extends not over the dominions of other sovereigns of the same sect. These states have each a Mufti or Cadi for its spiritual use.

Although the Imam be absolute, he is checked in the exercise of his authority by the supreme tribunal of Sana, of which he is only president. This tribunal, consisting of a certain number of Kadis, possesses the sole power of life and death. The Imam may not order any of his subjects for execution, but such as have been condemned in consequence of a criminal prosecution before this Court. The Kadis are generally esteemed to be perfons of incorruptible integrity, of blamelefs lives, and devoted to the faithful difcharge of their duties. They are not changed here fo often as in Turkey, but hold their offices ufually for life.

Yet, when one of thefe Monarchs is difpofed to abufe his authority, he can break through any reftraints impofed upon him by this tribunal. The affeffors are nominated by the Imam, and removeable at his pleafure. He has it thus in his power to extort their fuffrages by threatening them with difgrace. But, the fovereigns of Sana have never found their advantage in having recourfe to violent meafures. Acts of tyranny have commonly ended in the depofition of the Prince who hazarded them. This fate feems to await the prefent Imam, whofe cruelty and extortion have nearly wearied out the patience of his fubjects.

At the Imam's court, public offices are many, and titles of honour few. The firft Minifter has no other title but *Fakih ;* an appellation fo vague, that his fecretaries, and men of learning who think themfelves in any degree above the vulgar, affume it as well as the Minifter. The other Minifters, the Secretary of State, the Superintendant of pious eftablifhments, the Surveyor-general of public buildings, the Infpector of the camels, and, by confequence, all thofe who occupy the firft
em-

employments, are, in the same manner, only Fakihs, without any other title of honour to distinguish them.

Every petty district in the dominions of the Imam has its governor. If not a Prince, or one of the higher nobility, this governor is called *Wali* and *Dola;* or sometimes Emir, when he happens to be a person of low birth. I have already remarked, that the Sovereigns of Sana find it generally the best policy to confer those governments upon men who have risen merely by personal merit, rather than upon their nobles.

A Dola in Yemen is much such a another as a Pacha in Turkey, only acting upon a narrower stage. He commands the forces stationed in in his province, regulates the police, and collects the taxes. From lucrative governments, the Dolas are recalled every two or three years, to prevent their accumulating too much wealth. When the Imam continues a Dola in his office, he sends him a horse, a sabre, and robes. All are obliged to render an account, from time to time, of their administration; and, when guilty of high misdemeanors, or convicted of malverfations in office, they are punished by imprisonment, or by confiscation of their property, but seldom capitally. Sometimes a Dola, who has been thus disgraced, is raised from prison to an office

office of greater confequence than that of which he was divefted. This cuftom marks the character of defpotifm, where honour, and degradation by punifhment, of confequence, are utterly unknown.

In every little town, a Sub-dola, with a fmall garrifon, confifting fometimes of only five or fix foldiers, refide, to maintain order. The chief of a large village is a Schiech; he of a fmall one, a *Hakim.*

The Dolas of confiderable governments are attended by a *Bafkateb* or comptroller, whofe bufinefs is to keep a ftrict eye upon their conduct, and to inform the Imam of what is going forward. This fpy often fucceeds the Governor who has been removed upon his reprefentation; but another Bafkateb is, at the fame time, fent to do for him what he did for his predeceffor.

Every city in which a Dola refides has alfo a a Kadi, dependent on the chief Kadi of Sana. The Kadi is fole judge in civil and ecclefiaftical affairs; nor may the Dola interfere to contradict his fentences, or render them inefficacious. The Kadis in the provinces, no lefs than in the capital, are in high reputation for wifdom and integrity.

In the fea-port towns, the *Emir Bahrr*, who is infpector of the port, enjoys the chief authority under the Dola. In other towns, the chief Magi-
ftrate

ſtrate is denominated *Schiech el Belled*. He it is who levies the taxes, and determines what each individual muſt pay. The *Emir es Souk*, regulates ſales and markets. In Yemen the poſt of keeper of the priſon is honourable, and an object of ambition.

CHAP. VI.

Of the Revenues of the Imam.

IT is no doubt difficult for a traveller to gain any tolerably accurate knowledge of the public revenue of a ſtate in which he ſpends only a ſhort time. In Arabia it is peculiarly difficult; as he muſt here be very cautious in putting queſtions, that he may not render himſelf ſuſpected among a nation of whom ſo few have any knowledge of public affairs.

I however had the advantage of conſulting upon this head a man who had held employments, in which he could not avoid making himſelf acquainted with the ſtate of the Imam's finances. This perſon was *Orǣki* the Jew, ſurveyor-general of the buildings, who had been the favourite of two ſucceſſive Imams, and of whoſe adventures I have given ſome account in the narrative of our journey to Sana.

By

By this Jew's calculation, the revenues of Imam El Mahadi Mahomet amounted to 830,000 crowns in the month. But the reigning family having loft a number of provinces, *Kataba, Aden, Abu Arifch,* and *Taæs,* with part of *Bellad Anes* and *Harras,* and having beftowed the diftricts of *Ofab* and *Mechader* in fief, El Manfor's monthly income was thus reduced to 300,000 crowns. The prefent Imam had recovered fome of the difmembered territories, and had acquired others which had never before belonged to the empire. His revenue might therefore be nearly 500,000 crowns a-month.

But from this I cannot make an eftimate of the Imam's wealth; for Oræki the Jew could give me no information concerning his expenditure. In the provinces, I was told, every Dola pays the troops belonging to his government; defrays the charges of the police; and, after deducting all that the public expences require, remits the furplus to the Imam.

This revenue arifes from a land and a poll tax of long ftanding, and from duties payable upon articles of merchandife. Coffee affords a very confiderable tax. Before it can be put a-board a fhip for exportation, the Imam muft receive a fourth part of the price for which it was fold. It is remarkable, that Pliny even mentions it as

an

an old cuftom for the Arabs to grant their princes a fourth of the value of their productions (L.)

CHAP. VII.

Of the Military Force of Sana.

THE Imam keeps up a body of regular troops; but their precife number I could not learn. According to common opinion, it confifts ordinarily of four thoufand infantry, raifed chiefly in Hafchid-u-Bekil, and of one thoufand cavalry.

The principal commanding officers of this army were the four Schiechs of *Hamdan*, *Wada*, *Sefian*, and *Khaulan*. Befide thefe four general officers of high birth, many *Nakibs* or officers of inferior defcent, fome of whom had even been flaves in their youth, were alfo in the army. Nakib is the higheft title that the Imam can confer. Schiech is a title that can only come by defcent, and is peculiar to fovereign princes and independent lords.

In time of peace, a foldier ferving in the cavalry has nothing to do but to take care of his horfe, and attend the Imam or Dola to the mofque, according as he happens to be quartered at Sana, or in one of the provinces. The Arabs are extremely attentive to the breeding and management of their horfes. Each horfe is under

under the care of a particular groom. Their heads are left at liberty; but, to hinder them from kicking, they are confined almoft clofe to the ground by the legs. After conducting their mafter home from the mofque, the cavalry perform their exercife, which confifts merely in riding after one another at full gallop with their lances couched. As the nights are very cold in Yemen, cloths are always put upon the horfes, except when they are ridden.

Moft of thofe who ferve in the cavalry have likewife civil employments, in which they occupy themfelves in time of peace. Their arms are lances and fabres. Some carry piftols in the holfters of the faddle. They know nothing of the ufe of uniforms; every one dreffes after his own fancy.

The infantry in the garrifons are equally unemployed; they never ftand as centinels but at the gates of cities. The Dola is attended by foot-guards likewife to the mofque; they march in rank and file. Four men in arms leap before them with antic geftures. On his return from the mofque, they falute him with fome irregular difcharges of mufquetry. This too is all the exercife ufed by the infantry.

They are ftill more unfuitably clothed than the cavalry. The greater part wear nothing but a piece of linen about their loins, and a

handker-

handkerchief upon their heads. Some are a little better dreſſed, with a blue cap of linen and a ſhirt.

The Arabs have a ſingular way of diſplaying their courage in engagements, not unlike the *devotement* to the infernal gods among the ancients. A ſoldier willing to ſignalize his attachment to his maſter, binds up his leg to his thigh, and continues to fire away upon the enemy, till either they be routed, or he himſelf be ſlain upon the field of battle. I could take this only for a fable when it was firſt told me; but I was afterwards convinced of its truth, by a late inſtance in the caſe of a Schiech of Haſchid-u-Bekil, in the Imam's ſervice, who devoted himſelf in this manner, in a battle againſt his own countrymen. Six ſlaves charged muſkets for him, which he continued to fire upon the enemy, till being at laſt deſerted by the Imam's troops, and even by his own ſervants, he was cut in pieces.

Thoſe armies uſe no artillery. The Arabs know not how to manage cannons. In ſome towns they have renegadoes or vagabond Turks for gunners, little leſs ignorant than themſelves.

The Imam, as he has no dread of enemies or corſairs upon the Arabic Gulph, needs not to keep up a naval force. His ſubjects are in general

neral unſkilled in navigation, as I have had occaſion to remark. The fiſhermen only diſcover
ſome degree of courage and dexterity, ventu-
ring far out at ſea in ſmall canoes, ſcarcely fur-
niſhed with oars.

CHAP. VIII.

Of the Arts and Commerce of Yemen.

NOTWITHSTANDING the natural abilities of
the Arabs, the arts receive no encouragement,
and are totally neglected in the Imam's dominions, and no leſs throughout the neighbouring
countries. Books are ſcarce in Arabia, becauſe
the Arabs have a diſlike of printed characters.
Their intricate alphabetical writing is beſt performed with the hand; they can hardly read
books from our preſſes. It was for this reaſon,
that the attempt of *Ibrahim Effendi* to introduce
printing at Conſtantinople failed of ſuccefs, and
the renegado was ruined by the project. The
Hebrew characters indeed are much eaſier caſt,
and therefore the Jewiſh preſſes at Conſtantinople, Smyrna, and Salonica, may poſſibly maintain their ground (M.)

The devotees among the Muſſulmans, and
chiefly the ſect of the Sunnites, have a ſtrong
abhorrence againſt images; in conſequence of
which

which there is neither painter nor sculptor in Yemen; but a great many inscriptions are engraven.

The Turks have some musicians; but the Arabs never apply to music as a separate art. In Yemen, I never heard any musical instrument but the drum and the pipe.

Much gold and silver work is prepared here; but the workers in these precious metals are all Jews and Banians. All the current coin too is struck by Jews.

All Arabian workmen sit while they work; a habit not consistent with very great activity. In walking, they have their feet always bare; as the wearing of their sandals would be troublesome. Many work with their feet, with little less dexterity than with their hands.

The mills in Yemen are of a very simple construction. But I saw in Tehama an oil-press wrought by an ox; and it is surprising, that the same mode of operation has never yet been employed in the corn-mills.

The manufactures of a people of so little industry cannot but be very trifling. No sabres are manufactured in Yemen, nor any edged weapon, except a sort of crooked knives called *Jambea*. The making of match-firelocks has been attempted here within these few years; it succeeds but indifferently. It is only of late that

glassglafs-works have been eftablifhed at Mokha. Some coarfe cloth is manufactured here; but not fo much as is required for the ufe of the country. Broad-cloths are neither made nor worn here. The Englifh brought fome goods of this fort to Mokha, but were obliged to carry them back to India unfold.

A country, which affords fo few articles for fale, cannot have a great trade. Coffee is almoft the fole article exported from Yemen; a valuable commodity, in exchange for which many of thofe things which this country needs from abroad may well be obtained.

I have mentioned the imports in my account of the trade of Mokha. All the commerce of Yemen is carried on by this port, except only that fome fmall quantities of coffee are exported by Loheya and Hodeida. What has been faid, therefore, of the trade of Mokha, may be confidered as relating to the trade of all Yemen.

CHAP. IX.

Of the Principal Towns in the Imam's Dominions.

IN the travels of our whole party, and in my own feparate excurfions, I traverfed a great part of the Imam's dominions, which I have occafionally defcribed in the courfe of my narrative. I am now therefore only to speak of some places more remote from the coast, which I had not occasion to visit myself, and which yet seem to deserve notice. I shall mention nothing but what I learned from persons who had full access to certain information.

I have already given a general description of Tehama, that vast plain through which I travelled from one end of it to the other. I have therefore nothing to add to what has been said concerning the governments of *Mokha, Hæs, Jebid, Beit el Fakih, Hodeida,* and *Loheya.*

In the highlands I saw and have described the governments of *Sana, Damar, Jerim, Mechader, Dsjobla, Taæ, Bellad Aklan, Udden, Harras,* and *Mofhak.* The following are the other towns and districts, which I know only by hearsay.

Doran, in which several Imams reside, is a very ancient city, situate on the declivity of a mountain, not far from the roads between Sana and Damar. The district is under the goverment of a particular Schiech, as is also *Dsjebbe. Scherki,* a great mountain in its vicinity.

Kataba is a city governed by a Dola, and defended by a strong citadel, lying in a fertile country, through which passes a fine river, whose waters are discharged into the sea at Aden. In this
district

diftrict is a range of wild and lofty mountains, bordering on the territorities of the Imam.

Hodsjerie was originally a diftrict and government belonging to Sana; became afterwards the domain of the famous Schiech Abd Urrab; but is now reunited to the dominions of the Imam. It contains *Dimlu*, a ftrong city, upon a mountain, which *Abulfeda* calls the King's Treafury; and *Mukatera*, a fortrefs faid to be impregnable, which ftands upon a lofty and precipitous hill, acceffible only by one narrow path, which is fhut up by a gate; but fertile on the fummit in corn, and plentifully fupplied with water.

Ofab is a diftrict held in fief from the Imam by one of his relations. In it are a fmall village, and three ftrong caftles, upon hills.

Kufma is a fmall town, ftanding upon a high hill. Its confines I had occafion to fee, where it meets Tehama. The mountains in it produce coffee, and extend far through the interior country. They are free Arabs who inhabit them. *Dsjebi*, a town, with a diftrict of confiderable extent, in which are a number of independent Schiechs, lies farther northward. Thefe two diftricts form together the country of *Rema*; the merchants of which are often mentioned in ancient hiftory. It is a fertile tract of country, abounding chiefly in grapes and coffee.

Homranc,

Homran is an ancient city, with a ruinous citadel. In a hill, in its vicinity, there are said to be three hundred and sixty refervoirs for water, cut in the rock. The diftrict in which it lies, approaches near to the road between Sana and Beit el Fakih. *Burra,* a large and fertile mountain, is comprehended in it.

In the province of *Hofæfch,* extended over the mountains of *Melhan,* ftands *Sefekin,* a town of confiderable fize.

Manacha is alfo a confiderable town, and famous for its fairs. It is the feat of the Dola of *Harras.* In the heart of his government lies the diftrict of *Safan,* in which Schiech Mecrami has an almoft impregnable caftle, which he took, fome years fince, by furprife.

North-weft from Sana is a mountainous and extenfive tract of country, which is confidered as belonging to the Imam. But many Schiechs are in it, who acknowledge not this Prince for their Sovereign. He poffeffes, however, a number of towns in it, and governs thefe by Dolas, whofe authority is commonly confined within the walls of the places of their refidence. Such are the following:

Tulla, a ftrong town, with a citadel, in which a Dola refides, whofe jurifdiction extends over another fmall town with a citadel. The reft of the environs belongs to Schiechs. In this diſtrict is *Schhæhhava*, a large mountain, on which are more than three hundred villages, under the dominion of various Schiechs; famous, too, as having been the ſeat of *Khaſſem*, the founder of the reigning family.

Khamir, a fortified town, ſituate in the middle of the territories of the confederates of Haſchid-u-Bekil.—It coſt the Imam no ſmall trouble to retain poſſeſſion of this town.

Medem, the capital of *Hamdan*, in which the Schiech has a palace. This principality is two days journey in length, and one in breadth. It is reckoned among the dominions of Sana, becauſe the reigning chief has been made to acknowledge himſelf the Imam's vaſſal.

Amran, a town with a citadel in a fertile country, which once belonged to the allies of Hafchid-u-Bekil. *Saad el Khammel*, one of the moſt ancient and famous kings of Yemen, is interred in this diſtrict.

CHAP. X.

Of the Princes and Schiechs within the Dominions of the Imam.

ONE of the moſt ſingular and curious facts in the hiſtory of Arabia, is, its having always been, even from the moſt remote antiquity, parcelled

out

out among such a number of petty princes and independent lords. The history of Arabia exhibits, through its whole course, nearly the same political arrangements which appear to have prevailed in Europe, for some centuries, in the middle age; with this difference only, that the Schiechs have seldom been in a state of vassalage, and never knew the feudal government.

The nature and local circumstances of Arabia are favourable to the spirit of independence, which distinguishes its inhabitants from other nations. Their deserts and mountains have always secured them from the encroachments of conquest. Those inhabiting the plains have indeed been subdued; but their servitude has been only temporary; and the only foreign powers to whose arms they have yielded, have been those bordering on the two gulphs between which this country lies.

Independent Schiechs are therefore to be found among the *Bedouins*, or wandering Arabs, who escape oppression in consequence of the barrenness of their lands, and of the facility with which they retire into the deserts, whither no armies can follow them; and among the *Kobails*, or Arabian Highlanders, who inhabit wild and lofty chains of mountains, yet of sufficient fertility to afford subsistence to a frugal race

race, blocked up by their enemies in this retreat.

Of the latter are the Schiechs established within the Imam's dominions. The hills which they occupy are high and precipitous, yet cultivated up to their loftiest peaks, and abounding in productions of various sorts. These hills are very difficult of access; and the passes through the vallies are usually barred, either by fortifications, or by castles upon insulated rocks. A circumstance, to shew with what ease the Schiechs defend themselves, is, that the Imams, altho' they had little difficulty in expelling the Turks from the low country, have never been able, with all their efforts, to reduce those Highlanders, except only a small number who have been brought to recognize their territorial superiority.

I could not learn the names, either of all those Schiechs, or of their dominions. From the few, however, that came to my knowledge, one may conceive how numerous they are; since the domains of so many are intermixed through territories of no greater extent than those of the Imam of Sana.

There is not one independent Schiech in the Tehama. But, not far from the royal residence, in the province of Sana, is a tribe of Bedouins, denominated *Beni Dabbean.*

Niebuhr's Travels. P. 101

In the government of *Bellad Anes* are two Schiechs of eminence, the Schiech of *Bellad Anes*, and of the mountain of *Scherki*.

The lofty and extensive mountain of *Sumara* belongs in part to Schiech *Wadey*, and partly to the Schiech of *Beni Haffan:* Thefe are both vaffals to the Imam. But the town of *Hofæch*, in the vicinity of this mountain, is ruled by an independent Schiech.

The famous hill of *Sabbar*, which I mentioned in my account of Taæs, is faid to be parcelled out among more than a hundred free and hereditary Schiechs, perfectly independent of the Imam, although furrounded on all hands by his territories. This fertile mountain confifts of a chain of hills of various heights.

In the government of *Hodsjerie* are the Schiechs of *Manfora* and *Afæs*. The diftrict of *Beni Jufof*, and the hill of *Habbefchi*, contain alfo a good number of hereditary independent lords.

I have already fpoken of the prince of *Beni Aklan*, who refides at *Dorebat*, and of the independent Schiechs who poffefs Mount *Kamara*, lying within this principality. In giving an account of my excurfion through the highlands of Yemen, in company with Mr Forfkal, I at the fame time mentioned the prince of *Udden*, and his dominions. In nobility of family, and dignity

nity of rank, thefe two princes are inferior to none in Arabia.

The prince of *Ofab* is of the Imam's family, and a vaffal to that prince; his principality being a territory that has been detached from the dominions of Sana.

In no diftrict are there a greater number of confiderable Schiechs than in *Kufma*, the moft weftern range of the coffee mountains. This diftrict, confifting entirely of precipitous hills, planted with coffee-trees to the very fummits, is naturally populous, in confequence of affording fo profitable a produce as coffee, in fuch abundance. Hence it is, that thofe gentry are here fo rich and numerous. I was told of more than thirty, who draw large revenues from the markets within their dominions, at which an aftonifhing quantity of coffee is fold. Thefe Schiechs are all independent, and refide in fortified caftles upon the mountains.

The government of *Dsjebi* being, with refpect to external appearance, foil, and productions, precifely of the fame character as Kufma, is, like it, full of Schiechs of eminence. I learned the names of a dozen of them. They live in the fame ftyle as the others.

On Mount *Harras*, a large hill, fertile in vines, are likewife fome caftles, belonging to independent

dependent lords. This, among other diftricts, was feized by Schiech *Mecrami.*

In the territories which have been conquered by the Imams from the allies of Hafchid-u-bekil, are ftill many free domains. Among ten or a dozen of the moft eminent Schiechs, are the Schiechs *Beni Afchiab, Shemfan,* and *Marani.* Near *Tulla,* is alfo *Sejid Machfen* of *Hadsje,* a principality anciently held under the reigning family.

The mountain *Schæhhara,* with its three hundred villages, is fhared out among a great many Schiechs, moft of whom were related to the royal family before its elevation to throne of Sana.

The prince of Hamdan is diftinguifhed for his power, and the antiquity of his family; he being defcended from the tribe of Hamdan, which was known long before the days of Mahomet. Yet, with thefe advantages, he has been reduced to a ftate of vaffalage, probably becaufe his country was too plain and too narrow for defence againft an enemy. In this principality is *Muakeb,* a city of a fingular conftruction; its houfes are all cut out in the natural rock.

From this detail, it appears, that the ftate of Yemen is not unlike to that of Germany. The Arabs want only a head; they have princes, a body of nobility, and an ariftocratic league.
But

But their conftitution is not of recent origin; nor did it take its rife in the forefts. It is as ancient as fociety itfelf, and will probably laft while the country endures in which nature has eftablifhed it.

SECTION XX.

OF THE PROVINCE OF HADRAMAUT.

CHAP. I.

Of the General Character, and of the Commerce of this Province.

HADRAMAUT is bounded, on the weft by Yemen, on the fouth-eaft by the ocean, on the north-eaft by Oman, and on the north by a great defart. It comprehends a wide extent of country, efpecially if, with the Arabians, we include in it the diftrict of *Mahhra*. Mahhra feems to be like Tehama, a fandy plain, extending in breadth, from the fhores of the ocean backward to where the hill country commences.

Thefe

These plains have probably been once covered by the sea.

Such being the state of the coast, and of the Highlands, Hadramaut, like Yemen, exhibits great diversities of soil and surface. Some parts of it are dry and desart; but the hills are extremely fertile, and are interfected by well-watered vales.

The inhabitants of this province, too, are divided, like those of Yemen, into Arabs settled in towns, wandering Bedouins, and Kobails or Highlanders. A native of Hadramaut, with whom I had opportunities of conversing, described his country as the seat of science and religion. The other Arabs are less favourable in their accounts, and not without reason, if one may judge from the coarseness of the dialect spoken in this province. It differs so considerably from that of Yemen, that I needed an interpreter to assist me in conversing with the person who entertained me with the above pompous elogium of his country. The religion of his countrymen must be a tissue of fantastic pieces of superstition; for the Sunnites are the prevalent sect among them.

Arabia the Happy, comprehending, as I have above remarked, the two provinces of Yemen and Hadramaut, enjoyed, in the remotest times, a very extensive commerce. Its exports confifted not only in its own productions, but in thofe of India likewife, which were brought into its harbours, upon the fhores of the ocean, by veffels from India. As the navigation of the Arabic Gulph was always reckoned dangerous, thofe articles of merchandife were conveyed by land into Egypt and Syria. The caravans were a fource of wealth to the whole nation; the inhabitants of the towns gained by purchafes and fales, and the Bedouins by hiring out their camels. There is, therefore, the greateft truth in the accounts of the ancients, which defcribe fo pompoufly the opulence of the Happy Arabia, although its prefent ftate be far from flourifhing.

Since the Europeans have difcovered a different rout to India, the trade of South Arabia has neceffarily declined. To Yemen the lofs is made up by the exportation of fuch immenfe quantities of coffee; a traffic begun two centuries ago, and ftill encreafing: But Hadramaut, producing little coffee, has no fuch refource, and is therefore not likely to recover fuddenly from the difadvantages which it has fuffered by the lofs of its Indian trade.

Yet this province ftill carries on fome trade in its native productions; for thefe, fhips from *Mafkat* vifit its harbours upon the ocean. The little coffee which it affords, incenfe, gum Arabic,

bic, dragon's-blood, myrrh, and aloes, are the articles of this trade. The incenfe of Arabia is not of the very beft quality; but the aloes of *Soccatra*, an ifle belonging to the princes of Hadramaut, has been always in the very higheft eftimation.

The inhabitants of Hadramaut have likewife fome trivial manufactures. Yemen is furnifhed from this province with coarfe cloths, carpets, and the knives called *Jambea*, which are hung from the girdle. But the inhabitants of Hadramaut being averfe to a maritime life, the trade from their fea ports is all carried on in foreign bottoms (M.)

CHAP. II.

Of the Principal Towns in Hadramaut.

THERE are in Hadramaut a good many confiderable towns, which were known to the ancients, perhaps better than they are at prefent. Notwithftanding the pains which I took, I could learn the names only of a few of thofe places. What I know of the reft, I had from fome perfons not very well acquainted with the prefent ftate of Hadramaut. I fhall repeat what was told me concerning fome of thofe cities.

Schibam.

Schibam, a large city, and the feat of a powerful prince, is eight days journey diftant from *Sana*, and ten from *Mareb*. An Arabian from Mareb informed me, that he had not found a fingle village in *Dsjof*, on his way from his native city; but that, as he travelled through Hadramaut, he had been in feveral confiderable towns. *Schibam* feems to be the *Saba* of the ancients, from which the Sabeans were denominated. This people occupied the fouthern parts of Arabia, before Mareb became the capital of their empire.

Doan, in which a Schiech refides, is five and twenty days journey eaftward from Sana, and eleven from *Kefchim*. An inhabitant of Doan, whom I met with in Yemen, told me, that it was a larger and more elegant city than Sana.

Dafar is a well known fea-port town, from which incenfe, called in Arabia *Oliban* or *Liban*, is exported. This incenfe is not nearly fo good as that of India. The Arabians are blamed for felling both their incenfe and their gum without purifying them. This negle&t occafions a deterioration in the quality, and a reduction in the price. A Schiech likewife refides in *Dafar*.

Kefchim is a fea-port town, and the feat of a fovereign prince. Its inhabitants are faid to be highly civilized, and to receive all ftrangers hofpitably.

pitably. The English sometimes visit this harbour.

Merbat and *Hasek* are two cities, known only for the traffic which their inhabitants carry on in incense produced in that neighbourhood. The quantity of this incense is not so considerable as that which comes from Dafar; but it is better in quality than that from *Schæhhr*. The great consumption of incense in the Indian temples, and even in private houses, through some countries in the East, is what chiefly occasions the demand for this article. It is not used in the mosques.

Ainad is a considerable town, thirteen days journey from *Keschim*, and seven from Schæhhr. An inhabitant of this town whom I saw in Maskat, told me, what divers other Arabians confirmed, that the tomb of the ancient prophet *Kachtan* or *Jaktan*, mentioned in the Koran, stands within a day's journey of *Ainad*. Even before the days of Mahomet, pilgrims used to visit this tomb. The inhabitants of Hadramaut still assemble at a certain time to perform their devotions there. A famous fair is held at it. It is remarked, that all pilgrimages to one place, for so many centuries, owe their continued existence to commerce.

This same Arab from Ainad named to me more than a score of cities, in the interior parts
of

of the province, which he had vifited. As I know
nothing of them but their names, I fhall not fet
down the bare lift.

There are alfo feveral fea-ports, concerning
which I could obtain no particular information.
What was particularly ftriking in the lifts of
names mentioned to me, was the remarkable refemblance of the names of many of the prefent
cities in Hadramaut, to thofe of the cities of A-
rabia fpoken of by the moft ancient hiftorians.
Many of thefe eftablifhments, in this province,
muft have exifted in the fame ftate from the
moft remote antiquity.

Thefe obfervations lead me to think, that a
journey through this province might prove at
leaft no lefs interefting than our journey through
Yemen. The difficulties attending fuch an expedition, could not be greater than thofe which
we had to ftruggle with. I was acquainted with
a Turk, who related to me with what eafe and
fafety he had vifited the feveral fea-port towns
in South Arabia. The inhabitants of that coaft,
remembering the wealth which ftrangers ufed
to bring thither in former times, and long accuftomed to receive them well, would undoubtedly give Europeans a favourable reception at
prefent.

CHAP.

CHAP. III.

Of the Sovereign Princes in Hadramaut.

THE Bedouins, and inhabitants of the hills, have here, as well as through the reft of Arabia, a number of independent Schiechs; but, not knowing particulars, I can fay nothing of them.

The coafts, and the adjacent country, are shared among fovereigns of higher dignity, whom travellers have called Kings, although they take only the title of Schiech or Sultan. The Schiech of Schibam I have already mentioned as one of the moft powerful.

Doan belongs to a Schiech, whom I believe to be a defcendent of Mahomet, and of the family of the Imams; for he who reigned in 1763 was called *Sejid Ifa el Amudi.* In a neighbouring city, are the tombs of all the princes of the illuftrious houfe of Amudi.

The Schiech of Dafar is alfo a Sovereign Prince; but I know not either his name, or the extent of his power.

He of *Kefchim,* called by fome travellers, King of *Fartak,* is the moft powerful. His dominions comprehend a confiderable number of cities, among which is that of Fartak; and hence the
fancied

fancied kingdom of Fartak, reprefented in various maps. One of the Princes of Kefchim may have, fome time or other, refided in that city, and may thus have given rife to the idea of a Sovereign of Fartak. Befide his poffeffions on the continent, the Schiech of Kefchim is likewife Lord of the ifland of *Soccatra*, or *Soccatora*, famous for its aloes. The prefumptive heir to the reigning Schiech is always governor of this ifland, which feems to have belonged to thefe Arabian Princes from time immemorial. Arrian relates that, in the period concerning which he writes, it was fubject to the Sovereigns of the incenfe country. The firft Portuguefe who vifited Arabia found the Prince of Kefchim ftill in the undifturbed poffeffion of this part of the ancient dominions of his family.

The principality of *Ainad* muft be extenfive, if the account may be credited, which I received from a native of the city of the fame name. But I have reafon to fufpect, that the Sovereign of Ainad is one of thofe Sultans of Jafa who have conquered fome territories in Hadramaut.

There are probably ftill other fovereign ftates in this widely extended province. But I had not opportunities of acquiring farther knowledge of a country, which, for many reafons, deferves to be better known.

SEC-

SECTION XXI.

OF THE PROVINCE OF OMAN.

CHAP. I.

Of Oman in general.

THE province of Oman is bounded on the east by the Ocean; on the north, by the Persian Gulph; on the west, and the south, by extensive deserts. I visited no part of it, but the environs of Maskat; and, therefore, do not speak concerning it from personal observation.

It is possessed by a number of petty Sovereigns, the most considerable of whom is the Imam of Oman or Maskat. The Princes of *Dsjau, Gabria, Gafar, Rank, Gabbi, Dahhara, Makaniat,* and *Seer,* have the title of *Schiech.*

The whole western side of Oman is one sandy plain, a day's journey in length, and extending from the village of *Sib* to the town of *Sohar.* The Imam's territories are mountainous to the very brink of the shore. The rivers continue to flow throughout the year, all, except that near which Sohar ſtands, which, traverſing an arid plain, loſes itſelf among the ſands, and reaches the ſea only in the rainy ſeaſon.

The country affords plenty of cheeſe, barley, lentiles, with ſeveral different ſorts of grapes. Of dates ſuch abundance is here produced, as to yield an annual exportation of ſeveral ſhips lading ; and there is variety of other fruits, and of pulſe. Here are alſo lead and copper mines. Fiſhes are ſo plentiful upon the coaſt, and ſo eaſily caught, as to be uſed not only for feeding cows, aſſes, and other domeſtic animals, but even as manure to the fields.

The inhabitants are of different ſects in religion, and mutually regard one another as heretics. The ſubjects of the Imam follow one Muſfulman doctor ; thoſe of the Schiechs another.

CHAP. II.

Of the Territories of the Imam of Oman, or Maſkat.

THE territory poſſeſſed by the Imam of Oman is pretty extenſive, and contains a good many towns, moſt of which are but little known. I ſhall mention only ſome few particulars, which I learned concerning the more remarkable among them.

Roſtak, a city at ſome diſtance from the ſea, is the ſeat of the Sovereign. In its neghbourhood

is

is *Dsjebbel Akdar*, the higheſt and largeſt mountain in Oman, and diſtinguiſhed for its fertility in fruits, eſpecially grapes. Sohar is an ancient and celebrated city, but greatly decayed.

South from Roſtak, ſtands *Kalbat*, an ancient city, which was once in a flouriſhing condition.

The Imam of Oman poſſeſſes alſo *Kiloa* and *Sinsjibar*, upon the eaſtern coaſt of Africa, which were, not long ſince, conquered by one of his anceſtors.

The moſt important and beſt known city in the dominions of this Imam is Maſkat; in conſequence of which, he is, by many travellers, called King of Maſkat. It ſtands at one end of a beautiful plain, beſide a ſmall gulph, encompaſſed with ſteep rocks, forming an excellent harbour, in which the largeſt veſſels may find ſhelter. This harbour is likewiſe protected by forts; and the city thus fortified both by art and nature.

Arrian calls it *Moſca*, and ſpeaks of it as being, even then, a great emporium of the trade of Arabia, Perſia, and India. Maſkat has ever enjoyed this advantage, and even at preſent, poſſeſſes a conſiderable trade. The Portugueſe made themſelves maſters of it in 1508. Two churches, one of which is now a magazine, and the other the houſe of the *Wali* or Governor, ſtill remain to fhow that *they* were once eftablifhed here. An hundred and fifty years after their conqueft of Mafkat, the Portuguefe were driven hence by the Arabs, through the treacherous aid of a Banian, who had been robbed of his daughter by the Portuguefe Governor.

In no other Mahometan city are the Banians fo numerous as in Mafkat; their number in this city amounts to no fewer than twelve hundred. They are permitted to live agreeably to their own laws, to bring their wives hither, to fet up idols in their chambers, and to burn their dead. If a Banian intrigues here with a Muffulman woman, government does not treat him with the fame feverity as he would meet with elfewhere.

With refpect to the Imam's revenue, I could learn nothing, but that the duties levied upon merchant-goods amount to about an hundred thoufand rupees. At Mafkat, Europeans pay five per cent. upon imports; Mahometans fix and a half; and Jews and Banians feven per cent. The Imam's natural fubjects pay fix per cent. in kind, upon dates exported; which are the principal article that the country affords (N).

CHAP.

CHAP. III.

Of the Revolutions of Oman.

THERE are in Oman three very ancient and illustrious families; those of *Gafari, Hamani,* and *Arrabi.* The latter pretends to be descended from the Koreisch of Mecca, who were famous before the days of Mahomet. However this may be, the family of Arrabi have long reigned at Maskat, but are not at present in possession of the supreme power. The events which degraded them from the throne are connected with the history of *Nadir Schah,* the last Monarch of Persia. In order to convey distinct ideas of them, it will be necessary to go back to some things that happened in the last century.

Imam *Malek,* of the house of Arrabi, was master of all Oman, and added to his dominions, by conquest, *Kunk, Kischme, Hormus,* and *Baharein.* His son still extended these conquests, making himself master of Kiloa and Sinsjibar, in Africa. But, in the reign of his grandson *Ben Seif,* the new Monarch of Persia, Schah Nadir, sent an army to conquer Oman. The Persians lost many of their number among the hills, and were repulsed. Ben Seif accordingly

ingly continued to occupy the throne till his death.

Upon his deceafe, *Mohammed Gafari*, prince of *Gabrin*, made himfelf mafter of the greater part of Oman, and affumed the title of Imam. His fon El Nafer proved unable to maintain the conquefts of his father. *Seif el Afdi*, fon to the laft Imam of the family of Arrabi, made himfelf be proclaimed Imam, and forced Nafer to content himfelf with his patrimony, the principality of Gabrin.

Imam Seif el Afdi was an indolent voluptuous prince. Not content with a numerous Harem, he would occafionally attempt the chaftity of his fubjects daughters. He addicted himfelf to the ufe of wine and ftrong liquors. He neglected his affairs; and, not paying his foldiers, who were *Caffer* flaves, fuffered them to harrafs and pillage his fubjects. This conduct rendered him fo odious, that Sultan *Murfched*, one of his relations, eafily procured himfelf to be proclaimed Imam, and took poffeffion of almoft all Oman.

Mafkat ftill remained in allegiance to Imam Seif; and he maintained himfelf in it, by means of four fhips of war, and of the profits of its trade. But, becoming yet more odious to the few fubjects who ftill obeyed him, by perfeverance in his imprudent conduct, he foon found it impoffible to ftand out longer. In this extremity,

he

he refolved rather to yield up his dominions to the Perfians, than to his relation Imam Murfched.

Sailing to Perfia, with fome veffels which ftill remained to him, he obtained from Nadir Schah a fleet, under the command of *Mirza Taki Khan*, Governor of Schiraz. The Perfian Admiral, upon arriving at Oman, made Imam Seif drunk, and feized Mafkat, with its citadels. Seif not knowing well what to do, purfued his rival Murfched with the Perfian forces, till Murfched, reduced to defpair by the lofs of his friends, died by a voluntary death. Imam Seif died himfelf foon after, at Roftak, oppreffed with the mortification of finding himfelf duped by the Perfians.

Taki Khan, on his return to Schiraz, revolted againft Nadir Schah, and fought to eftablifh himfelf in the fovereignty of *Farfiftan*. It is well known, how that the Perfian Monarch quafhed this rebellion, and punifhed its author. But thefe difturbances withdrew the attention of the Perfians from the affairs of Arabia, and made them neglect to keep up the garrifon in Marfkat.

CHAP.

CHAP. IV.

Of the Reigning Imam.

AT the period of Tœki Khan's expedition into Oman, there was at *Sohar* a governor of the name of *Achmed ben Sajid*, a native of a small town within the Imam's dominions. This Achmed, being a man of ability and enterprife, and feeing that, after the death of the two Imams, he fhould be under a neceffity of fubmitting to fuch potent enemies as the Perfians, made his peace with the invaders, and managed matters fo well, that Tœki Khan confirmed him in his government.

During the civil wars in Perfia, a prince of *Rank*, of the houfe of *Arrabi*, the Prince of *Seer*, and a Nobleman named *Bel Arrab*, had fhared among themfelves the fpoils of the laft Imam. Bel Arrab had even affumed the title.

Achmed, feizing the Perfian officers in Mafkat by furprife, forced the garrifon to furrender, and made himfelf mafter of the city, without any effufion of blood. Gaining to his intereft the firft Cadi, who officiates as Mufti in Oman, he obtained from him a decifion, that he, as the deliverer of his country, deferved to be
raifed

raised to the dignity of its Sovereign. In virtue of this decision, Achmed was proclaimed at Maſkat, Imam of Oman.

As ſoon as Imam Bel Arrab heard this news, he prepared to attack his rival with an army of four or five thouſand men. Achmed, too weak for reſiſtance, retired into a fortreſs among the hills, in which he was inveſted by his enemy, and would have been obliged to ſurrender himſelf, had he not happily eſcaped in the diſguiſe of a camel-driver. Being beloved in his former government, he found means to aſſemble ſome hundreds of men, and with theſe marched againſt Bel Arrab, whoſe army was ſtill encamped among the hills. He divided his little troop into detachments, who ſeized the paſſes of the vallies, and ſounded their trumpets. Bel Arrab, ſuppoſing himſelf to be circumvented by a ſtrong army, was ſtruck with a panic, fled, and was ſlain in his flight by a ſon of Achmed.

After the defeat and death of Bel Arrab, no perſon gave Imam Achmed ben Sajid any further diſturbance in the poſſeſſion of the throne of Oman, except a ſon of Imam Murſched, who has made ſome unſucceſsful efforts to deprive him of the ſovereign authority. Notwithſtanding theſe attempts, the reigning Imam has yielded up to his rival the town of *Nahhel*, with the territory belonging to it. A brother and two fons of the laft Imam, of the ancient family, are ftill living, in a private ftation indeed, but in circumftances fo opulent, that they maintain three or four hundred flaves. The reigning Imam has married the daughter of one of thofe princes; thus connecting his own family with the moft illuftrious perfons in his dominions. It may be prefumed, therefore, that the reigning family, although but newly royal, may continue to keep poffeffion of the throne.

In 1765, Imam Achmed had reigned fixteen years, to the full fatisfaction of his fubjects. He faw juftice promptly and uprightly adminiftered, without partiality to rank or religion. Theft was fcarce ever heard of. At Mafkat goods remained fafely in the ftreets by night; and few were at the pains to bolt their doors. The reigning Imam's troops confift chiefly of Caffre flaves, who are well paid, armed with matchfirelocks, and ftrictly difciplined. Imam Seif's flaves and foldiers were very thievifh; ftrangers had moft to fear from them who were guardians of the public fecurity.

To eke out his fcanty revenue, the Prince does not difdain to deal himfelf in trade. He keeps four fhips of war, and a number of fmall veffels, which, in time of peace, he employs in the conveyance of goods, chiefly to and from

the

the eastern coast of Africa, where he possesses still Kiloa and Sinjibar. Some other ships are kept to guard the coast; but this they do so negligently, or fearfully, that pirates venture into the very road of Maskat.

The inhabitants of Oman, although not fond of sea-fights, are nevertheless the best mariners in all Arabia. They have several good harbours, and employ many small vessels in the navigation between Jidda and Basra. To this last town there come annually fifty such vessels, called *Trænkis;* the structure of which I described in the account of our passage from Jidda to Loheya. They are sewed together without nails, the planks being bound with cords.

Two numerous tribes of Arabs are chiefly employed in carrying coffee by sea. One of these tribes once dwelled on the shores of the Persian Gulph; but, being harassed by turbulent neighbours, at length sought refuge in the dominions of the Imam of Omam.

CHAP. V.

Of the Principality of Seer.

THIS petty sovereignty extends from Cape *Musfendom* along the Persian Gulph. The Persians call it the country of *Dsjulfar,* another cape near

near Muffendom. The Europeans alfo have thus learned to call thefe people the Arabs of Dsjulfar.

The other Arabs call it *Seer*, from the town of the fame name, which has a good harbour, and is the feat of the Schiech. He formerly poffeffed, and indeed ftill retains, the ifle of *Scharedsje*, with fome confiderable places upon the oppofite fide of the Gulph, among which are *Kunk* and *Lundsjc*.

This country not long fince acknowledged the fovereign authority of the Imam; but it has withdrawn itfelf from this condition of dependence; and the Schiech often goes to war with his old mafters. Yet he is not ftrong enough to defend himfelf without affiftance; and therefore takes care to live in a good underftanding with the other independent Schiechs, efpecially with the Schiech of *Dsjau*, whofe dominions lie weftward from Oman.

The Prince of Seer makes fome figure among the maritime powers in thefe parts. His navy is one of the moft confiderable in the Perfian Gulph. His fubjects are much employed in navigation, and carry on a pretty extenfive trade.

SECT.

SECTION XXII.

OF THE PROVINCES OF LACHSA AND NEDSJED.

CHAP I.

Of Lachfa, in particular.

This country is bounded towards the eaft by the Perfian Gulph, towards the fouth by Oman, weftward by the province of Nedsjed, and northward by the territories of the wandering Arabs in the neighbourhood of Bafra.

It is alfo denominated *Hadsjar,* and fometimes *Bahhrein.* The latter of thefe names, in ftrict propriety, belongs only to the ifland of *Aual,* and the fmall ifles depending upon it.

Lachfa affords no great variety of productions. Its affes and camels are efteemed to be of an excellent breed; and, of the latter, fome thoufands are annually fold into Syria. In the interior parts of this province, the inhabitants live much upon dates: Upon the coafts, pearl-fifhing fishing is followed with advantage; and there is a considerable trade in foreign commodities.

With respect to religion, the inhabitants of Lachsa are divided. Those living in the towns are Shiites; but the peasants are, like the Bedouins, Sunnites. Here are also Jews, and a great many *Sabæans*, or Christians of St John.

This country was once a province of the Ottoman empire. The Arabs have long since, however, shaken off the Ottoman yoke. Many Turks, descended from the ancient Pachas, still remain in the province, and enjoy considerable estates, but have no share in the government.

The province of Lachsa belongs in sovereignty at present to the Schiech of the Arabian tribe of *Beni Khaled.* The reigning Schiech, in 1765, was *Arar.* The tribe of Beni Khaled is one of the most powerful in Arabia. They are so far spread through the desart, as often to harrass the caravans passing between Bagdad and Kaleb. The greater part of Lachsa is inhabited by Bedouins, and other petty tribes; but these all acknowledge the dominion of the Schiech of Beni Khaled.

I could learn nothing concerning the cities in the interior parts of this province. Lachsa, the seat of the reigning Schiech, is probably a large city, containing considerable buildings.

Katif,

Katif, a town of some magnitude, stands upon the coast, at the distance of about five German miles from the isle of Bahhrein. The inhabitants earn their subsistence by the pearl-fishery. When any are too poor to fish at their own risk and expence, they hire their labour to stranger-adventurers, who resort hither in the hotter months of the year, the season for the fishing. The air of this country is, however, believed to be very insalutary in summer. The ruins of an old Portuguese fortress are still to be seen near this place.

Koueit or *Græn*, as it is called by the Persians and Europeans, is a sea-port town, three days journey from *Zobejer*, or old Basra. The inhabitants live by the fishery of pearls and of fishes. They are said to employ in this species of naval industry more than eight hundred boats. In the favourable season of the year, this town is left almost desolate, every body going out either to the fishing, or upon some trading adventure. Græn is governed by a particular Schiech, of the tribe of *Othema*, who is a vassal to the Schiech of Lachsa, but sometimes aspires at independence. In such cases, when the Schiech of Lachsa advances with his army, the citizens of Græn retreat, with their effects, into the little island of *Feludsje*. Near Græn are the remains of another Portuguese fortress.

Between the territories of the Schiech of Lachfa, and the dominions of the Sovereign of O-
man, are a numerous tribe, denominated *Al Mu-
fillim*, and poffeffing feveral confiderable towns,
the names of which are unknown to me.

CHAP. II.

Of the Province of Nedsjed.

THIS. province is of vaft extent. It comprehends all the interior parts of Arabia, lying between the provinces which I have above briefly
defcribed, and the defart of Syria. The foil is
various ; among the hills fertile, and bearing a-
bundance of fruits, efpecially dates ; but, being
bounded by arid tracts of country, its rivers are
only fhort ftreams, which, after paffing through
the vallies, have their waters abforbed in the fandy plains, before they can reach the ocean. Upon
this account, the inhabitants are, in many places,
obliged to dig deep wells; and cultivation is
there difficult, or almoft impoffible.

The Bedouins inhabit a great part of this province. The remainder is mountainous, full of
cities and villages, and parcelled out among fo
many petty Sovereigns, that almoft every little
town has its own Schiech. Formerly, when the
power

power of the Sherriffes was at its height, many of these Schiechs, who were fituate in the vicinity of Hedsjas, were obliged to pay tribute to the Sherriffe of Mecca. At prefent, they pay nothing.

The inhabitants of this vaft country refemble the other Arabs in their moral qualities; they are at once robbers and hofpitable. As thofe petty Sovereigns are fo numerous in Nedsjed, it is impoffible for any traveller to pafs fafely thro' this country; the firft Schiech whofe territory he enters, will be fure to rob him, if it were only to prevent a neighbour with whom he is at war from profiting by this act of rapacity, if he himfelf fhould abftain from it. The caravan indeed travels fafe between Oman and Mecca, becaufe it confifts of beggars from whom nothing is to be gained. But the Schiechs of Nedsjed levy a contribution upon the caravan from Bagdad, on its way to Mecca, in the fame manner as the Schiechs of Hedsjas levy contributions upon thofe from Syria and Egypt. I have, however, learned that the inhabitants of Nedsjed carry on a confiderable trade among themfelves, and with their immediate neighbours; and it is therefore not improbable that an European might travel in fafety, even through this remote part of Arabia.

The people appear to be of a very warlike character, and are almoft conftantly in arms.

It is faid that none of their young men is fuffered to marry till after he has performed fome gallant action.

Nedsjed is divided into two wide diftricts; *El Arad*, which joins Oman; and *El Kherdsje*, ftretching to the confine of Yemen. Several of the towns in El Ared were named to me; among others, *El Aijæne*, the birth-place of the new prophet *Abd ul Wahheb*, of whom I fhall fhortly fpeak.

In the diftrict of *El Kerdsje*, extending northward from *Hedsjas* to the defart, is the city of Imam, famous, even before the days of Mahomet, for being the native city of Mofeilama, who fet himfelf up for a prophet. This diftrict contains alfo many other cities.

North from Nedsjed, and about ten days journey from Bagdad, is the famous mountain of *Schamer*, of confiderable extent and fertility. Between this mountain and Syria is a hilly tract of country, denominated *Dsjof al Sirhan*, populous and cultivated.

CHAP. III.

Of the new Religion of a Part of Nedsjed.

In this province are Sabæans, or Chriftians of St John, and a few Jews. Its other inhabitants
are

are all Mahometans, and were once rigid Sunnites. Some time fince, a new religion fprang up in the diftrict of El Ared. It has already produced a revolution in the government of Arabia, and will probably hereafter influence the ſtate of this country ſtill farther.

The founder of this religion was one Abd ul Wahheb, a native of Aijæne, a town in the diſtrict of El Ared. This man, in his youth, firſt ſtudied at home thofe fciences which are chiefly cultivated in Arabia; he afterwards fpent fome time at Bafra, and made feveral journies to Bagdad, and through Perfia.

After his return to his native place, he began to propagate his opinions among his countrymen, and fucceeded in converting feveral independent Schiechs, whoſe ſubjects confequently became followers of this new prophet.

Thefe Schiechs, who had hitherto been almoſt conſtantly at war among themfelves, were now reconciled by the mediation of Abd ul Wahheb, and agreed to undertake nothing in future without confulting their apoſtle. By this affociation, the balance of power in Nedsjed was deſtroyed: Thoſe petty Schiechs, who could maintain their independence againſt any of the members of the league feparately, were unable to refiſt the whole acting together. Wars alfo became, from the fame caufes, more keen and frequent, religion now intermingling itfelf with other grounds of difpute.

Abd ul Wahheb having thus reduced great part of El Ared, the Schiechs who were worfted, called in to their affiftance Arar, Schiech of Lachfa. That Prince, from motives as well of policy as of religion, complied with their requeft, and fent an army into El Ared. This army being defeated by Abd ul Wahheb, Schiech Arar marched thither himfelf, at the head of four thoufand men, with a train of artillery, confifting of three old pieces of cannon and a mortar. He laid fiege to a fortrefs ftanding on a hill; but, as he could make no ufe of his artillery, he was compelled, after fuffering fome loffes, to return to Lachfa.

I have already given fome account of the adventures of Schiech Mecrami of Nedsjeran; and I at the fame time mentioned that he was in fome fort the head of a particular fect. An Arabian of Lachfa told me, that there was a great fimilarity between the principles of Abd ul Wahheb, and thofe of Shiech Mecrami. It feems to be fo. At leaft thofe two innovators in religion muft have been good friends; otherwife Schiech Mecrami could not have paffed through Nedsjed with a fmall army, to attack the potent chief of Lachfa, as he did in 1764. It fhould feem, that he had joined Abd ul Wahheb, or rather

his

his son Mahomet, who had by this time succeeded his father, in order to reduce the Sunnite Schiechs. I was even told, that these two acting in concert, had subdued many of their neighbours. The rest wrote to all the Arabs in the neighbourhood of Basra, during the time of my stay in that city, begging their assistance.

After the death of Abd ul Wahheb, his son retained the same authority, and continued to prosecute his views. He sustains the supreme ecclesiastical character in El Ared. The hereditary Schiechs of the small states in that country, which were once independent, do indeed still retain a nominal authority; but Mahommed is, in fact, sovereign of the whole. He exacts a tribute, under the name of *Sikka*, or aid, for the purpose of carrying on the war against the Infidels.

The Sunnites complain of his persecution. But, more probably, this bigotted and superstitious sect hate and calumniate Mahomet for his innovations in religion. However the matter be, certain it is, that such of the inhabitants of Nedsjed as are unwilling to embrace the new religion are retiring to other parts of the country. *Zobayer*, the ancient Basra, which had decayed to little better than a hamlet, has been peopled by these refugees, and is now a large town.

As

As I had no opportunity of becoming acquainted with any of the difciples of this new religion, I can fay nothing pofitive with refpect to its tenets. I had a converfation upon this head indeed with an Arabian Schiech, who had been accuftomed from his youth to travel with merchants through all Arabia, and had vifited the principal cities in Nedsjed. This Bedouin Schiech, who appeared to be an intelligent man, gave me the following account of the religion in queftion.

Abd ul Wahheb taught, that God is the only proper object of worfhip and invocation, as the creator and governor of the world. He forbade the invocation of faints, and the very mentioning of Mahomet, or any other prophet, in prayer, as practices favouring of idolatry. He confidered Mahomet, Jefus Chrift, Mofes, and many others, refpected by the Sunnites in the character of prophets, as merely great men, whofe hiftory might be read with improvement; denying, that any book had ever been written by divine infpiration, or brought down from heaven by the angel Gabriel. He forbade, as a crime againft Providence, the making of vows, in the manner of the Sunnites, to obtain deliverance from danger.

This account of the Schiechs does not entirely accord with what was told me by fome

Sunnites,

Sunnites, of the doctrines of Abd ul Wahheb. But, upon this head, it would be unfair to give credit to the disciples of a superstitious sect, whose false opinions are all combated by the new religion.

The Musulman religion, as professed by the Sunnites, is surely far different from what it was instituted by Mahomet. This sect follow the authority of some commentators, who explain the Alcoran by their own whimsies, and exalt their private opinions into doctrines of the Mahometan system. It acknowledges a long train of saints, who are invoked in cases of necessity, and to whom many absurd miracles are ascribed, and these said to have been wrought in favour of persons who addressed themselves to the saints, in preference to God. It gives faith to the virtues of amulets, and the efficacy of foolish vows. In short, it has gradually adopted many pieces of superstition, which are condemned in the Alcoran, and justified only by the strained interpretations of the Doctors. Other sects, such, for instance, as that of the Zeidites, have corrupted the religion of Mahomet less; although even among them it is far from remaining in its original purity.

The new religion of Abd ul Wahheb deserves therefore to be regarded as a reformation of Mahometism, reducing it back to its original
simplicity,

simplicity. He has gone farther, perhaps, than some other reformers; but an Arab can hardly be expected to act in such matters with a delicate hand. Experience will here shew, whether a religion, so stripped of every thing that might serve to strike the senses, can maintain its ground among so rude and ignorant a people as the Arabs.

The imposture of Schiech Mecrami is nowise inconsistent with the spirit of reformation. The Schiech, taking advantage of the rudeness of his countrymen, has impressed them with a fanatical idea of the efficacy of his prayers, giving out, that he obtains in this way whatever he asks from God. This confidence in the power of prayer is not inconsistent with simplicity of doctrine. We have among ourselves instances, that it is apt to seize upon the mind, in an age illuminated by science, and professing the purest of religions.

CHAP.

SECTION XXIII.

OF THE INDEPENDENT ARABIAN STATES UPON
THE SEA-COAST OF PERSIA.

CHAP. I.

Of the Arabs inhabiting around the Perſian Gulph.

Our geographers are wrong, as I have elſewhere remarked, in repreſenting a part of Arabia as ſubject to the Monarchs of Perſia. So far is it from being ſo, that, on the contrary, the Arabs poſſeſs all the ſea-coaſt of the Perſian empire, from the mouths of the Euphrates, nearly to thoſe of the Indus.

Theſe ſettlements upon the coaſt of Perſia belong not, indeed, to Arabia properly ſo called. But, ſince they are independent of Perſia, and uſe the ſame language, and exhibit the ſame manners, as the native inhabitants of Arabia, I ſhall here ſubjoin a brief account of them.

It is impoſſible to aſcertain the period at which the Arabians formed their ſettlements upon this coaſt. Tradition affirms, that they have been eſtabliſhed here for many centuries. From a variety of hints in ancient hiſtory, it may be preſumed, that theſe Arabian colonies occupied their preſent ſituation in the time of the firſt kings of Perſia. There is a ſtriking analogy between the manners aſcribed to the ancient *Ichthyophagi*, and thoſe of theſe Arabs.

They live all nearly in the ſame manner, leading a ſeafaring-life, and employing themſelves in fiſhing, and in gathering pearls. They uſe little other food but fiſh and dates; and they feed alſo their cattle upon fiſh.

They prize liberty as highly as do their brethren in the deſart. Almoſt every different town has its own Schiech, who receives hardly any revenue from his ſubjects; but, if he has no private fortune, muſt, like his ſubjects, ſupport himſelf by his induſtry, either in carrying goods, or in fiſhing. If the principal inhabitants happen to be diſſatisfied with the reigning Schiech, they depoſe him, and chooſe another out of the ſame family.

Their arms are a match-firelock, a ſabre, and a buckler. All their fiſhing-boats ſerve occaſionally as ſhips of war. But a fleet like this, that muſt frequently ſtop to take fiſh for food, when they ſhould purſue the enemy, can never perform any very great exploits. Their wars

are

are mere skirmishes and inroads, never ending in any decisive action, but producing lasting quarrels, and a state of continual hostility.

Their dwellings are so paultry, that an enemy would not take the pains to demolish them. And as, from this circumstance, these people have nothing to lose upon the continent, they always betake themselves to their boats at the approach of an enemy, and lie concealed in some isle in the Gulph till he have retreated. They are convinced that the Persians will never think of settling on a barren shore, where they would be infested by all the Arabs who frequent the adjacent seas.

These Arabs are Sunnites. They regard the Persians, who are Shiites, with abhorrence, and shun all alliance with them. The mutual hatred of the two sects, was even one cause of the failure of Nadir-Shah's attempt to subdue these Arabs. In the prosecution of this object, the usurper had, at immense expence, equipped a fleet of twenty-five large ships upon the Persian Gulph. But, as he had no Persian sailors, he was obliged to take Indians, who were Sunnites. These refusing to fight against their brethren of the same orthodox faith, massacred their Shiite officers, and carried off the ships. Towards the end of his life, Nadir-Shah was meditating to seize these Arabs, to transport them to the shores

shores of the Caspian Sea, and to settle a colony of Persians in their room. His tragical death prevented the execution of this project; and the disturbances in Persia have ever since prevented all incroachments from that quarter upon the liberty of these Arabs (o).

Their government and present political situation seem to me to bear a great resemblance to those of ancient Greece. Hostile engagements are continually a-fighting, and important revolutions happening upon the Persian Gulph; but the Arabs have no historian to spread their fame beyond their own narrow confines.

CHAP. II.

Of Places subject to the Dominion of Persia.

THE kings of Persia, although not masters of these coasts, yet retained some places upon them. In later times, the Persian governors of these places have shaken off their allegiance, and have, in some measure, erected them into independent sovereignties. The chief of these are *Gambron*, and *Hormus*.

Gambron, a sea-port town in the province of Laristan, belonged anciently to the Persian Monarch. After the death of Nadir-Schah, a Persian

Dancing Girls in Egypt

fian, named *Nafer Khan*, made himfelf mafter of the province, and, by confequence, of the city. He acknowledges himfelf vaffal to *Vakeel Kerim Khan* of Schiraz, yet pays no tribute, and refpects not the Vakeel's authority, unlefs when he comes with his army to compel him.

The city of Gambron, which has been alfo called *Bender Abbas*, was famous through all the laft century, and in the beginning of the prefent, as the port of Schiraz, and of all the fouth of Perfia. Its trade was, at that time, very extenfive. At prefent it is very low; nor is there a fingle European counting-houfe in the city. This decline has been occafioned by the domeftic difturbances in Perfia, and the wars and difputes between the French and the Englifh. The Dutch for a while continued to carry on a petty trade here. But, fince they formed a fettlement in the ifle of Karek, they have entirely deferted Gambron.

The ifle of Ormus, fo celebrated of old, now retains nothing of its ancient fplendour. It belongs at prefent to *Mulla Ali Shah*, a Perfian, who made himfelf mafter of it immediately after the death of Nadir-Shah, whofe admiral he had been. This Prince of Ormus poffeffes likewife a part of the ifle of *Kifhme*, the other part being fubject to the Prince of *Seer*.

South

South from Lariftan is *Minau,* a confiderable inland town, fix leagues diftant from the feafhore. The inhabitants of the diftrict in which it lies are Shiites, and are chiefly employed in agriculture; from thefe circumftances, they are fometimes induced to acknowledge the authority of the Chan of Lariftan.

A tribe of Arabs, denominated *Belludge,* inhabit between Minau and Cape *Jafke.* They are mafters of a good many veffels, and carry on a confiderable trade with Bafra, upon the Arabic Gulph, and even venture as far as to the coafts of India. Thefe Arabs are Sunnites; and unity of religious fentiments has occafioned their joining the party of the *Afghans* in the late revolutions of Perfia.

Some geographers reprefent thefe Belludge as inhabiting all along the Perfian coaft, to the mouths of the Indus, and have defcribed them as a warlike people, addicted to piracy. I know not whether they are to be confidered as independent, or as tributary to Perfia. More probably, they acknowledge no fovereign authority but that of their own Schiechs. Some narratives of travels, performed in the laft century, relate the extraordinary adventures of a Prince of Jafke, who withftood the power of Shah Abbas, till he was, at length, taken off by treachery. His widow continued to refift the Perfian King,

and

and performed deeds worthy of the heroines in the ages of chivalry. But, it is to a Schiech of the Belludge that the ſtory is properly to be referred.

The country from Bender Abbas, northward to *Delam*, reſembles the Tehama in Arabia; it is an arid plain, and is called by the Perſians *Kermeſir*, or the hot country.* In this diſtrict I know no place but *Khamir*, a caſtle ſituate on a precipitous rock, which, with a ſmall tract adjoining, is the property of a particular Schiech. Ships come hither for cargoes of ſulphur, of which there is abundance in the neighbourhood.

CHAP. III.

Of the Territories of the Tribe of Houle.

This numerous tribe are maſters of all the coaſt from Bender Abbas to Cape Berdiſtan, and poſſeſs all the ports in this extent of coaſt. One part of the tract is parched and barren; but a range of hills, like *Dahr Aſban*, extend nearly to the ſea, and afford wood, which is cut down and exported by the inhabitants.

Notwithſtanding theſe natural advantages, the Arabs of Houle do not cultivate their lands, but live by hunting and fiſhing. They are Sunnites;
and

and are esteemed among their neighbours for valour. If their forces could be brought to act in combination, they might easily conquer all the cities upon the Persian Gulph: But almost every city is subject to a particular Schiech; and, although these Schiechs are all descendents from the same family, they choose rather to remain petty and poor, than to raise themselves to a more opulent and respectable condition, by submitting to act in concert, under the direction of one Grand Schiech.

The following are the Schiechs or Princes of the tribe of Houle:

The Schiech of Seer, whom I mentioned in the description of Oman; but who, being originally from this country, and of the tribe of Houle, possesses, in the neighbourhood of Gambron, the cities of *Kunk*, *Lundsje*, and *Ras Heti*. His subjects export wood for fuel and charcoal.

The Schiechs of *Mogho* and *Tsjærack*. The inhabitants of the latter of these districts also export wood; and are said to be the bravest of all the tribe of Houle.

Lastly, the Schiechs of *Nachelo*, *Nabend*, *Aaloe*, *Tahhrie*, *Schilu*, and *Konkoun*. The inhabitants of Nachelo are esteemed to be very skilful divers. In the city of Konkoun, the inhabitants of which are of a more pacific charac-

ter

ter than the other branches of the tribe of Houle, both Jews and Banians reside.

Persians, who have no ships, but live by husbandry, occupy the tract between the principality of *Abu Schæhhr* and Cape *Berdiftan*.

CHAP. IV.

Of the Principalities of Abu Schæhhr and Bender Rigk.

ABU SCHÆHHR, the capital of the independent state of the same name, possesses a commodious harbour, in which ships can come up close to the houses. This circumstance induced Nadir Shah to station a fleet here, of which some remains are to be still seen. Since that time, this city has been better known, and more considerable, It is at present the sea-port town of Schiraz; and the English, the only European nation who continue to trade with Persia, have a factory here.

The Arabs inhabiting the district of Abu Schæhhr are not of the tribe of Houle. There are among them three eminent families; the two first of which have been, from time immemorial, settled in this country. The third, named *Matarisch*, came lately from Oman, where they were employed in fishing, entered into alliance with the other two, and found means to usurp the sovereign authority, which they have now held for several years.

The present Schiech, *Nafer*, of the family of *Matarifch*, possesses likewise the isle of Bahhrein, upon the coast of Arabia, by which he is enabled to keep on foot some shipping. He also has considerable domains in *Kermesir*, which he holds from Kerim Khan, with whom Nafer's children are placed as hostages for their father's fidelity. It is a happy circumstance for Schiraz, that the Prince of Abu Schæhhr can thus be retained in the interests of Persia by means of his possessions in Kermesir.

Schiech Nafer was a Sunnite; but, in hopes of being appointed Admiral of the Persian fleet, he became a Shiite, and married a Persian lady. These two steps have proved very injurious to him and his family. He is odious to his subjects and neighbours; and his children are no longer counted among the Arabian nobility.

Bender Rigk, the seat of the prince of this name, is a city encompassed with walls in an indifferent state, and lies north from Abu Schæhhr. The petty state, of which this is the capital city, comprehends several other places in Kermesir, which render its Sovereign in some measure dependent upon *Kerim Khan*. The Arabs of this principality are chiefly addicted to a seafaring-life; the Persians inhabiting its back parts are husbandmen.

The reigning family of Bender Rigk are of the Arabian tribe of *Beni Saab*, and are originally from Oman; but the grandfather of the present prince, having become a Shiite, and married a Persian lady, this family are no longer counted by the Arabs among their genuine nobility.

The reigning Prince of Bender Rigk, *Mir Mahenna*, is distinguished through this country for his vices and cruelties, as one of the most execrable tyrants that ever existed. He made servants murder his father in his own presence, because the old man had a predilection for his eldest son. He killed his mother, because she reproached him for his crimes. He caused his brother, and sixteen of his other relations, to be assassinated, that he might establish himself in unquestioned possession of the throne. He drowned two of his sisters, because a neighbouring prince had asked one of them in marriage. He exposes all the female children that happen to be born to him. In 1765, this detestable monster was under the age of thirty years.

Mir Makenna had fallen twice into the hands of Kerim Khan. From his first captivity he made his escape, upon a defeat which the Governor

vernor of Perfia fuffered. He obtained his liberty the fecond time, by the good offices of his fifter, who was married to a Perfian officer. Upon returning into his own dominions, he immediately began to pillage the caravans which travelled between Schiraz and Abu Schæhhr, and to practife piracy. Kerim Khan prepared to chaftife him, and befieged his capital, but without fuccefs.

In the year 1765, the fame Kerim Khan fent to demand payment of the tribute due for his poffeffions in Kermefir; but Mir Mahenna maltreated the officer who was fent on the errand, and caufed his beard to be fhaven. Kerim Khan then fent a ftrong army againft him, which conquered *Bender Rigk*, and all his territories. Mir Mahenna had, however, prudently retired, before it was too late, with his troops, and a part of his fubjects, into a defart ifle called *Khoueri*, where he waited till the Perfian army fhould retire from his country. After they were gone, he returned out of the ifland, expelled the garrifon from Bender Rigk, and recovered poffeffion of his dominions.

The tyrant had abandoned himfelf to drunkennefs; and had begun to exercife his cruelties upon his troops to fuch excefs, as to cut off the nofe and ears of fome of the principal officers; yet his foldiers were ftill fo fteadily attached

tached to him, that, even in the period of his exile, he took the ifle of Karek from the Dutch. A band of robbers never abandon their chief, while he continues to fhare the plunder among them.

CHAP. V.

Of the Tribe of Kiab, and their Schiech Soliman.

THE Arabian tribe of *Kiab,* or, as the Perfians pronounce it, *Tsjab,* inhabit the fartheft point upon the fide of the Perfian Gulph. They were in fmall confideration before the reign of their prefent Schiech Soliman, whofe fame hath even reached Europe, in confequence of a quarrel he had with the Englifh, in which he took fome of their fhips.

This Schiech took advantage of the troubles of Perfia, and of the defects in the government of Bafra. He began with fubduing his petty independent neighbours; after which he made himfelf mafter of feveral large diftricts in Perfia, and promifed tribute to the Khans who were contending for the throne of that diftracted empire. None of them ever attempted to exact tribute but *Kerim,* and he contented himfelf with a fmall fum. Soliman then extended his
conquefts

conquests towards Bafra. He cultivated the friendship of the *Ajals*, the chief people of that country; and at last made himself master of all the isles between the mouths of the Euphrates, commonly called the country of *Schat el Arrab*.

Having pushed his conquests to the navigable rivers, he endeavoured to form a naval force. He built his first vessel in 1758; and, in 1765, he had ten large, and seven small ships.

In the same year, 1765, Kerim Khan sent a force against him, too powerful for him to resist. He then transported his treasures and troops from isle to isle, till he had carried them to the west of *Schat el Arrab*. The Persians could not pursue him for want of ships, and were therefore obliged to retire. The Pacha of Bagdad then ordered his forces to attack Soliman; but he retreated among the isles, and escaped the Turks now, as he had before avoided the Persians.

The territory of the tribe of Kiàb extends from the desart of Arabia to the country of Hindean, and northward to the principality of *Havifa*. It is watered by several rivers, large and small. It abounds in dates, rice, grain, and pasture. Its principal cities are *Damek*, lying within Persia, *Hafar*, and *Ghoban*, the seat of a Schiech, near one of the mouths of the Euphrates.

CHAP. VI.

Of some other independent States.

H*INDIAN*, north from Bender Rigk, and bordering on the possessions of the tribe of *Kiab*, is a small district, subject to a particular Sovereign. The Arabs who inhabit it live upon the produce of their lands, and their cattle.

Havisa, a city and district in the back parts of the country bordering on the Persian Gulph, belongs to a descendent from Mahomet. This Prince is named *Maula*, and enjoys the privilege of coining money.

Upon the eastern coast of the Persian Gulph are many isles, and most of them inhabited. Except Ormus, none of them constitutes an independent state. The different princes on the continent possess the isles adjoining to their respective dominions.

On the western side of the Gulph is an isle, or rather a cluster of isles, known to the Europeans by the name of *Bahhrein*. The Arabs call the largest of these isles *Aval;* and each of the smaller has its particular name. As this isle is famous for the pearl-fishery, and has undergone

gone many revolutions, and often changed its master, I must say a few words of it.

Bahhrein is a fortified city, upon the isle, known either by the same name, or by the name of *Aval.* In this isle were once three hundred and sixty towns and villages. At present it contains, beside the capital, only sixty wretched villages. A long series of wars have ruined the others.

This isle produces great abundance of dates. But its chief dependence is upon the pearl-fishery, as the best pearls are found here in great abundance. The duties upon the two articles of dates and pearls afford its Sovereign a lack of rupees, or 300,000 French livres. Out of this revenue he is obliged to maintain a garrison in the city.

Bahhrein belonged once to the Portuguese. When they were driven out of the Persian Gulph, it fell into the hands of the Schiech of Lachsa, but was taken from him by the Persians. The Imam of Oman then made himself master of it, but gave it up again to the Persian Monarch for a sum of money. After some time, during the inroad of the *Afghans*, the Persian Governor gave it up to the Schiech of Nabend, of the tribe of Houle. Another Houlite, the Schiech of *Tahhri*, expelled him of Nabend. Nadir Shah's admiral then seized it; but, after his

his departure, the Schiech of Tæhhrie recovered it. During the late troubles in Perfia, the Schiech of *Afloe* made himfelf mafter of this ifle, but was immediately difpoffeffed by the Princes of Abu Schæhhr and Bender Rigk, who conquered it together. The firft of thefe princes drove out the fecond, and was in his turn expelled by the Beni Houle. In 1765, it had returned again into the poffeffion of the Schiech of Abu Schæhhr, and he was then fole Monarch of the ifle of Bahhrein.

From this narrative, the reader may form an idea of the continual revolutions which take place among this multitude of petty princes. At Bafra I learned fome particulars concerning their complicated quarrels, which I could not well comprehend: I was told, that every Arab Prince was always at open war with two or three others of his own nation.

The navigation is continually difturbed and interrupted by thefe ftrong quarrels. On board any Arabian veffel, paffengers are always in danger of falling into the hands of one enemy or another. It is only on board a European fhip, which the Arabian fmall craft dare not attack, that one can perform this voyage in fafety.

CHAP. VII.

Of the Ifle of Karek.

This ifle, which lies on the eaſt coaſt of the Perſian Gulph, between Abu Schæhhr and Bender Rigk, contains only a ſingle village; but the aqueducts cut in the rocks, which ſtill remain, ſhew it to have been once more populous in proportion to its extent, which is about five leagues in circumference.

Karek has become famous, in conſequence of the ſettlement lately formed upon it by the Dutch, and ſince given up by them. As this event has made ſome noiſe in the world, I ſhall give a brief account of it.

The Dutch carried on a great trade to Baſra, and had for the principal director of their factory there a Baron Kniphauſen, who was much reſpected in that city. This German having embroiled himſelf with the Governor, in conſequence of ſome affair of gallantry, was caſt in priſon, and might have loſt his head, had he not paid a large ſum of money for his liberty. Before he ſailed for Batavia, he obtained from the factory at Baſra a written atteſtation of the innocence of his conduct; and the Dutch Eaſt-India Company approved of all he had done.

In

In confequence of his difference with the Governor of Bafra, Mr Kniphaufen had agreed with Mir Nafer, Prince of Bender Rigk, to whom Karek belonged, that the Dutch fhould, for a certain annual rent, be allowed to feat their factory there. The government at Batavia relifhed the project, which was, in fact, a very wife one, and fent the Baron, with two great fhips, to carry it into execution.

Upon arriving at Karek, he feized fome fhips from Bafra, and detained them, till he received reftitution of the fum which he had paid for his liberty. He built a large fquare magazine upon the ifland, and raifed, by degrees, four towers at its corners, each of which he furnifhed with fix cannons. Mir Nafer, diffatisfied at the erection of thefe fortifications, attacked the Dutch, who attacked him in his turn, but could not follow him into his faftneffes. This petty war proved, however, very expenfive to the company.

Baron Kniphaufen, after governing Karek with fovereign authority for five years, was fucceeded by Mr Vanderhulft, who having been previoufly employed at Bafra, and knowing the Arabs, thought it his duty to profecute, with *Mir Mahenna,* the new Prince of Bender Rigk, the war which had been waged againft his father. Mir Mahenna, by a ftratagem, feized two armed veffels belonging to the Dutch, and

unsuccessfully attempted a descent upon the
island. Mr Vanderhulst then enlarged his fortifications, and formed the plan of a town,
which was soon peopled with Persians and Arabs.

This settlement might be lucrative to the officers employed about it; but the expences of
the war and the garrisons consumed the Company's profits, and they determined to abandon
it; but the prospect of an advantageous trade
with Persia induced them to hold it some time
longer. The new Governor, Mr *Buschmann*,
therefore concluded a peace with Mir Mahenna;
after which the trade met with no interruption.

His successor, Mr *Van Houting*, although in
other respects a man of merit, did not conduct
himself so prudently, being a stranger to the
genius and temper of the Arabs, and having no
experienced officers under him. He was not
careful to observe a neutrality in the quarrels
between the Prince of Abu Schæhhr and Mir
Mahenna; but, in concert with the former, attacked the latter in his retreat in the island of
Khoneri. Mir Mahenna allowed his enemies
to approach; and, when he saw them in security, fell upon them with his cavalry, and entirely
discomfited the troops of the Dutch, and of Abu
Schæhhr.

Em-

Emboldened by this fuccefs, Mir Mahenna made a defcent upon the ifle of Karek, and befieged the town. Mr Van Houting fuffered himfelf to be outwitted by a Perfian, by whom he was perfuaded to permit Mir Mahenna to enter the fort with a fmall retinue, in order to agree upon terms for an accommodation. The Arab then made the Dutch garrifon prifoners, and fent them to Batavia. This event happened in the end of December 1765.

It is not probable that the Dutch Eaft-India Company will put themfelves to the trouble of expelling the conqueror, and renewing their eftablifhment on the ifle of Karek.

SECT

SECTION XXII.

OF THE BEDOUINS, OR WANDERING ARABS.

CHAP I.

Peculiarities in the Manners of the Bedouins.

THE Arabs fettled in cities, and efpecially thofe in the fea-port towns, have loft fomewhat of their diftinctive national manners, by their intercourfe with ftrangers; but the Bedouins, who live in tents, and in feparate tribes, have ftill retained the cuftoms and manners of their earlieft anceftors. They are the genuine Arabs, and exhibit, in the aggregate, all thofe characteriftics which are diftributed refpectively among the other branches of their nation.

I have repeatedly noticed the different acceptations in which the word *Schech* or *Schiech* is ufed. Among the Bedouins it belongs to every noble, whether of the higheft or the loweft order. Their nobles are very numerous, and compofe in a manner the whole nation; the plebeians

beians are invariably actuated and guided by the Schiechs, who fuperintend and direct in every tranfaction.

The Schiechs, and their fubjects, are born to the life of fhepherds and foldiers. The greater tribes rear many camels, which they either fell to their neighbours, or employ them in the carriage of goods, or in military expeditions. The petty tribes keep flocks of fheep. Among thofe tribes which apply to agriculture, the Schiechs at leaft live always in tents, and leave the culture of their grounds to their fubjects, whofe dwellings are wretched huts.

It is the difference in their ways of living that conftitutes the great diftinctions which characterife the different tribes. The genuine Arabs difdain hufbandry, as an employment by which they would be degraded. They maintain no domeftic animals but fheep and camels, except perhaps horfes. Thofe tribes which are of a pure Arab race live on the flefh of their buffaloes, cows, and horfes, and on the produce of fome little ploughing. The former tribes, diftinguifhed as noble by their poffeffion of camels, are denominated *Abu el Abaar ;* and the fecond *Moædan.* The latter are efteemed a middle clafs, between genuine Arabs and peafants. I have heard fome tribes mentioned contemptuoufly, becaufe they kept buffaloes and cows. The
Moædan

Moædan transport their dwellings from one country to another, according as pasturage fails them; so that a village often arises suddenly in a situation where, on the day before, not a hut was to be seen.

The genuine Bedouins, living always in the open air, have a very acute smell. They dislike cities, on account of the fœtid exhalations produced about them. They cannot conceive how people, who regard cleanliness, can bear to breathe so impure air. I have been assured, by persons of undoubted veracity, that some Bedouins, if carried to the spot from which a camel has wandered astray, will follow the animal by smelling its track, and distinguish the marks of its footsteps, by the same means, from those of any other beasts that may have travelled the same way. Those Arabs, who wander in the desart, will live five days without drinking, and discover a pit of water by examining the soil and plants in its environs. They are said to be addicted to robbery; and the accusation is not entirely unfounded; but may be laid equally to the charge of all nations that lead an erratic life. The Schiechs ride continually about on their horses or dromedaries, inspecting the conduct of their subjects, visiting their friends, or hunting. Traversing the desart, where the horizon is wide as on the ocean, they perceive travellers at a distance.

As travellers are seldom to be met with in those wild tracts, they naturally draw nigh to those whom they discover, and are tempted to pillage the strangers when they find their own party the strongest. Besides, travellers passing through these desarts go generally in caravans; and a single person, or a small party, has a singular and suspicious appearance, which is a temptation to the Bedouins.

In Arabia, as in all other thinly inhabited countries, robbery is practised; but the Arabian robbers are not cruel, and do not murder those whom they rob, unless when travellers stand upon the defensive, and happen to kill a Bedouin, whose death the others are eager to revenge. Upon all other occasions they act in a manner consistent with their natural hospitality. Upon this head I have heard some anecdotes, which it may not be amiss to introduce here.

A Mufti of Bagdad, returning from Mecca, was robbed in Nedsjed. He entered into a written agreement with the robbers, who engaged to conduct him safe and sound to Bagdad for a certain sum, payable at his own house. They delivered him to the next tribe, those to a third; and he was thus conveyed from tribe to tribe, till he arrived safe at home.

An European, belonging to a caravan which was plundered, had been infected with the plague upon his journey. The Arabs, feeing him too weak to follow his companions, took him with themfelves, lodged him without their camp, attended him till he was cured, and then fent him to Bafra.

An Englifhman, who was travelling exprefs to India, and could not wait for the departure of a caravan, hired two Arabs at Bagdad, who were to accompany him to Bafra. By the way he was attacked by fome Schiechs, againft whom he at firft defended himfelf with his piftols; but, being hard preffed by their lances, was forced to furrender. The Arabs, upon whom he had fired, beat him till he could not walk. They then carried him to their camp, entertained him for fome time, and at laft conducted him fafe to Bafra. When Mr Forfkal was robbed by the Arabs in Egypt, a peafant, who accompanied him, was beaten by the robbers, becaufe he had piftols, although he had made no attempt to defend himfelf with them.

The pillaging of the caravans is not always owing merely to the propenfity which the Arabians have to robbery. Their pillaging expeditions are commonly confidered by themfelves as lawful hoftilities againft enemies who would defraud the nation of their dues, or againft rival tribes, who have undertaken to protect thofe illegal traders.

In

In one of those expeditions, a few years since, undertaken against the Pacha of Damascus, who was conductor of the Syrian caravan to Mecca, the tribe of *Anæse*, which gained the victory, showed instances of their ignorance, and of the simplicity of their manners. Those who happened to take goods of value knew not their worth, but exchanged them for trifles. One of those Arabs having obtained for his share a bag of pearls, thought them rice, which he had heard to be good food, and gave them to his wife to boil, who, when she found that no boiling could soften them, threw them away as useless.

CHAP. II.

Of the political Constitution of the wandering Arabs.

TREATING of the government of the Arabs in general, I said a few words occasionally concerning that of the Bedouins. To avoid unnecessary repetition, I shall add here only a few particulars concerning chiefly their political interests, in respect to the neighbouring nations.

The dignity of Schiech is hereditary, but is not confined to the order of primogeniture. The petty Schiechs, who form the hereditary nobility, choose

choose the grand Schieeh out of the reigning family, without regarding whether he be more nearly or more diftantly related to his predeceffor.

Little or no revenue is paid to the grand Schiech; and the other Schiechs are rather his equals than his fubjects. If diffatisfied with his government, they depofe him, or go away with their cattle, and join another tribe. Thefe emigrations, which happen pretty frequently, have reduced fome tribes, which were once potent, to a low and inconfiderable ftate; and have greatly augmented the numbers and power of fome petty tribes.

Perfonal flavery is eftablifhed among the Bedouins; but none of them are *afcripti glebæ*. A peafant, when diffatisfied with his mafter, may quit his fervice, and remove any where elfe.

The Bedouins, who live in tents in the defart, have never been fubdued by any conqueror; but fuch of them as have been enticed, by the profpect of an eafier way of life, to fettle near towns, and in fertile provinces, are now, in fome meafure, dependent on the Sovereigns of thofe provinces.

Such are the Arabs in the different parts of the Ottoman empire. Some of them pay a rent or tribute for the towns or pafturages which they occupy. Others frequent the Banks of the Euphrates, only in one feafon of the year; and, in winter,

winter, return to the defart. Thefe laft acknowledge no dependence on the Porte.

Neither are, properly fpeaking, fubject to the Turks; to whom, on the contrary, they would be dangerous neighbours, if the Pachas did not find means to fow diffentions among the tribes and great families, when there are more than one pretender to the dignity of Schiech of Schiechs.

The policy of the Turks occafions frequent wars among the Bedouins; but thefe are neither long nor bloody.

Whenever the Turks interfere in their quarrels, all the tribes combine to repulfe the common enemy of the whole nation.

Every Grand Schiech juftly confiders himfelf as abfolute lord of his whole territories; and accordingly exacts the fame duties upon goods carried through his dominions as are levied by other princes. The Europeans are wrong in fuppofing the fums paid by travellers to the Grand Schiechs to be merely a ranfom to redeem them from pillage.

The Turks, who fend caravans through the defart to Mecca, have fubmitted to the payment of thefe duties. They pay a certain fum annually to the tribes who live near the road to Mecca; in return for which, the Arabs keep the wells open, permit the paffage of merchandize, and efcort the caravans.

It

If the Bedouins fometimes pillage thofe caravans, the haughty perfidious conduct of the Turkifh officers is always the firft caufe of fuch hoftilities. Thofe infolent Turks look upon all the Arabs as rebels; that is, in the modern fignification of this word, as a people who, although weak, have the audacity to withftand the oppreffion of their ftronger neighbours. In confequence of this felfifh reafoning, they violate their engagements; and the Arabs take their revenge by pillaging the caravans.

The famous *Ali Bey*, when he conducted the Egyptian caravan to Mecca, would not pay all the duties on his way to Mecca, but promifed to pay the reft, on his return, and forgot his promife. On the year following, the Arabs affembled in greater numbers, and obliged the Captain of the caravan to pay for himfelf and Ali Bey both. The Turks exclaimed againft this as an act of robbery; yet the Arabs had only done themfelves juftice.

The conduct of *Abdalla*, Pacha of Damafcus, who commanded the Syrian caravan in 1756, was ftill more odious. When the Schiechs of the tribe of Harb came to meet him, to receive the ftipulated toll, he gave them a friendly invitation to vifit him; but, inftead of paying the toll, cut off their heads, and fent them to Conftantinople, as a proof of his victory over the rebel Arabs. The ftroke which thofe fuffered by the death of

their

their chiefs hindered them from attempting any thing in revenge, on either that or the following year: The caravans travelled in triumph to Mecca; and the Turks boasted of the valour and prudence of Abdalla Pacha. But, in the third year, the Arabs avenged the slaughtered Schiechs, and, with an army of eighty thousand men, raised out of all the tribes, routed the Turks, and pillaged the caravan. The tribe of *Anæfe*, under the command of their Schiech, distinguished themselves particularly in this expedition.

There is a certain subordination among the tribes. The petty tribes, being unable to defend themselves, place themselves under the protection of the greater, and are governed by their laws. Thus are powerful tribes formed by the union of several small tribes.

The Arabian nation are much more numerous, and wider spread, than they are generally supposed to be. They occupy countries, once cultivated and populous, whose ancient inhabitants have disappeared. The period at which these Arabian settlements were formed, cannot now be ascertained; nor is it known whether they may not have been anterior to the reign of the Caliphs. The ancients did not distinguish accurately between different nations. The Kings of Palmyra, who have been supposed to be Jews, were more probably Arabs.

CHAP.

CHAP. III.

Of the Bedouins on the confines of the Dejari.

THE moſt ancient and powerful tribes of this people are thoſe which eaſily retire into the deſart when attacked by a foreign enemy. Theſe too have preſerved the national character in its greateſt purity, and have maintained their liberty unimpaired. Of this number are the following tribes, of whom I ſhall mention ſuch particulars as have come to my knowledge.

The *Beni Khaled* are one of the moſt powerful tribes in all Arabia, on account of their conqueſts, their wealth, and the number of other tribes ſubject to them. From the deſart of Nedsjed, they have advanced to the ſea, and have conquered the country of Lachſa, as I mentioned in the proper place. The Schiech of this tribe does not live always in the city of Lachſa, but ſometimes in tents in the deſart.

The tribe of *Kiab*, who inhabit north from the Perſian Gulph, and of whom I have already ſpoken, rarely encamp; they have poſſeſſions in the province of *Suſiſtan*, in Perſia.

In this province of Suſiſtan, near the principality of Haviſa, and in the neighbourhood of the city of Schuſter, five different conſiderable

able tribes of independent Bedouins. From the exiftence of thefe eftablifhments, I fhould judge the authority of the Perfians in this country to be precarious, and Sufiftan to be interfperfed with defarts.

Beni Lam, are a great tribe between *Korne* and *Bagdad*, upon the banks of the Tigris, the Arabic name of which river, in conftant ufe among the inhabitants of the country, is *Didsjele*. They receive duties upon goods carried between Bafra and Bagdad. Thefe Arabs fometimes pillage caravans. The Pacha of Bagdad then fends troops againft them, and fometimes chaftifes them by beheading their chiefs. But the fucceffors of the Schiechs, who have been beheaded, are always as great enemies to the Turks, and as zealous to maintain their liberty, as their predeceffors have been.

Montefidfi, or Montefik, are the moft powerful tribe north from the defart, whether in refpect to the extent of their territories, or the great number of the fubaltern tribes who acknowledge their authority. They poffefs all the country upon both fides of the Euphrates, from *Korne* to *Ardje*.

In fummer, when the grafs in the defart is in a manner burnt up, the reigning Schiech refides at *Nahhr el Antar*, a town upon the banks of the Euphrates. In winter, they drive their cattle to feed in the defart, and encamp in tents. The inhabitants of the villages, who apply to agriculture, and are for this reafon held in contempt by the Bedouins, pay a tribute. They are poor, as muft naturally be the condition of the fubjects of thofe Schiechs who live comfortably themfelves, but are not difpofed to fuffer their peafantry to grow rich.

The Arabs of this tribe often plunder travellers going between *Helle* and *Bafra*. The Pacha of Bagdad commonly chaftifes them; fometimes even depofes the reigning Schiech, and advances another prince of the fame family in his room. Thefe Arabs fubmit to this flight degree of dependence on the Turks, becaufe they are unwilling to lofe their eftablifhments on the fertile banks of the Euphrates. In the late troubles of thefe provinces of the Ottoman empire, frequent notice was taken of this tribe, and they acted no unimportant part.

The tribe derive their name from one *Montefik*, who came from Hedsjas, and was defcended from a family who were illuftrious before the days of Mahomet. One thing certain is, that the defcendents of this *Montefik* have been fovereigns in this country from time immemorial. They are divided into many branches; and, in my time, the reigning family confifted of one
hun-

hundred and fifty perfons, all of whom might afpire to the fupreme power.

In 1765, the reigning Schiech, who was not of the eldeft branch, was named *Abdallah*. The other princes of his family enjoyed, at the fame time, a certain fhare of authority; each having his own fubjects, with whom, in time of war, they all join the troops of the Schiech of Schiechs; in fome diftricts they levy taxes and cuftoms upon their own account.

There were named to me more than a fcore of inferior tribes, who live all in fubjection to that of Montefik, which, of itfelf, is not extremely numerous. Among thefe fubordinate tribes, are fome who have others again ftill lefs confiderable, dependent upon them. The Arabs call thofe dependent tribes *El Araye.*

All thefe tribes upon the confines of the defart, whofe names I have mentioned, are genuine Arabs, who breed fheep and camels, and live in tents. But this defcription is, with more peculiar propriety, applicable to the reigning tribes; for, I believe, that fome of the inferior tribes have loft their nobility, by intermixing the practice of agriculture with the habits of paftoral life.

CHAP.

CHAP. IV.

Of the Bedouins of Mesopotamia.

The rich plains of Mesopotamia and Assyria, which were once cultivated by a populous nation, and watered by surprising efforts of human industry, are now inhabited, or rather ravaged, by wandering Arabs. As long as these fertile provinces shall remain under the government, or rather anarchy of the Turks, they must continue desarts, in which nature dies for want of the fostering care of man. A hereditary Sovereign, seated at Bagdad, and none else, might restore this country to its once flourishing state.

The Pachas, not knowing how to improve the value of these depopulated districts, and not being able to drive away the Arabs, permit them for an annual rent to cultivate those lands, or feed their flocks upon them. But that people are passionately fond of liberty, and shew by their conduct that they consider not themselves as subject to the Turkish yoke. The frequent wars, in which several of the tribes are engaged with the Pacha of Bagdad, although viewed as rebellion by the Ottoman officers, are proofs of the independence of the Arabs.

So rich a tract of country, naturally invites its inhabitants to cultivate it. The lands between the Tigris and the Euphrates are interfected by numerous canals, and are inhabited only by tribes practifing agriculture, or *Moædan.* Such are the

Beni Hæhkem, a tribe fituate eaftward from the Euphrates, whofe prefent Schiech is named *Fontil,* and who rules feveral petty tribes of hufbandmen.

Khafaal, a powerful tribe of hufbandmen, likewife on the eaft fide of the Euphrates. They have a great many petty tribes of Arabs, who live in villages, fubject to them. One of thefe petty tribes comprehends five and twenty inferior tribes, and two others forty each. The tribes which practife hufbandry appear therefore to be lefs numerous than the Bedouins, who often unite into very large bodies. The tribe of Khafaal can mufter two thoufand cavalry, and a proportionate number of infantry. The Pacha of Bagdad has lately made war on thefe people, with various fuccefs. Thefe Arabs are Shiites; and this is one motive more to fet them at variance with the Turks. The reigning Schiech is named *Hammoud,* and levies cuftoms from veffels coming up the Euphrates.

All

All the Arabs within the territories of the government of Bagdad are not hufbandmen. South from that city are fome Bedouins, who breed camels. Of thefe are the tribes of *Beni Temim,* and *Dafafa,* as well as fome other tribes between Bagdad and Moful. The tribe of *Al Tobad* have become very confiderable, through the favour of the Pacha of Bagdad, one of whofe principal officers was a near relation to the reigning Schiech. All that tract of country between Bagdad and Moful is poffeffed by hordes of Bedouins; one of which, occupying the range of hills adjacent to the Tigris, lately made an attack upon the troops of the Pacha; and another, denominated *Al Buhamdan,* pillaged a caravan when I was in Moful.

Thay are a great and powerful tribe of Bedouins between Merdin and Moful. The reigning Schiech, who is of the family of *Salie,* for a fmall annual tribute, poffeffes the large and fertile plain of Affyria. Were it not for the ufual Turkifh policy of fowing diffention among the neighbours, the Pachas would find it impoffible to maintain any fhadow of authority over this tribe. But, the Pacha of Bagdad fends the *Togk,* or horfe's tail, fometimes to one Schiech, fometimes to another; and thus is a conftant rivalry kept up among them, which weakens their common ftrength. This horfe's tail is not merely an enfign of empty honour. It confers the dignity of *Beg*, with the right to the poffeffion of the plain, which is held to be with the Turks. The depofed *Beg* quits his place of refidence between *Moful* and *Niffibin*, and retires with his partizans to the banks of the river *Khabour*, and there waits an opportunity to fupplant his rival.

All travellers complain of the robberies of thefe Bedouins of Affyria. The reftleffnefs and thievifh difpofition of thefe people feem to increafe the farther they recede from their native defarts, and approach the country inhabited by the plundering *Kurdes* and *Turcomans*.

I was told of ten wandering tribes, *Arak Arabi*. The moft confiderable encamps in the environs of *Helle;* its name is *Solæd;* and its branches are fpread even into the governments of Aleppo and Damafcus.

An Arabian Schiech, with whom I was acquainted at Aleppo, gave me the names of eight tribes of Bedouins who live towards the head of the Euphrates, in diftricts comprehended within the government of the Pacha of *Orfa*. But, as he could give me no farther information concerning thefe tribes, I pafs them by in filence.

CHAP.

CHAP. V.

Of the Bedouins of Syria.

The Pachas of this province have as much to do with the wandering Arabs, as the Turkish governors on the Persian frontier. It is of great consequence to the cities of Aleppo and Damascus, that their caravans, travelling to Bagdad or Basra, be suffered to pass in safety through the desart. Without escorting them with an army, the Pachas could not protect them from insult and pillage, did they not artfully contrive to employ one tribe of Arabs against the rest.

With this view, the Pacha gives the title of Emir to the most powerful Schiech in the neighbourhood. This emir is obliged to guide the caravans, to keep the other Arabs in awe, and to levy the dues from those who feed their cattle on the Pacha's grounds. As payment for his trouble, and to reimburse his expences, he receives a certain sum yearly. But the Arabs having little confidence in Turkish promises, the Pacha settles upon the Emir a number of villages, the revenues of which make up the stipulated sum. These villages were miserable enough before, but have been absolutely

ruined

ruined by the precarious government of the Arabs.

Upon a calculation of the fcanty revenue which the Porte derive from this part of their dominions, and the trivial rents paid by the Arabs for the liberty of ravaging whole provinces; and, on the other hand, a comparative eftimate of the fums expended in maintaining that vagabond race in a fpecious fubjection; it is plain, that they are lofers by the fhadow of authority which they pretend to have over the Arabs; but Ottoman vanity is pleafed with the vain fancy of poffeffing immenfe territories, from which the Sultan derives no revenue, and in which his orders are not refpected.

The moft powerful tribe near Aleppo, are the *Mauali*, whofe reigning Schiech is of the family of *El Burifche*. The Pachas put fometimes one, fometimes another of the Schiechs of this family in poffeffion of the villages and revenues belonging to the dignity of *Emir*. He whom they depofe, retires commonly with his party to the banks of the Euphrates, and there awaits an opportunity to foften the new Pacha by prefents, and recover his place. A few years fince, an Emir forefeeing that he was to be depofed, plundered a caravan, carried away 30,000 head of cattle from the paftures about Aleppo, and conveyed his booty to a place of fafety near the Euphrates.

phrates. Some time after, he furprifed and pillaged the city of *Hæms*. It was fuppofed, when I was in Aleppo, that the Pacha would be obliged to recal and reinftate him in the office of Emir.

A nephew of the Emir, or reigning Schiech of the tribe of Mauali, named to me fifteen confiderable tribes who inhabit the neighbourhood of Aleppo. Another Schiech, a great traveller, mentioned five others, fomewhat farther diftant, and near the road from Aleppo to Baf,ra. All thefe Bedouins pay each a trifle to the Emir, for liberty to hire out or fell their camels, and to feed their cattle through the country. The neighbouring tribes in the *defart of falt*, who are fubject to the Pacha, pay fomething to a farmer (of the tax) for liberty to gather the falt formed in that defart.

I was furprifed to fee among thofe tribes the tribes of *Thay* and *Sobæd*, which muft of confequence be fpread very widely over the country. The tribe of *Rabea* boafts of its antiquity, and pretends to have come from Yemen to fettle in the north, at the time when the dyke of the refervoir of the Sabæans at Mareb was broken down.

As my ftay at Damafcus was very fhort, I could not acquire enough of information concerning the Bedouins in the government of Damafcus

mafcus or Scham. I learned only the names of a dozen of their tribes, one of which named *Abu Salibe*, confifts, as I was told, folely of Chriftians. Another, *Beni Hamjar*, pretend that they are defcended from the old Arabian kings of this name.

Several circumftances lead me to prefume, that, of the other nations in Syria, *Kurdes*, *Drufes*, *Metuaeli*, *Naffaries*, and *Tfchinganes*, fome are of Arabian anceftry.

The tribe of *Anæfe* are efteemed to be the greateft tribe in the defart of Syria. They have even fpread into Nedsjed, where they are reckoned the moft numerous tribe in the heart of Arabia. The caravans of Turkifh pilgrims pay them a confiderable duty for their free paffage through the country. This tribe too, when diffatisfied, plunder the caravans. They often make war on the Pacha of Damafcus. They lately routed and killed the Pacha of *Ghaffa* in his own government.

In my time, the departure of a caravan from Bagdad was retarded by news received of thofe Arabs being on ill terms with the Pacha of Damafcus. Two Turkifh lords, who were very much beloved in Arabia, refolving to attend the caravan, the merchants ventured to pack up and fend off their goods. But, I not choofing, after fo many dangers, to expofe myfelf anew

and

and unneceffarily, took the road from Bagdad to Moful, and intrufted a trunk to an Arab, a camel-driver in that caravan, directing him to deliver it to a certain man at Aleppo. Within a day's journey of Damafcus, the whole caravan were plundered by the tribe of *Anæfe*. The trunk was opened. The Bedouins took what they chofe, but left me my books, papers, a box of medals, and two watches. The cameldriver collected the broken pieces of my trunk, and brought the whole honeftly to Aleppo. Thus had I, at the fame time, a proof of Arabian rapacity and Arabian integrity.

CHAP. VI.

Of the Bedouins of Arabia Petræa, and Paleftine.

THE name of *Arabia Petræa* is ufed in a vague manner by our geographers. It feems to be a denomination given to thofe countries which are moftly defart, between Egypt, Syria, and Arabia properly fo called. It would be difficult to determine exactly the limits of thofe countries, which are little known, and but thinly inhabited; the inhabitants of which wander among dry fands and rocks, feeking here and there a few fpots which afford fome fcanty food for

their

their cattle. None but Bedouins haunt thefe
defarts.

In the account of my journey to *Mount Sinai*, I fpoke of three tribes whom I found fettled by the highway. Thofe are no doubt of that clafs which acknowledge the fuperiority of a greater tribe. On the other fide of that chain of mountains, and in the environs of *Akaba*, there muft be other tribes, but the names of thefe I know not.

I have already mentioned the great tribe of *Harb*, who live to the north of *Hedsjas*. In this province are alfo the ancient tribes of *Beni Ottæba, Hodeil, Jom*, and others, which the inhabitants of Mecca call bands of robbers, feemingly for no other reafon, but that their Sherriffe has frequent quarrels with thofe Bedouins.

There are alfo feveral confiderable tribes upon the confines of Nedsjed, and the great defart. The tribe of *Beni Temim*, among thefe, were famous in the days of the fucceffors of Mahomet, for a prophetefs named *Sedsjay*, who did honour to the tribe. Schiech *Dahher*, Mafter of Acca, and the greater part of Paleftinè, is alfo an Arab, but I know not to what tribe he belongs.

I could learn nothing of confequence concerning the Arabs of Paleftine. They feem to be poor neglected hordes, who inhabit that barren and difmal country.

I was told of the tribe of *Dsjærhamiè*, between *Rama* and Jerusalem. The European monks, who are now the only pilgrims that visit the Holy Land, describe those Arabs as devils incarnate, and complain dolefully of their cruelty to the poor Christians. Those lamentations, and the superstitious pity of good souls in Europe, procure large alms to the convent of Franciscans at Jerusalem. The exaggerated relations of the sufferings of the pilgrims, from those inhuman Bedouins, will therefore be continued as long as they can serve the purpose for which they are intended.

It must be confessed, however, that this tribe of *Dsjærhamie* form, in one instance, a remarkable exception from the ordinary national character of the Arabs, who, in general, never maltreat a stranger, unless they have first received provocation. But, those Arabs in the neighbourhood of Jerusalem have a rooted aversion to the monks; in other respects, they are honest enough people.

They convey every year, from Jafa to Jerusalem, money and goods, sent to the monks from Europe, to a considerable amount, without ever touching or embezzling the smallest article. They know that the superior of the convent at Jerusalem pays the travelling expences of the pilgrims,

grims, and that they are poor monks, who have nothing to lose. Yet they wait to intercept those indigent caravans, not to pillage them, but that they may have the pleasure of venting their hatred against the monks.

It would be a gross mistake, therefore, if any European should fancy that he might travel safely through Judea, in consequence of putting himself under the protection of the monks. A young Frenchman had a trial of this when I was in that country. Passing the river Jordan, he was severely beaten by the Bedouins, solely for being found in company with the monks, which made the Arabs view him in a suspicious light.

SECT.

SECTION XXV.

OF THE RELIGION AND CHARACTER OF THE ARABS.

CHAP. I.

Of the different Sects of Mahometans in Arabia.

It might be expected that the Mahometan religion should be preserved in its highest purity in Arabia, which was its cradle; and that no contrariety of opinions, or diversity of sects, should have arisen there. An old tradition records a saying of Mahomet's, from which he appears to have foreseen that it was impossible for his followers to remain in perpetual harmony of doctrine and worship. He is said to have predicted that his new religion should be divided into seventy different sects, as the Christians of his time were.

This prediction is in part accomplished; for there are at present several Mahometan sects in Arabia.

The doctrines and rites of the Mussulman religion are in general sufficiently known. I

shall

shall satisfy myself with mentioning some remarkable peculiarities which distinguish the sects established in Arabia, and which have an influence on the moral character or political state of the nation.

The most considerable sects among the Arabian Mahometans, are,

1. That of *Sunni*, to which the Turks also belong. This forms the most numerous sect in Arabia; its opinions being professed by the inhabitants of the holy cities of Mecca and Medina, and by the Sherriffes of those cities who are reputed the successors of Mahomet.

2. The sect of *Schya*, of which the whole Persian nation profess themselves. In the eastern parts of Arabia are some disciples of this sect; and it prevails all along the borders of the Persian Gulph. The *Metaueli*, or *Mut-Ali*, in Syria, are likewise Shiites.

3. The sect of *Zeidi*, which prevails in Yemen, and of which the Imam of Sana is a follower.

4. The sect of *Beiasi*, *Beiadi*, or *Abadi*, is the principal sect in *Oman*. It is said to owe its origin to the enemies of the Caliph Ali, two of whom went into Oman after a defeat, which only nine of them had survived.

5. The sect of *Meſſalich*, of which I have already taken notice in describing the Bedouins settled between the provinces of Hedsjas and Yemen.

Yemen. I fufpect this rather to be a different religion, than a fect of the Muffulman.

6. The fect of *Mecrami* and *Abd ul Wahheb*. I have already given my opinion of this little known fect in the defcriptions of Nedsjeran and Nedsjed.

7. The fect of *Dsjedsjal*, of which the inhabitants of *Mecran*, a maritime province of Perfia, are followers.

8. Laftly, the fects of *Schabreari* and *Merdinar*, of which are the *Belludsje*, Arabian tribes on the confines of the province of Mecran, as I have above obferved.

All thefe different fects acknowledge Mahomet their prophet, and regard the Koran as their code of civil and ecclefiaftical laws. However, they mutually treat each other as *Chauaredsji* or *Rafidi*, that is to fay, heretics.

The *Sunnites* allow only the four fects, which they confider as orthodox; thofe of *Schafei*, *Hanefi*, *Malcki*, and *Hanbali*, to have houfes of prayer about the *Kaba*. The Zeidites, however, to make themfelves amends for the exclufion they fuffer, have reared for themfelves an invifible houfe of prayer in the air, immediately over the Kaba, by which means they are, in their own opinion, put into poffeffion of thefe facred places. Notwithftanding thefe lofty pretenfions, every pilgrim of this fect is obliged to pay a

high

high capitation to the Sherriffe, who has, for these several years, made the Shiites likewise pay dear for permission to visit Mecca.

The Zeidites seem to be less rigid and superstitious than the Sunnites, who are much addicted to the worship of saints, and believe in the most ridiculous miracles. The former trouble not themselves with the controversy about Mahomet's successors, which has occasioned the schism between the Sunnites and the Shiites. Nor are they so rigid and exact in respect to prayers and other ceremonies; they make no mention of saints; and the Imam of Sana, who is a Zeidite, suffers useless mosques to fall into ruins, and sometimes even demolishes them, to the great offence of his Sunnite subjects in the Tehama.

All these sects venerate the descendants of Mahomet, except the *Beiasi*, who treat them with no greater respect than other Arabs, and believe all the families in the nation to have the same right to the sovereign power.

For this reason, the Prince of Maskat, who is of the sect of *Beiasi*, takes the title of Imam, although not descended from Mahomet. This sect abstain, not only from strong liquors, like the other Mussulmans, but even from tobacco and coffee; although, out of hospitality, these are offered to strangers in *Oman*. The *Beiasi* pique

pique themselves on great austerity of manners, and simplicity in their mode of living. Even the most opulent among them avoid every thing like magnificence in their dress, houses, and mosques. The Prince administers justice in person, and permits all his subjects to be seated in his presence. It was in consequence of this severity of manners, that the last Imam, who was a tyrannical and voluptuous prince, became odious to his subjects. In the description of O-man, I have taken notice of the revolution by which that prince was driven from the throne.

At Maskat, I received an account of the miraculous origin of the sect of *Dsjedsjal*, in the province of Mecran. Its first author was a venerable old man, who was found by some wood-cutters shut up in the middle of a tree, and having a book in his hand. Each sect indeed tells ridiculous stories of the other sects to bring them into contempt.

I saw or heard of no convents of monks among the Zeidites in Yemen, or among the Beiasi in Oman. The Sunnites, and among them the Turks especially, are known to have a great number of religious orders, the members of which are distinguished by the names of *Dervises* and *Santons*, and discriminated from one another by diversities of dress and manners. At Mokha were beggars, who sang through the streets,

streets, called Dervifes; as well as some other poor creatures, who, for any trifle, were ready to read the paffages of the Koran infcribed on the tombftones. As the Zeidites and Beiafi are not worshippers of faints, they cannot have Dervifes and Santons; who, on the other hand, are very numerous in Egypt, where they perform many extravagant fooleries.

The Turks and Perfians have been almoft conftantly at war; and their refpective Princes have generally contrived to reprefent to their fubjects difputes which originated from their ambition, as prompted by religious confiderations. This is the reafon of the violent hatred with which the Shiites and Sunnites are animated againft one another. In Turkey and Perfia, Chriftians are permitted to build churches, and the Jews, fynagogues; but in Perfia, no Sunnite mofque is allowed; and the Turks tolerate the Shiites in the exercife of no other part of their worfhip, except their pilgrimage to their Prophet's tomb in the vicinity of Bagdad; and for this permiffion they pay very dear to the Ottoman Porte. In Yemen, the Sunnites and Zeidites live happily together; for the latter, who are the more tolerant of the two, are the predominant fect.

The Muffulmans in general do not perfecute men of other religions, when they have nothing to to fear from them, unlefs in the cafe of an intercourfe of gallantry with a Mahometan woman. A Chriftian, convicted of blafphemy, would alfo be in danger of lofing his life. In fuch a cafe, it is true, a Mahometan would as little be fpared. While I was at Bagdad, a Janiffary urged a citizen for a debt; the latter always anfwered with a devout air, that he fhould remember God and the Prophet, and wait patiently for payment, without putting himfelf in a paffion. The Janiffary was at laft provoked to utter a blafphemous expreffion; the artful citizen attefted witneffes; and the Janiffary was accordingly convicted, expelled out of his corps, and next day hanged.

All the Muffulman fects are not alike abhorrers of images. In Oman, the Banians are allowed to fet up their images openly in their apartments. The Sunnites even appear to have loft fomewhat of their averfion for thefe material reprefentations of Deity. Thofe in India keep paintings; and I even faw two of thefe in a villa of the Sultan's near Conftantinople. At Kahira I found prints, and a plafter buft in the houfe of a learned Sunnite.

CHAP.

CHAP. II.

Of the other Religions tolerated in Arabia.

THROUGH all Arabia are Jews, who are held in much greater contempt than the Chriftians. I have already mentioned the Jewifh tribes fettled in the neighbourhood of *Kheibar*, where they are not barely tolerated, but have the fovereign authority in their own hands.

The Jews difperfed through different cities have fynagogues, and enjoy a great deal of freedom. They are fond of living together, and commonly form a village near every principal town. In Oman they are ftill better treated, and permitted to wear the drefs of Mahometans.

The Chriftians were once numerous in Arabia. I know of no Chriftian church remaining at prefent in all this country. In the province of Lachfa are many Sabæans, or Chriftians of St John. But, the Chriftianity of this fect feems to be a confufed medley of the opinions and ceremonies of feveral different religions.

Banians from India are fettled in great numbers in the commercial cities. At Mokha they fuffer many mortifications. But, at Mafkat, among the tolerant fect of the Beiafi, they are

are permitted to obferve the laws, and cultivate the worfhip of their own religion without difturbance. In Perfia there are alfo fome of thefe Indians; but the Turks, who are auftere Sunnites, fuffer none of them in their provinces.

I never faw that the Arabs have any hatred for thofe of a different religion. They, however, regard them with much the fame contempt with which Chriftians look upon the Jews in Europe. Among the Arabs this contempt is regulated. It falls heavieft upon the Banians; next after them, upon the Jews; and, leaft of all, upon the Chriftians, who, in return, exprefs the leaft averfion for the Muffulmans. A Mahometan, who marries a Chriftian or Jewifh woman, does not oblige her to apoftatize from her religion; but the fame man would not marry a Banian female, becaufe this Indian fect are fuppofed to be ftrangers to the knowledge of God, having no book of divine authority. The Mahometans in India appear to be even more tolerant than thofe of Arabia. They live in a good underftanding with the Banians, and treat them with lefs contempt than their Arabian brethren.

This progrefs towards general toleration preferves the Arabs from the rage of making profelytes. They feek neither to entice nor conftrain

Scene in the Wilderness, on the way to Mount Sinai.

ſtrain any perſon, except ſometimes their young ſlaves, whom they compel to embrace Mahometiſm: But, when a proſelyte voluntarily preſents himſelf, they are, by the laws of their religion, obliged to receive him, and even to provide for his maintenance. The converts who moſt commonly offer themſelves are deſerters from the crews of European ſhips, who take this ſhift to eſcape puniſhment. As they are known to be moſtly very bad ſubjects, government allows them but a very ſcanty penſion, ſcarcely ſufficient for their maintenance. They are not confined, either from intercourſe with Chriſtians, or from taking voyages into diſtant countries. We had in our ſervice in Arabia a French renegado, who, when he left us, went to India.

It may not be improper to remark, in this place, that the Indians are ſtill leſs anxious about making converts than the Arabs. The Bramins, Rajaputs, and Banians, receive nobody into their communion, but, on the contrary, expel all of their members who render themſelves obnoxious by irregularity of life, and by this means afford proſelytes to the Chriſtians. Thus the European miſſionaries, who run ſo indecently through the Eaſt, and profane the ſacrament of baptiſm, by caſting it at the head of every

one, have little reafon to boaft of the conver‑
fions they effect, efpecially as they ufe fo much
importunity to accomplifh them.

CHAP. III.

Of the Character of the Arabs.

CLIMATE, government, and education, are, un‑
doubtedly, the great agents which form and
modify the characters of nations. To the firft
of thefe the Arabs owe their vivacity, and their
difpofition to indolence; the fecond increafes
their lazinefs, and gives them a fpirit of dupli‑
city; the third is the caufe of that formal gra‑
vity which influences the faculties of their mind,
as well as their carriage and exterior afpect.

No two things can differ more than the edu‑
cation of the Arabs from that of the Europeans.
The former ftrive as much to haften the age of
maturity, as the latter to retard it. The Arabs
are never children; but many Europeans conti‑
nue children all their life.

In Arabia, boys remain in the Haram, among
the women, till the age of five or fix, and du‑
ring this time follow the childifh amufements
fuitable to their years; but, affoon as they are
removed from that fcene of frivolity, they are ac‑
cuftomed

customed to think and speak with gravity, and to pass whole days together in their father's company, at least if he is not in a condition to retain a preceptor, who may form them. As music and dancing are esteemed indecent among the Arabs, women are also excluded from all assemblies, and the use of strong drink is forbidden. The Arabian youth are strangers to the pretended pleasures which are so eagerly pursued by the youth of Europe. The young Arabs, in consequence of being always under the eyes of persons advanced to maturity, become pensive and serious even in infancy.

Yet, under this air of gravity and recollection, the nation have in reality a great degree of vivacity in their hearts, which varies through the different provinces. The inhabitants of Yemen, living in a mild climate, and an agreeable air, have more animation in their character than those of Hedsjas and Arabia Petræa, whose imagination receives a more gloomy cast 'from the continual prospect of barren desarts and bare rocks. I have seen young Arabs in Yemen dance and leap, with arms in their hands, to the sound of small drums; yet, even the inhabitants of the desart, shew greater vivacity than the Turks. As for the melancholy Egyptians, I never saw them discover any mark of genuine joy, even at their festivals, however splendid.

This

This vivacity in the Arabians makes them fond of company, and of large affemblies, notwithftanding their feeming ferioufnefs. They frequent public coffee-houfes, and markets, which are fo numerous through Yemen, that every village, of any confiderable magnitude, has a weekly market. When the villages lie at too great a diftance, the country people meet in the open fields, fome to buy or fell, and others to converfe, or amufe themfelves as fpectators of the bufy fcene. Artifans travel through the whole week from town to town, and work at their trade in the different markets. From this fondnefs of theirs for fociety, it may be inferred, that the nation are more civilized than they are commonly fuppofed to be.

Several travellers accufe them of being cheats, thieves, and hypocrites. An arbitrary government, which impoverifhes its fubjects by extortion, can have no favourable influence indeed upon the probity of the nation; yet, I can fay, from my own experience, that the accufations laid againft them have been exaggerated above the facts. The Arabs themfelves allow that their countrymen are not all honeft men. I have heard them praife the fidelity with which the Europeans fulfil their promifes, and exprefs high indignation againft the knavery of their

own

own nation, as a difgrace to the Mufulman name.

CHAP. IV.

Of the Vengeance of the Arabs.

A LIVELY, animated people, of quick and violent paffions, are naturally led to carry the defire of vengeance for injuries to its higheft excefs. The vindictive fpirit of the Arabs, which is common to them with the other inhabitants of hot climates, varies, however, with the varying modifications of the national character.

The Arabs are not quarrelfome; but, when any difpute happens to arife among them, they make a great deal of noife. I have feen fome of them, however, who, although armed with poignards, and ready to ftab one another, were eafily appeafed. A reconciliation was inftantly effected, if any indifferent perfon but faid to them, Think of God and his Prophet. When the conteft could not be fettled at once, umpires were chofen, to whofe decifion they fubmitted.

The inhabitants of the Eaft in general ftrive to mafter their anger. A boatman from Mafkat complained to the governor of the city of a merchant who would not pay a freight due for the carriage of his goods. The governor always put off hearing him, till fome other time. At laſt the plaintiff told his cafe coolly, and the governor immediately did him juſtice, faying, I refufed to hear you before, becaufe you were intoxicated with anger, the moſt dangerous of all intoxications.

Notwithſtanding this coolnefs, on which the people of the Eaſt pique themſelves, the Arabs ſhew great fenſibility to every thing that can be conſtrued into an injury. If one man ſhould happen to fpit befide another, the latter will not fail to avenge himſelf of the imaginary infult. In a caravan I once faw an Arab highly offended at a man, who, in fpitting, had accidentally befpattered his beard with fome fmall part of the fpittle. It was with difficulty that he could be appeafed by him, who, he imagined, had offended him, even although he humbly afked pardon, and kiſſed his beard in token of fubmiſſion. They are leſs ready to be offended by reproachful language, which is, befides, more in ufe with the lower people than among the higher claſſes.

But the moſt irritable of all men are the noble Bedouins, who, in their martial fpirit, feem to carry thofe fame prejudices farther than even

the

the barbarous warriors who issued from the North, and overran Europe. Bedouin honour is still more delicate than ours, and requires even a greater number of victims to be sacrificed to it. If one Schiech says to another, with a serious air, 'Thy bonnet is dirty,' or, 'The wrong side of thy turban is out,' nothing but blood can wash away the reproach; and not merely the blood of the offender, but that also of all the males of his family.

At Barra I heard the story of an adventure, which had happened about a dozen of years since, in the neighbourhood of that city, and which may afford an idea of the excess to which the spirit of revenge often rises among this nation. A man of eminence, belonging to the tribe of *Montefidsi*, had given his daughter in marriage to an Arab of the tribe of *Korne*. Shortly after the marriage, a Schiech of an inferior tribe asked him, in a coffee-house, Whether he were father to the handsome young wife of such a one, whom he named? The father, supposing his daughter's honour ruined, immediately left the company to stab her. At his return from the execution of this inhuman deed, he who had so indiscreetly put the question was gone. Breathing nothing now but vengeance, he sought him every where; and not finding him, killed in the mean time several of his relations,

relations, without sparing even his cattle or servants. The offender offered the governor of Korne a great sum if he would rid him of so furious an adversary. The governor sent for him who had been offended, and endeavoured by threats, and a shew of the apparatus of punishment, to force him to a reconciliation; but the vengeful Arab would rather meet death than forego his revenge. Then the governor, to preserve a man of such high honour, soothed him to an agreement, by which the first aggressor gave his daughter, with a handsome portion, in marriage to him whom he had offended. But the father-in-law durst never after appear before his son-in-law.

The thirst for vengeance discovers itself likewise in the peculiar manner in which murther is prosecuted here. In the high country of Yemen, the supreme court of Sana commonly prosecutes murthers in the mode usual in other countries; but, in several districts in Arabia, the relations of the deceased have leave either to accept a composition in money, or to require the murtherer to surrender himself to justice, or even to wreak their vengeance upon his whole family. In many places, it is reckoned unlawful to take money for the shedding of blood, which, by the laws of Arabian honour, can be expiated only by blood. They think

little

little of making an affaffin be punifhed, or even put to death, by the hand of juftice; for this would be to deliver a family from an unworthy member, who deferved no fuch favour at their hands.

For thefe reafons, the Arabs rather revenge themfelves, as law allows, upon the family of the murderer, and feek an opportunity of flaying its head, or moft confiderable perfon, whom they regard as being properly the perfon guilty of the crime, as it muft have been committed through his negligence in watching over the conduct of thofe under his infpection. In the mean time, the judges feize the murderer, and detain him till he has paid a fine of two hundred crowns. Had it not been for this fine, fo abfurd a law muft have been long fince repealed. From this time, the two families are in continual fears, till fome one or other of the murderer's family be flain. No reconciliation can take place between them, and the quarrel is ftill occafionally renewed. There have been inftances of fuch family feuds lafting forty years. If, in the conteft, a man of the murdered perfon's family happens to fall, there can be no peace till two others of the murderer's family have been flain.

This deteftable cuftom is fo exprefsly forbidden in the Koran, that I fhould not have been perfuaded persuaded of its existence, had I not seen instances of it. Men, indeed, act every where in direct contradiction to the principles of religion; and this species of revenge is not merely impious, but even absurd and inhuman. An Arabian of distinction, who often visited us at Loheya, always wore, even when he was in company, both his poignard and a small lance. The reason of this, he told us, was, that a man of his family had been murdered, and he was obliged to avenge the murder upon a man of the inimical family, who was then actually in the city, and carried just such another lance. He acknowledged to us, that the fear of meeting his enemy, and fighting with him, often disturbed his sleep. In the narrative of my journey from Beit el Fakih to Mokha, I have related an instance of a family feud of this kind, in the country through which we passed.

Among the Bedouins in the East of Arabia, every family strive to right themselves, whenever they think that they have suffered an injury. When the two hostile families happen to belong to two powerful rival tribes, formal wars sometimes follow in consequence of such accidental quarrels: But, on the other hand, the public peace is not at all interrupted by a private feud, when the persons at variance belong to two petty tribes, both subject to the same

great

great tribe. Laſtly, when the two contending parties are ſubjects of the ſame Schiech, and are, of conſequence, held to be of the ſame family, the Schiech and the principal ſubjects join to reconcile the parties, and to puniſh the murderer.

The tribes upon the confines of Oman, and the ſhores of the Perſian gulph, are alſo acquainted with theſe family wars, and more harraſſed even than the Arabians by them. A great part of theſe tribes earn their ſubſiſtence by carrying coffee from Yemen to the Perſian gulph, and by the pearl fiſhery; and, from this circumſtance, parties at variance have more frequent opportunities of meeting and fighting at ſea. Weak tribes are thus often obliged to quit their way of life, and fall into obſcurity and miſery (P).

CHAP. V.

Of the Arabian Nobility.

THE Arabs are accuſed of being vain, full of prejudices with reſpect to birth, and ridiculouſly attentive to records of genealogy, which they keep even for their horſes. This reproach cannot affect the great body of the nation, who
know

know not their family names, and take not the trouble of keeping a regifter of births. Moft of thofe, even in the middle ftation of life, know not who were their grandfathers, and would often be as much at a lofs to know their fathers, if it were not regulated by cuftom, that the fon fhall join his father's name with his own.

All thofe petty princes who govern in Arabia are, undoubtedly, very proud of their birth, and with fome reafon, fince their families have, from time immemorial, enjoyed independence and fovereign power. The nobility, who are free, or dependent only on the chiefs of their tribes, are equally fo. They enjoy privileges which the traditional hiftory of the nation reprefents as having always belonged to certain families. The Schiechs are excufeable, therefore, although they value themfelves upon advantages which are peculiarly theirs.

What adds to the high conceit the Bedouin Schiechs have of their nobility, is its being incommunicable, and not to be conferred by any fovereign prince, or even by the Caliphs. As it is founded on the cuftoms of a paftoral people, who know no diftinction of rank, but that of the heads of families, no fovereign can augment the number of thefe chiefs. Nobles can be created only in countries where the nobility

form

form a diftinct clafs, enjoying certain civil privileges, which may be equally conferred on others. The Bedouin nobility may be compared to the chiefs of the clans among the Scotch highlanders, who are in a very fimilar condition with refpect to their honours and authority (Q).

The defcendents of Mahomet hold, with fome reafon, the firft rank among the great families in Arabia. Mahomet was fprung from one of the nobleft families in the country, and rofe to the rank of a potent prince. His firft profeffion of a dealer in camels, proves him to have been a Schiech of the genuine and pure nobility of his nation. It may be inferred, however, from the fingular veneration in which his family are held, that religious opinions have contributed to gain them the pre-eminence which they hold, above even the moft ancient fovereign houfes. A fect naturally refpect the pofterity of their founder, as a race bearing an indelible character of fanctity.

Thefe defcendents of Mahomet have received different titles. In Arabia they are called Sherriffes, or *Sejids;* in the Mahometan countries fituate northward, Sherriffes or Emirs; and in the Arabian colonies in the Eaft, fimply Sejids. The prince of *Havifa,* on the frontiers of Perfia, takes the title of *Maula,* which has, I believe, been alfo affumed by the Emperor of Morocco.

Morocco. In some countries, this family are distinguished by a green turban. Nay, on the coasts of Arabia, ships hoist a green flag, when fitted out by a Sejid. Yet the green turban is not invariably a distinctive mark of a descendent of Mahomet. Beggars sometimes wear turbans of this colour; and one of our servants did the same, and was blamed by nobody.

The Sherriffes of Hedsjas are esteemed the noblest of Mahomet's descendents, because they have made fewer intermarriages with strangers than the rest of the Prophet's posterity. In that province, they are treated with almost incredible respect. A Sherriffe may venture into the midst of a fray, without the smallest fear of being intentionally hurt or killed. He needs not to shut his doors against thieves. In the Ottoman provinces, the family of the Prophet are less regarded. In my time, a Sejid, who had been guilty of divers crimes, and although warned and reproved by an indulgent governor, had not corrected his bad habits, was condemned to suffer capital punishment.

Having heard a distinction frequently made between a Sherriffe and a Sejid, I made inquiry into its nature. I learned that Sherriffes are constantly devoted to a military life, and are descended from *Haffan;* but that the Sejids are the posterity of *Hoffein*, and follow the

pursuits

purſuits of trade and ſcience, although they have ſometimes riſen to ſovereign power in ſome parts of Arabia.

There are, in all Mahometan countries, an aſtoniſhing number of Sherriffes. I ſaw whole villages peopled with this family ſolely. To thoſe who know not in what manner this title is tranſmitted, the numbers of thoſe who enjoy this high rank muſt undoubtedly appear ſurpriſing; but polygamy naturally multiplies families, till many of their branches ſink into the moſt wretched miſery. In my account of *Jebid*, I have mentioned my acquaintance with a Sherriffe in that city, who was in extreme poverty. A peculiar cuſtom tends to the farther increaſe of the race of Sherriffes. The ſon of a woman of the family of Mahomet is eſteemed a Sherriffe, and tranſmits the honour to all his poſterity. I travelled through Natolia with a Turk, who was called ſimply *Achmed*, and wore the common turban, while his ſon was honoured with a green turban, and with the title of Sherriffe, becauſe his mother was a *Sherriffa*. Other ſimilar inſtances came within my knowledge in the provinces of Turkey; and, from various circumſtances, I was led to infer, that many perſons enjoy this title who are not at all connected with the Prophet's family. The genuine Sherriffes, to ſtrengthen their party againſt the Caliphs

liphs, have acknowledged kindred with various powerful families who were entire strangers to them.

In Turkey, where the Sherriffes are not numerous, they enjoy various privileges, and, among others, that of being subject, in every considerable town, not to the Pacha, but to a man of their own family, who is denominated *Nakib*, or general of the Sherriffes. The Turkish government seems, however, to be suspicious of their ambition, and never intrusts them with any public office. They are commonly called *Emirs*; an indeterminate title, which is bestowed equally upon persons of the highest quality, and upon subordinate officers.

Of all the titles in use among the Arabian nobility, the most ancient and most common is that of Schiech. The Arabian language, which is in other respects so rich, is however poor in terms expressive of the distinctions of rank. The word *Schiech* has, in consequence of this circumstance, various significations. Sometimes it is the title of a prince or noble; at other times, it is given to a professor in an academy; to a man belonging to a mosque, to the descendent of a saint, to the mayor of a town, and in Oman, even to the chief of the Jewish synagogue. Although thus seemingly prostituted, yet is not this title despised by the great. A

Schiech

Schiech of an ancient Arabian family would not change the name for that of *Sultan*, which has been assumed by some petty princes in the highlands of Hadramaut and Jafa.

The Schiechs of illustrious families among the Bedouins have reason for considering their genealogy as a matter of some consequence. Some of them are descended from ancestors who were princes before the days of Mahomet, and the first Caliphs. As it would be difficult, among a people who have no public registers or historians, to make out regular tables of genealogies reaching farther than ten centuries backwards, the Arabians have contrived a compendious mode of verifying their lines of descent. From among their later ancestors, they select some illustrious man from whom they are universally allowed to be descended. This great man, again, is as universally allowed to be descended from some other great man; and thus they proceed backwards to the founder of the family. The Sherriffes and Sejids, by the same expedient, prove the origin of their family to have been with Mahomet, and thus abbreviate their genealogy, without rendering it doubtful.

Beside these Schiechs and princes, there are, at Mecca, some families not less concerned to preserve preferve their genealogies, with all poffible exactitude. Thefe are the families defcended from the tribe of *Koraifch*, which have held certain employments, by hereditary right, fince the days of Mahomet and his firft fucceffors. Their employments are, 1*ft*, the office of keeper of the key of the *Kaba*, which was conferred by Mahomet on the family of *Othman ibn Tælha*: 2*d*, That of Mufti of the fect of *Schafei:* 3*d*, That of Mufti of the fect of *Hanbali;* and, *laftly*, That of a learned *Schech* to attend in the holy mofque.

There are alfo, in Mecca, twelve other families, defcended from the illuftrious tribe of *Koraifch*. If any where in the world, a faithful lift of genealogy, for more than ten centuries, may be found, it is certainly among thefe families of *Koraifchites*, who are conftantly obliged to prove the genuinenefs of their defcent, in order to preferve their envied privileges.

I never heard the diftinction between the genuine and naturalized Arabs formally explained. Such a diftinction is made, however; for the Bedouins value themfelves fo much on the purity of their defcent, that they look very contemptuoufly on the Arabs who live in cities, as a race debafed by their intermixture with other nations. No Schiech will marry the daughter

of

of a citizen, unless he happen to be driven by poverty to contract so unequal an alliance. At Bagdad I saw a Schiech of eminence from the desart, who, from motives of this nature, had married the daughter of the Mufti of that city.

The Arabs seem still to have a vanity in the use of those long names which are so disgusting in their history; but this length of names and titles is occasioned by the difficulty of distinguishing individuals among a nation who know not the use of family names. Thus an Arab named Ali, if his father's name was *Mohammed*, takes the name of *Ali Ibn Mohammed* ; if from Basra, he adds the name of his country, *el Basri* ; and, if a man of letters, the name of his sect, as *Schafei* ; and his name at length will thus be, *Ali Ibn Mohammed el Basri el Schafei* ; so that he cannot be confounded with any other of his countrymen. An illustrious man never takes these long names in his lifetime, but has all this pomp of epithets conferred on him after his death.

Some men, whose fathers have not been much known, adjoin to their own names that of their eldest son. A Turk of the name of *Salech*, who furnished me for hire with mules to perform the journey from Aleppo to Konie, called himself
Fatime

Fatime Ugli, the son of Fatime. I asked several Turks, if it were common among them to take the name of the mother. They replied, that there were some instances of it, but that no man in his senses would name himself after a woman.

SECTION XXVI.

OF THE MANNERS AND USAGES OF THE ARABIANS.

CHAP. I.

Of Marriage among the Arabians.

THE Europeans are mistaken in thinking the state of marriage so different among the Mussulmans from what it is with Christian nations. I could not discern any such difference in Arabia. The women of that country seem to be as free and happy as those of Europe can possibly be.

Polygamy

Polygamy is permitted, indeed, among Mahometans, and the delicacy of our ladies is shocked at this idea; but the Arabians rarely avail themselves of the privilege of marrying four lawful wives, and entertaining at the same time any number of female slaves. None but rich voluptuaries marry so many wives, and their conduct is blamed by all sober men. Men of sense, indeed, think this privilege rather troublesome than convenient. A husband is, by law, obliged to treat his wives suitably to their condition, and to dispense his favours among them with perfect equality: But these are duties not a little disagreeable to most Muffulmans; and such modes of luxury are too expensive to the Arabians, who are seldom in easy circumstances. I must, however, except one case; for it sometimes happens that a man marries a number of wives in the way of a commercial speculation. I knew a *Mullah*, in a town near the Euphrates, who had married four wives, and was supported by the profits of their labour.

Divorce, the idea of which is also regarded as horrid by the fair sex in Europe, is not nearly so common as is imagined in the East. The Arabians never exercise the right of repudiating a wife, unless urged by the strongest reasons; because this is considered a dishonourable step, by persons who value their reputation, and

throws

throws disgrace on the woman and her relations. Wives are entitled to demand a divorce when they think themselves ill used by their husbands. Only profligate and impudent men, who have married without consideration, will divorce their wives for slight causes.

An Arabian, in moderate circumstances, seldom marries more than one wife. And even the most considerable persons in the nation are often contented with one for life. Rich men, who are in a condition to maintain as many wives as they please, have often confessed to me, that although they had begun to live with several wives, they had at last found that they could be happy only with one.

The Arabian women enjoy a great deal of liberty, and often a great deal of power, in their families. They continue mistresses of their dowries, and of the annual income which these afford, during their marriage; and, in the case of divorce, all their own property is reserved to them. Hence it happens, that when a man in narrow circumstances marries a woman of fortune, he is entirely dependent on his wife, and dares not divorce her.

It is absurd to say, as some travellers have, that the Mahometan wives are all slaves, and so entirely the property of their husbands, that they are even inherited by his heirs. In this representation, reprefentation, flaves purchafed with money have been confounded with women of free eftate, who difpofe of themfelves in the Eaft juft as in Europe.

The opinion, that women are flaves in Arabia, feems to have arifen from the miftaken notion, that fathers there fell their daughters to the higheft bidder. It many times happens, no doubt, that a poor man, who has an handfome daughter, is pleafed to match her with a rich man, from whom he may receive occafional prefents. And rich voluptuaries, who choofe to marry more wives than one, are obliged to take young women of low condition, who are compelled by interefted parents, or feduced by fplendour, to accept a hufband who affociates them with other wives, and at length divorces them.

Inftead of felling his daughter, every man, in tolerably eafy circumftances, ftrives to give her a dowry, which may continue her own property. The marriage is made out by the Cadi, and figned in his prefence; and in it not only is her dowry fecured to the wife, but alfo a feparate maintenance, in cafe of a divorce. The rich often give their daughters, in preference, to poor men, and confider their children as more likely to be happy, when thus fettled, than if they were married to rich men. The wife is then miftrefs of all the property, and even of the

the houfe of her hufband, and is not in danger of being fent away.

Many ridiculous ftories have been told of the marks of virginity which an Arab expects when he marries a young woman. But moft of thefe ftories greatly exaggerate the truth. The Bedouins, and the highlanders of Yemen, a rude and almoft favage race, do indeed regard the want of thofe marks as a proof of difhonour, and think themfelves obliged to fend a woman back to her relations, when her chaftity cannot be thus evinced. But the inhabitants of the towns, being more civilized, never concern themfelves about fuch a trifle; only, in cafe of fuch an accident, a fon-in-law forces an addition to the dowry from his father-in-law, by threatening to fend his daughter home again, although he never actually does fo. At Bafra I heard of a fingle inftance of divorce upon this ground, and the man was of the loweft clafs of the people.

Many fuperftitious obfervances, refpecting marriage, ftill prevail in Arabia. The Arabs ftill believe in the virtue of enchantments, and in the art of tying and untying the knots of fate. The miferable victim of this diabolical art addreffes fome phyfician, or fome old woman; for the old women are always fkilled in forcery. The Chriftians of the Eaft have a ftill more

certain

certain remedy againſt the effects of witchcraft. They ſay maſſes for the perſon afflicted; and when, at laſt, the imagination of the poor patient has had time to recover, the honour of the cure is always aſcribed to the powerful influence of the maſſes.

We imagine in Europe, that the inhabitants of the Eaſt keep Eunuchs for the guardians of their harams; yet Eunuchs are not common through the Eaſt, and in Arabia there are none. The Turkiſh Monarch keeps more Eunuchs in his ſeraglio at Conſtantinople than are in all the reſt of his dominions. The Pacha of Aleppo had two, and he of Moſul one, whom he kept, becauſe he had belonged to his father. It is wrong, therefore, to regard Arabia as the ſeat of Eunuchiſm. They are brought from Upper Egypt, but are moſtly natives of the interior and little known provinces of Africa. The Arabians abhor the cruel operation which is requiſite to render a man a fit guardian of the chaſtity of a haram.

Eunuchs born in a climate which has a tendency to inflame the blood, are not abſolutely void of all paſſion for the fair ſex. On the ſea, between Suez and Jedda, I met with a Eunuch who travelled with his ſeraglio; and at Baſra I heard of another rich Eunuch, who kept female ſlaves for his private amuſement.

Much has been said in Europe concerning the origin of the practice of polygamy, so generally prevalent through the East. Supposing that the plurality of wives is not barely allowed by law, but takes place in fact, some of our philosophers have imagined, that, in hot countries, more women than men are born; but I have already stated, that some nations avail not themselves of the permission given by the Mussulman law for one man to marry several wives. It would be unfair to judge of the manners of a whole people by the fastidious luxury of the great. It is vanity that fills seraglios, and that chiefly with slaves, most of whom are only slaves to a few favourite women. The number of female servants in Europe, who are, in the same manner, condemned in a great measure to celibacy, is equal or superior to that of those who are confined in the harams of the East.

It is true, that European clergymen and physicians settled in the East have presumed that rather more girls than boys are born here. I obtained some lists of Christian baptisms in the East; but some of those were filled with inconsistencies; and, in the others, the number by which the females born exceeded the males was indeed very trifling. I have reason, therefore, to conclude, that the proportion between the male and the female births is the same here as elsewhere.

This

This proportion varies fometimes in Europe, as is proved by a recent inftance of a town in England, in which, for fome part of this century, more girls than boys have been born.

There are, it muft be allowed, a good many Mahometans, who marry more wives than one, and at the fame time keep female flaves; but to fupply thefe men's harams a furplus of females is not neceffary. Different accidents carry off a number of men, and thofe accidents are fuch as the women are not expofed to. In the Eaft, women are more impatient for marriage than in Europe. According to the ideas of Eaftern manners, nothing is more difgraceful to a woman than to remain barren. Confcience obliges the women of thofe regions to defire that they may become mothers. A woman will, therefore, rather marry a poor man, or become fecond wife to a man already married, than remain in a ftate of celibacy. I have mentioned the inftance of the poor Mullah, who married four wives, and lived by the profits of their labour. The men are equally difpofed to marry, becaufe their wives, inftead of being expenfive, are rather profitable to them. Nothing is more rarely to be met with in the Eaft, than a woman unmarried after a certain time of life.

The Shiites are, by their law, permitted to live for a certain time, by agreement, but without

out a formal marriage, with a free Mahometan woman. The Perfians frequently avail themfelves of this permiffion; but the more rigid Sunnites think this an illicit connection, and do not tolerate it. In Turkey, a man who fhould cohabit with a free woman, without being married to her, would be punifhed by law.

CHAP. II.

Of the Domeftic Life of the Arabs.

ARABIA affords no elegant or fplendid apartments for the admiration of the traveller. The houfes are built of ftone, and have always terrace roofs. Thofe occupied by the lower people are fmall huts, having a round roof, and covered with a certain herb. The huts of the Arabs on the banks of the Euphrates are formed of branches of the date tree, and have a round roof covered with rufh mats. The tents of the *Bedouins* are like thofe of the *Kurdes* and *Turcomans*. They have the afpect of a tattered hut. I have formerly remarked, that they are formed of coarfe ftuffs prepared by the women.

The palaces and houfes of Arabians of rank difplay no exterior magnificence. Ornaments are

are not to be expected in the apartments of men who are strangers to all luxury, except what consists in the number and the value of the horses, servants, and arms which they keep. The poor spread their floors with straw mats, and the rich with fine carpets. No person even enters a room, without having first put off his shoes. A Frenchman boasts of having maintained the honour of his nation, by wearing his shoes in the governor of Mecca's hall of audience. It is just such another boast, as if an Arabian envoy should vaunt of trampling on the chairs of an European Lord.

The men of every family always occupy the fore part of the house, and the women the back part. If the apartments of the men are plain, those of the women are, on the contrary, most studiously set off with decorations. Of this I saw a specimen in a haram, which was nearly finished for a man of rank. One room in it was wholly covered over with mirrors; the roof, the walls, the doors, the pillars, presented all so many looking glasses. The floor was to be set with sofas, and spread with carpets.

Arabians, in circumstances which admit not of their having separate apartments for the females of the family, are careful, whenever they carry a stranger into the house, to enter before him, and cry *Tarik*, retire. Upon this notice,

given

given by the mafter of the houfe, the women inftantly difappear, and even his very beft friends fee not one of them. A man muft, indeed, deny himfelf this fight; for it is reckoned highly impolite to falute a woman, or even to look her ftedfaftly in the face. To avoid receiving ftrangers in their houfes, fhopkeepers and artifans expofe their wares, and follow their refpective trades, in the open ftreets.

The retired life of the women difpofes them to behave refpectfully to the other fex. I met a Bedouin lady, who, purely out of refpect, left the road, and turned her back upon me; and I faw her do the fame to other men. I feveral times have feen women kifs the hands of a man of diftinction, or kneel to kifs his feet.

The great often have in their halls bafons with *jets d'eau*, to cool the air. I have mentioned that which we faw in the Imam of Sana's hall of audience. The edges of the bafon were coated with marble, and the reft of the floor was covered with rich carpets.

As the people of the Eaft wifh to keep their floors very clean, they fpit very little, although they fmoke a great deal. Yet to fpit is not reckoned a piece of impolitenefs. I have feen fome perfons of rank ufe a fpitting-box, and others fpit on the bottom of the wall, behind the cufhions on which they fat.

As

As the floors are spread with carpets, and cushions are laid round the walls, one cannot sit down, without inconvenience, on the ground; and the use of chairs is unknown in the East. The Arabians practise several different modes of sitting. When they wish to be very much at their ease, they cross their legs under the body. I found indeed, by experience, that this mode of sitting is the most commodious for people who wear long clothes, and wide breeches, without any confining ligatures. It seems to afford better rest, after fatigue, than our posture of sitting upon chairs. In presence of superiors, an Arab sits with his two knees touching each other, and with the weight of the body resting upon the heels. As in this position a person occupies less room than in the other, this is the posture in which they usually place themselves at table. I often tried it, but found it extremely uneasy, and could never accustom myself to it. In many parts of Arabia, there are long, low chairs, made of straw mats; but they sit crosslegged on them, as well as on the carpets.

The life which the Arabians lead in their houses, is so vacant and unvaried, that they cannot help feeling it irksome. Their natural vivacity prompts them to seek amusements out of doors. They frequent coffee-houses and markets, and are fond of assembling in public meetings

ings as often as poffible. Yet they have not the fame means of diverfion as other nations. What I have formerly faid concerning the amufements of the inhabitants of the Eaft, refpects the Arabians only in part. They are often obliged to take up with fedentary and domeftic amufements, which to Europeans appear very infipid.

It is, no doubt, to divert the tædium of a fedentary life, that the people of the Eaft make fo much ufe of tobacco. The Arabians, notwithftanding the natural drynefs of their conftitution, and the warmth of their climate, fmoke ftill more than the inhabitants of the northern provinces of Afia. They ufe the long Perfian pipe, which I have already defcribed. A cuftom peculiar to Arabia, is, that perfons of opulence and fafhion carry always about them a box filled with odoriferous wood. They put a bit of this wood into any perfon's pipe, to whom they wifh to exprefs particular refpect; and it communicates to the tobacco a fragrant fmell, and a very agreeable tafte.

I never faw the Arabians ufe opium, like the Turks and the Perfians. Inftead of taking this gratification, they conftantly chew *Kaad*. This is the buds of a certain tree, which are brought in fmall boxes from the hills of Yemen. Perfons who have good teeth chew thefe buds juft as they come from the tree: For the use of old men it is first brayed in a mortar. It seems to be from fashion merely that these buds are chewed; for they have a disagreeable taste; nor could we accustom ourselves to them. I found likewise that Kaad has a parching effect upon the constitution, and is unfavourable to sleep.

The lower people are fond of raising their spirits to a state of intoxication. As they have no strong drink, they, for this purpose, smoke *Haschisch*, which is the dried leaves of a sort of hemp. This smoke exalts their courage, and throws them into a state in which delightful visions dance before the imagination. One of our Arabian servants, after smoking *Haschisch*, met with four soldiers in the street, and attacked the whole party. One of the soldiers gave him a sound beating, and brought him home to us. Notwithstanding his mishap, he would not make himself easy, but still imagined, such was the effect of his intoxication, that he was a match for any four men.

CHAP. III.

Of the Food of the Arabians, and their Manner of Eating.

As the people of the East squat themselves upon the ground when they sit, so their manner of eating at meals is conformable to this way of sitting. They spread a large cloth in the middle of the room, put upon this cloth a small table only one foot high, and upon the table a large round plate of tinned copper. Upon this are set different copper dishes, neatly tinned within and without. Instead of table napkins, Arabians of rank use a long linen cloth, which those at table put under their knees. Where this linen cloth is wanting, every one uses a small handkerchief of his own. They use no knives nor forks. The Turks have sometimes wooden or horn spoons; but the Arabians use their fingers with great dexterity, and eat all dishes with the hand.

Were we to judge them by the standard of our own manners, the people of the East behave very indecently at an European table. I could not help being much struck by the behaviour of the first Turk I saw eat, who was the comptroller of the customs of the Dardanelles, in company

with

with whom I happened to fup at the French Conful's table. That Turk tore his meat in pieces with his fingers, and wiped them with his napkin. My furprife at this mode of eating ceafed when I became more familiar with the manners of thofe people. They know not the ufe of table napkins, and fuppofe them to be handkerchiefs, with which they are to wipe themfelves. They are much at a lofs when a piece of meat is to be cut; for they think it indecent to make ufe of the left hand in cutting it, as with it they perform their ablutions. They manage better when the meats are, after their own fafhion, cut into fmall bits, before being fet down on the table. We, Europeans, were at firft fhocked to fee fo many hands in the difh together. But, as the Mahometans are obliged, by the laws of their religion, to pay the utmoft attention to perfonal cleanlinefs, and are habituated to it, there is in reality little difference, in point of delicacy, between their mode of eating and ours.

The more eminent Schiechs in the defart eat of nothing but *Pilau*, or boiled rice. It is ferved up in a very large wooden plate. The company fit down and eat, one after another, till the whole contents of the plate be exhaufted, or they are fatisfied. In the houfes of perfons of diftinction in the towns, feveral of thefe plates are

are fet, one upon another, in a pyramidical form. When the mafters rife, the fervants fit down at the fame table, and eat up what remains.

The meal was ferved up in a different ftyle at *Merdin*, where I dined with fifteen of the *Waiwode's* officers. A fervant ftood in the middle of the company, to fet down and remove the difhes which were brought in by the other fervants. Hardly was a plate fet down upon the table, when fixteen hands were thruft into it, all at once, and foon emptied it of its contents, efpecially when this was paftry, which the inhabitants of the Eaft, whofe drink is water, are paffionately fond of. They eat with amazing quicknefs in the Eaft. At Merdin we emptied more than fourteen plates within lefs than twenty minutes.

The Muffulmans in general, and particularly the Arabs, repeat always a fhort prayer before fitting down to a meal, " In the name of the moft merciful God." When any one has done eating, he rifes, without waiting for the reft, and fays, " God be praifed." They drink little while they eat ; but, as they rife from the table, after wafhing, they drink fome cold water, and a cup of coffee.

The Arabians, in the eaftern part of this country, are not lefs fond than the Turks of coffee,

coffee, which they alfo call *Kahwe*. They prepare it in the manner which we have adopted from them. The only difference, between their mode of preparing it and ours, is, that they, inftead of grinding their coffee-beans, pound them in a mortar. We carried a coffee-mill with us into Arabia, but foon found the tafte of the pounded coffee much fuperior to that of the ground, and left off ufing our mill. The pounding feems better to exprefs the oily parts of the bean, which give the coffee its peculiar relifh. The people of the Eaft always drink their coffee without either milk or fugar.

It is odd enough that, in Yemen, the proper country of which the coffee plant is a native, there fhould be fo little coffee drunk. It is there called *Bunn*, and is fuppofed to have heating effects upon the blood. The favourite drink of the Arabians of this province is prepared from the hufks of coffee-beans, flightly roafted, and pounded. It is called *Kahwe*, or more commonly *Kifcher*. It taftes like tea, and is thought refrefhing. People of diftinction drink it out of porcelain cups, and the lower fort out of cups of coarfe earthern ware.

Although the Muffulmans are forbidden the ufe of all intoxicating liquors, yet many of them are paffionately fond of thefe, and drink them privately, and at night, in their own houfes.

houses. Our physician saw, in the house of a rich merchant at Loheia, all the necessary instruments for distilling brandy. On the frontiers of Arabia, where there are Christians, both wine and spiritous liquors are to be found; but in Arabia, none of these are to be obtained, except from the Jews of Sana, who have great plenty, and that of excellent quality. They supply their countrymen; but, having no casks, they are obliged to carry their wine and brandy in copper vessels, which renders the use of them dangerous to the health. The English, too, sometimes bring *Arrack* from India to Mokha.

At Loheya, we bought a sort of wine, prepared from an infusion of dry grapes in water, in a pot which is buried in the ground, to make the liquor ferment. We had also offered to us a thick, white liquor, called *Bufa*, which is prepared from meal mixed with water, and brought into a state of fermentation. It is used at Basra, and is still more common in Armenia, where the inhabitants keep it in large earthern pots, half buried in the ground, and draw it out for use by the insertion of reeds. A proof of the permanency of national customs is, that Xenophon found this same liquor used in Armenia, and preserved in this very manner (R).

The

The Arabians are, in general, a sober, frugal nation, which is probably the cause of their leanness, and seemingly stinted growth. Their usual articles of food are rice, pulse, milk, butter, and *Keimak*, or whipped cream. They are not without animal food; but they seldom eat of it; for it is thought very unwholesome in these hot countries. Mutton is the most common species of animal food used here; and on it the Arabians of the desart chiefly live. As the castration of animals, though not forbidden by the Mussulman law, is little practised here, wedder-mutton is never used by the Arabians.

The common people in Arabia have little other food, but bad bread made of *Durra*, a sort of coarse millet, by kneading it with camel's milk, oil, butter, or grease. I could not eat of this bread at first, and would have preferred to it the worst bread I had ever eaten in Europe; but the people of the country, being accustomed to it, prefer it to barley bread, which they think too light.

The modes of baking bread are different in different places of Arabia. In the ship in which we sailed from Jidda to Loheya, there was a saillor, whose task every afternoon was to prepare Durra for next day's bread. He broke and bruised the grain between two stones, one of which

which was convex, the other concave. Of the meal thus prepared, he formed dough, and then divided it into fmall cakes. In the meantime, the oven was heated; but it was fimply an earthen pot glazed; and a fire of charcoal was kindled up within it. When the oven was fufficiently heated, the cakes were laid againft the fides of the pot, without removing the coals, and in a few moments the bread was taken up half-roafted, and was eaten hot.

The Arabians of the defart ufe a heated plate of iron, or a gridiron, in preparing their cakes. When they have no gridiron, they roll their dough into balls, and put it either among live coals, or into a fire of camels dung, where they cover it till it is penetrated by the heat. They then remove the afhes, and eat the bread, while it is fcarcely dry, and ftill hot. In the towns, the Arabians have ovens like ours; their bread is of barley-meal, and of the form and thicknefs of our pancakes; but they never give it enough of the fire.

It is fingular that the Arabs, who are no ftrangers to the invention of mills, fhould ftill continue the old and troublefome practice of bruifing their grain with ftones, without machinery. But I fufpect that they find bread made of meal prepared in this way to tafte more agreeably than that which is made of meal that
has

has been ground in a mill. The negroes, of certain countries in Africa, are said to prefer the mode of bruising their maize upon a stone, even after they have lived long among Europeans.

CHAP. IV.

Of the Dress and Fashions of the Arabians.

WHEN speaking of the dress of the inhabitants of the East in general, I communicated some idea of the dresses used by the Arabians. I described the dress of people of distinction in Yemen, when I had occasion to mention the dress of ceremony with which I was favoured by the Imam of Sana. But there is a great variety in the national dresses of the Arabians, and various fashions prevail among them, which I must not leave unnoticed.

Nothing can be more inconvenient or expensive than the head-dress worn by Arabians of fashion. They wear fifteen caps, one over another, some of which are indeed of linen, but the rest of thick cloth or cotton. That which covers all the rest is usually richly embroidered with gold, and has always some sentence of the Koran embroidered upon it. Over all these caps they wrap a large piece of muflin, called a *Safch*, ornamented at the ends, which flow loofe upon the fhoulders, with filk or golden fringes. As it muft be very difagreeable, in a hot country, to have the head always loaded in this manner, the Arabians, when in their own houfes, or with intimate friends, lay afide this ufelefs weight, all to one or two of the caps. But, before perfons whom they are obliged to treat with ceremony or refpect, they dare not appear without their turbans. Thofe who defire to pafs for men of learning, difcover their pretenfions by the bulk of their turbans.

Arabians of rank wear one piece of drefs, which is not in ufe among the other inhabitants of the Eaft. This is a piece of fine linen upon the fhoulder, which feems to have been originally intended to fhelter the wearer from the fun and rain, but is now merely ornamental.

The common clafs of Arabs wear only two caps, with the *Safch* carelefsly bound on the head. Some have drawers and a fhirt; but the greater number have only a piece of linen about their loins, a large girdle with the *Jambea*, and a piece of cloth upon the fhoulders; in other refpects they are naked, having neither fhoes nor ftockings. In the highlands, where the climate is colder, the people wear fheep fkins. The fcanty clothes which they wear through the

day,

day, are also their covering by night; the cloth swaddled about the waist serves for a mattrass; and the linen garment worn about the loins is a sheet to cover the Arab while he sleeps. The highlanders, to secure themselves from being infested by insects, sleep in sacks.

Persons in a middle rank of life wear, instead of shoes, sandals, being merely single soles, or sometimes thin pieces of wood, bound upon the foot with a strap of dressed leather. People of better fortune use slippers, like those worn through the rest of the East; and this is also the dress for the feet worn by the women.

The ordinary dress of the Arabs is indeed simple enough; but they have also a sort of great coat, without sleeves, called *Abba*, which is simpler still. I was acquainted with a blind taylor at Basra, who earned his bread by making *Abbas*; so that they cannot be of a very nice shape, or made of many pieces. In Yemen they are worn only by travellers; but in the province of Lachsa, the Abba is a piece of dress commonly used by both sexes.

In several places in Arabia, the men wear no drawers; but these with a large shirt are all the dress used by the lower women. In the Tehama, women of this class wrap a linen cloth about their loins in the manner of drawers. The women of Hedsjas veil their faces, like those of Egypt,

Egypt, with a narrow piece of linen, which leaves both the eyes uncovered. In Yemen, they wear a larger veil, which covers the face fo entirely, that the eyes can hardly be difcerned. At Sana and Mokha, they cover the face with a gauze veil, which is often embroidered with gold. They wear all rings on their fingers, arms, nofe, and ears. They ftain their nails red, and their hands and feet of a brownifh yellow colour, with the juice of the plant *Elhenne*. The circle of the eyes, and even the eye-lafhes, they paint black, with a preparation of lead ore called *Kochhel*. The men fometimes imitate this mode of painting the eyes with *Kochhel;* but perfons of fenfe laugh at fo effeminate a practice.

This mode of ftaining the fkin of a brown colour, is poffibly ufed by the women of the low country, in confequence of the natural fallownefs of their complexion. They fancy, that, when the whole body is brown, the peculiar darknefs of the countenance will efcape obfervation. I conjecture this much concerning the women, from the practice of the men; they going almoft naked, rub the body all over with *Elhenne*, and thus become entirely brown.

The women of Yemen alfo make black punctures in their face to improve their beauty. Their natural complexion is a deep yellow; but,

among

among the hills, are perfons of fair complexions and fine faces, and there even among the peafantry. In the towns, thefe women, who think themfelves handfome, lift up their veils to fhew their beauty, whenever they think they can do it unobferved.

Fafhion fhews its influence, in a particular manner, in the modes in which the hair and beard are worn in Arabia. In the Imam of Sana's dominions, all men, of whatever ftation, fhave their heads. In other parts of Yemen, all men, even the Shiechs, preferve their hair, wrap it in a handkerchief, and knot it up behind; caps and turbans are not in ufe there. Some of the highlanders keep their hair long and loofe, and bind the head with fmall cords.

Every body, without exception, wears the beard of its natural length; but the Arabs keep their muftachios very fhort. In the highlands of Yemen, where few ftrangers are ever feen, it is difgraceful to appear without a beard. Our fervant wore only his muftachios; and thofe good highlanders fancied that we had fhaven him by way of punifhment for fome fault.

The Turks, on the contrary, fhave their beards, and keep only their muftachios long. Among this nation, the beard is an enfign of honour and dignity; and therefore the flaves and domeftic fervants of great men are obliged to keep themselves close shaven. The Persians wear long mustachios, and clip their beards in an aukward enough fashion. The *Kurdes* shave their beards, but preserve their mustachios, with a list of hair upon each cheek.

The Arabians have all black beards. Some old men, when their beards are whitened by time, dye them red; but this practice is generally disapproved. The Persians blacken their beards, although naturally black, and continue to do so, till a very advanced age. Turkish gravity could not endure the use of this fashion of ornament. Some young noblemen are indeed beginning to imitate this Persian mode, in order to disguise the whiteness of their beards; for this colour of their hair is more common in Turky than in the southern regions of Asia. A white beard is thought by the Turks to be very unbecoming for a man of rank.

When Turks, who have had themselves shaven in their youth, determine upon suffering their beards to grow, they observe the ceremony of pronouncing a *Fatha*, which is considered as a vow to preserve their hair untouched by a razor through the rest of life. The Mahometans perhaps fancy, as some travellers have represented, that angels occupy their beards. It is at least certain, that a man who cuts his beard, after having once determined to preserve it long, is severely punished ed for the breach of his vow. At Bafra, he would be condemned to receive three hundred blows with a ftick, but might indeed, for a round fum, efcape the punifhment. An inhabitant of that city, who had, twelve years before I vifited it, fhaven himfelf in a drunken fit, fled to India, and durft never return, for fear of the difgrace, and the punifhment, which he had merited both by his fhaving and his drunkennefs.

The Jews, through all the Eaft, preferve their beards from their youth. They wear the beard not in the fame form as the Muffulmans and Chriftians, fhaving none of it about the temples and the ears. To diftinguifh themfelves ftill more from the reft of mankind, they retain two tufts of hair hanging over their ears. Thefe Jews of Arabia refemble thofe of Poland; only they have a more decent and lefs beggarly afpect. They dare not wear the turban, but are obliged to content themfelves with a fmall bonnet. Neither are they fuffered to drefs in any colour but blue; all their clothes are of blue cloth. They are alfo forbidden the ufe of the *Jambea*.

As there are many *Banians* fettled in Arabia, I fhall add a few words refpecting their drefs. It confifts of a turban of a particular form, a piece of linen upon the fhoulders, another piece of linen fixed by a ftring about their loins, and flippers.

pers. Some alfo wear over thefe pieces of drefs a long white robe, which plaits upon the haunches, and fits clofe upon the body and the arms. Thefe Indians ufed to drefs entirely in white; but they received, fome years fince, an order from Sana, enjoining them to wear red clothes. To obtain a difpenfation from this change of drefs, they paid a confiderable fum to the Imam, and the order was revoked. They were foon after enjoined, by another edict, to wear a red, inftead of a white turban: But, not choofing to buy off in this inftance, they obeyed, and now wear a red turban, with the reft of their drefs white,

CHAP. V.

Arabian Politenefs.

In Yemen, Oman, and Perfia, an European is treated with as much civility as a Mahometan would find in Europe. Some travellers complain of the rude manners of the inhabitants of the Eaft; but it muft be allowed that the Europeans often involve themfelves in embarraffments in thefe countries, by being the firft to exprefs contempt or averfion for the Muffulmans. A proof of the defire of thefe governments to obtain

tain the friendship of Europeans, is their exacting easier duties of custom from them than from other nations, as I had occasion to remark, both in Persia, and throughout all Arabia.

In Turkey they are less kindly treated. A comparison of the manners of the Turks with those of the Arabians will best prove the superior politeness of the latter nation.

The Turks in general hate Europeans; probably from an indistinct remembrance of the bloody wars which they have at different times waged with the inhabitants of the West. Children are, with them, as much terrified at the name of European as with us at the name of Turk. Turks, in the service of Europeans, consider their masters as indebted to them for protection, yet are despised by their countrymen for eating the bread of Christians, and at Constantinople are nicknamed swine-herds. The Europeans are held in particular abhorrence at Damietta, Damascus, and Kahira. The Arabians, having never had any quarrels with the inhabitants of Europe, have not the same reasons for viewing them with aversion.

Neither are the Christians of the East treated equally well in all the different parts of Asia. The Armenians and Georgians are not ill looked upon in Persia; and may aspire to the first posts in the army, without changing their religion.

religion. I was myself acquainted at Shiraz with a Khan, and several officers, who were Christians, and natives of Georgia. The Turks again admit no Christian soldiers into their armies, and regard their Christian fellow subjects with the most insolent contempt.

In Arabia, the Christians are called *Naſſara* or *Nuſrani*. As they are incapable of any honourable office in this country, the most respectable among them are merchants. The Arabians, for this reason, give every Christian of a decent appearance the title either of *Chauadſje*, or of *Barſagan*, two appellations both signifying merchant. A Christian of more ordinary dress and equipage is called *Mallim*, or master, as they suppose such a one to be an artisan. I had assumed the name of *Abdallah*, and was accordingly called in Arabia *Chauadsje Abdalla*, and in Persia *Abdalla Aga*. In Natolia, where the Turkish language prevails, and civility seems to be unknown, the Turks call the Christians of the East *Dsjaurler*, a term extremely contemptuous. A Turk, who had hired me his mules for the journey between Aleppo and Konie, and was consequently in my service, never gave me another name than *Dsjaur*. I told him indeed, that I was not a *Dsjaur*, but a Frank; and he afterwards gave me the name of Frank or Abdallah.

The

The behaviour of the Turks to the Chriftians correfponds to the reproachful language in which they addrefs them. In the Turkifh empire, Chriftians are obliged to wear a badge, which marks their fervile condition, and to pay a poll-tax. In Conftantinople, Chriftians, as they pafs, are required either to fweep the ftreets, and remove the filth, or to pay money, that they may be excufed. Thefe vexatious impofitions are not warranted by the government; but fo abject is the condition of the Chriftians, that they dare not complain of an injury fuffered from a Mahometan. They are in danger of being infulted if they appear in the ftreets on days of public feftivity. I fhall mention one inftance, out of many, which I witneffed, of the infolence of the Turks. In Natolia, we met in the high way with a Turk, who being about to mount his horfe, compelled an honeft Greek merchant to alight from his mule, and hold the ftirrup to him. An Arab would blufh for fuch rudenefs. A Schiech, from whom we had hired camels, ufed often to prefent his back for a ftep by which I might mount my dromedary.

I know enough of the Chriftians of the Eaft, to induce me to believe that their own conduct often draws upon them the contempt of the Turks; at leaft, the Greek merchants whom I faw saw in Natolia were mean, flattering, babbling creatures; qualities which could not but render them contemptible to a haughty and serious nation. They would eagerly run to hold the stirrup, not only to a Turk, but even to their own *Katerdsjis* or horse-hirers, with whom they condescend to cultivate a shameful familiarity. A Turk, who was servant to two Greeks, called his masters *Dsjaurlers*, and they him *Bekir Aga*, or Mr *Bekir*. In the presence of the Turks, they call themselves *Dsjaurlers*, and give the Turks the pompous titles of *Bascham*, *Effendum*, *Sultanum*, &c. exclusively; but, on the contrary, in the absence of the Turks, they discover an insufferable degree of vanity, and the softest names they give them are *Kafr* and *Kopek*. The Armenians indeed are of a different character. They are grave and sincere, behave with a degree of dignity, and know better how to command the esteem of the Turks, who treat them better than the Greeks. They sometimes, or indeed pretty often, hear themselves called infidels; but this reproach they laugh at, and confidently name themselves Christians, by which means they come to receive the same name from the Mahometans.

In Arabia and Persia, the Jews are held at least as much in contempt as in Europe. In Turkey they are very numerous, and practise

all

all different trades. Among those of them who are employed in commerce, are some rich bankers, who often rise into credit with people in power, and afford protection to their brethren. The Arabians call them *Jehudi*. In Turkey, where they are insulted alike by the Mussulmans and the Christians, they receive the denomination of *Tschefied*, which is still more opprobrious than than that of *Dsjaur*.

The chief part of Arabian politeness is hospitality; a virtue which is hereditary to the nation, and which they still exercise in its primitive simplicity. An ambassador sent to any prince or Schiech has his expences defrayed, and receives presents, according to the custom of the East. A traveller of any distinction, who should go to see any great Schiech in the desart, would receive the same treatment. I have spoken occasionally of the *Kans* and *Manfales*, or houses of hospitable entertainment, in which I was received on my travels. What appears to distinguish the Arabians from the other inhabitants of the East, is, that they exercise hospitality to all, without respect of rank or religion.

The Arabians invite all who come in while they are at table, to eat with them, whether great or small, Mahometans or Christians. In the caravans, I have often had the pleasure of seeing a poor muleteer prefs paffengers to fhare his meals, and, with an air of fatisfaction, diftribute his little ftore of bread and dates to whofoever would accept any part of it from him. I have, on the other hand, been fhocked at the behaviour even of rich Turks, who retired to a corner to eat by themfelves, that they might avoid afking any one to partake of their fare.

When a Bedouin Shiech eats bread with ftrangers, they may truft his fidelity, and depend upon his protection. A traveller will always do well therefore to take an early opportunity of fecuring the friendfhip of his guide by a meal. When two Arabians falute each other, he who fpeaks firft lays his right hand on his heart, and fays, " *Salam Aleikum,*" or, " peace be with you;" the other replies, " *Aleikum effalam,*" or, " with " you be peace." Old perfons commonly add their bleffing, or rather, "the mercy and bleffing " of God." The Mahometans of Egypt and Syria never falute the Chriftians in thefe words; but content themfelves with faying to them, " *Se-* " *bachel chair,* good day," or, " *Sahheb falamat,* " friend, how art thou?" In Yemen, this diftinction is not obferved. The inhabitants of the highlands of Yemen ufe a form of falutation, of which I could never learn the meaning.

I long imagined that the ufe of a peculiar form of falutation to Chriftians was owing to the orthodox

thodox zeal of the Mahometans; but I have since underſtood that it is rather owing to a fuperſtitious averſion in the oriental Chriſtians for the Muſſulman form of ſalutation. They would not ſuffer me to uſe thoſe words, and would not reply in them to ſome Turks who miſtook them for men of their own nation; a circumſtance which eaſily happens, as Chriſtians ſometimes uſe the white turban to procure reſpect, and to make robbers ſuppoſe them Turks.

Two Arabs of the deſart meeting, ſhake hands more than ten times. Each kiſſes his own hand, and ſtill repeats the queſtion " how art thou?" In Yemen, perſons who value themſelves on their good-breeding uſe many compliments. Each does as if he wiſhed the other's hand, and draws back his own to avoid receiving the ſame honour. At length, to end the conteſt, the eldeſt of the two ſuffers the other to kiſs his fingers. People of rank embrace their equals; and all treat one another with a degree of politeneſs that ſurpriſes ſtrangers.

At viſits, they obſerve nearly the ſame cuſtoms as the other inhabitants of the Eaſt. When the viſit is an ordinary and familiar one, pipes of *Kircher* and *Kaad* are always preſented; on a viſit of ceremony, roſe-water and perfumes are added. When it is time for the viſitor to retire, a ſervant comes in with a flaſk of roſe-water, and
beſprinkles

besprinkles the company; another perfumes the beard of the visitor, and the wide sleeves of his gown. When we first saw the ceremony used, which was at *Raschid*, we were a good deal surprised to see a servant sit down beside us, and cast water upon our faces.

CHAP. VI.

Of some peculiar Customs.

IN hot countries, cleanliness is indispensibly necessary to health. The common people, who reason little, might forget or neglect a care so necessary to their welfare. For this reason, as it should seem, have the founders of several sects enjoined purifications and ablutions as a religious duty.

The Arabians are obliged to be extreme cleanly by the laws equally of their climate and their religion; and they observe these precepts with the most scrupulous exactitude. They not only wash, bathe, and pair their nails very often, but cut away all hairs from the body; and pluck them from those parts upon which the razor cannot be employed, that not the least impurity may remain upon them. Those are held in contempt who excercise uncleanly trades, such as the servants

A Woman selling bread.

vants at the public baths, barbers, cooks, tanners, &c. This contempt, however, falls upon the employment, without operating to the exclufion of the perfon exercifing it from fociety.

Much has been faid concerning the origin of the cuftom of circumcifing infants, which feems, at a firft view, fo abfurd. Some have referred it to men's difpofition, to offer to the Deity a part of what they hold deareft, and value as moft precious. But this feems to be an aukward attempt at pleafantry, and befides, is not true; otherwife circumcifion would be practifed among all nations, in all climates, and would be regarded as a religious ceremony; whereas it fubfifts only in hot countries, and there not as a religious inftitution, but as an old cuftom.

It is true that feveral nations, in hot climates, do not practife it, fuch as the Perfians, the Indians, and many of the inhabitants of Africa; but there are others who obferve it, although not enjoined by the precepts of their religion. Such are the Chriftians of Abyffinia, and many of the idolatrous people of Africa. The Mahometans do not confider circumcifion as a religious duty, but merely as a laudable cuftom of their anceftors, worthy of being kept up. None but the fuperftitious Jews appear to attach ideas of religious fanctity to an obfervance which is purely civil.

The cuftom of circumcifing infants certainly owes its origin to the phyfical nature of thefe climates. There are fome corporeal defects and infirmities more common in fome countries than in others, which this practice has a tendency to remedy; and, where thefe prevail, circumcifion is ufed. Nothing is more effectual in preventing thofe difeafes, which, in hot countries, are liable to attack certain parts, than the keeping of thofe parts very clean by frequent ablution. Circumcifion renders this ablution neceffary, and reminds thofe, who might otherwife neglect it, of its utility. Legiflators have accordingly thought it their duty to make people take fuitable precautions for the prefervation of health, by giving this ufeful cuftom the fanction of laws civil and religious.

This conjecture will appear the more probable, when it is confidered that the practice of circumcifing girls is general in the fame countries in which boys are circumcifed. In Oman, on the fhores of the Perfian Gulph, among the Chriftians of Abyffinia, and in Egypt among the Arabs and Copts, this latter cuftom is prevalent. At Bafra and Bagdad, all the women of Arabian blood circumcife their daughters as well as their fons. At Kahira, the women who perform this operation are as well known as midwives. They are openly called into houfes from the ftreets,

without

without any secret being made of the intention with which they are invited.

In Egypt, we mentioned to a nobleman, who had invited us to his country seat, our curiosity to know in what manner girls were circumcised. He immediately made a young Arabian girl, who had been circumcised, and was then eighteen years of age, to be called in, and allowed us to examine, in the presence of his servants, what changes had been produced by the operation, upon the parts, and even to make a drawing of them. I was convinced, that it is also out of cleanliness, and to render ablution easier, that the practice of circumcising women has been first adopted. No law has appointed it, any more than that of boys; it is a usage, not a religious duty.

The corruption of dead bodies has the most destructive effects upon the health in hot countries; more so than in more temperate climates. It was therefore necessary to secure the inhabitants, from its noxious influence, by increasing, through religious motives, their natural aversion for dead carcases. Mahomet, and some other founders of sects, have for this reason affixed ideas of spiritual impurity to the act of touching a dead body. Some Mussulmans require great purification to cleanse a man thus defiled, and separate him for some time from society.

The

The Arabians are lefs rigid; when a perfon of this nation has had the misfortune to touch a carcafe, he wafhes himfelf carefully, and, when no mark of external impurity remains, he then returns to the ordinary intercourfe of life.

A frugal nation, who regard even fobriety as a virtue, muft naturally affix ideas of fhame to every thing that indicates any degree of intemperance. The Arabians are greatly fhocked when that accident happens to a man, which is the natural confequence of the fulnefs of the inteftines after too copious a meal, and of the indigeftion of windy articles of diet. The *Chevalier D'Arvieux* has been blamed as guilty of exaggeration in what he fays concerning the delicacy of the Arabs upon this fcore; but I have found all that he fays of the manners and ufages of this nation to be ftrictly true. I am therefore inclined to believe equally what he relates concerning things which I could not obferve or verify myfelf. It fhould feem that the Arabs are not all equally fhocked at fuch an involuntary accident. Yet, a Bedouin, guilty of fuch a piece of indecency, would be defpifed by his countrymen. The inftance of an Arab of the tribe of *Belludsje* was mentioned to me, who, for a reafon of this fort, was obliged to leave his country, and never durft return.

The

The ignorance of the Arabians subjects them to all the illusions of superstition. They wear almost all amulets upon their arms; on their fingers they have ordinary rings. Their religion is said to oblige them to take off their rings, which are of gold, or set with precious stones, whenever they say their prayers, which, if this precaution were neglected, would be of no efficacy. They seem to think, that, in order to be heard, they must appear before the Deity in the utmost humiliation and abasement.

SECTION XXVII.

OF THE LANGUAGE AND SCIENCES OF THE ARABIANS.

CHAP. I.

Of the Language and Writing of the Arabians.

THE Arabian language, one of the most ancient and general in the world, has had the fate of other living languages, which have been spoken through

through many ages, and by the inhabitants of different provinces and countries remote from one another. It has gradually undergone such an alteration, that the Arabic spoken and written by Mahomet may now be regarded as a dead language.

From religious prejudices, perhaps the Mussulmans in general believe, and the Arabians assert, the language of the Koran, and consequently the dialect spoken at Mecca in the days of Mahomet, to be the purest and most perfect of all. That dialect, however, differs so widely from the modern language of Arabia, that it is now taught and studied in the college of Mecca just as the Latin is at Rome. The same is done through Yemen; and is so much the more necessary, because the dialect of that province, which differed from that of Mecca eleven centuries since, has suffered new and very considerable changes since that period. The dialect of the highlands of Yemen is said to have the strongest analogy to the language of the Koran; for those highlanders have little intercourse with strangers. The old Arabic language is, through all the East, just like Latin in Europe, a learned tongue, to be acquired only in colleges, or by the perusal of the best authors.

There is perhaps no other language diversified by so many dialects as that of Arabia. The

nation

nation having extended their conquests, and sent out colonies through great part of Asia, and almost over the whole coasts of Africa; the different people conquered by them have been obliged to speak the language of their new masters and neighbours; but those people retained at the same time terms and phrases of their former language, which have debased the purity of the Arabic, and formed a diversity of dialects.

These different dialects in Arabia bear a considerable resemblance to those of Italy; beyond the confines of Arabia, their reciprocal relations to each other are the same as those of the languages of Provence, Spain, and Portugal, and all the others derived from the Latin. Even in the narrow extent of the Imam of Sana's dominions, this diversity of dialects is very considerable. Not only does the language of the Tehama differ from that spoken in the highlands; but, even in the same parts of the country, people of rank use words and phrases entirely unknown to the rest of the people. These dialects of Yemen differ still more widely from those used by the Bedouins in the desart, than from one another.

The pronunciation of one province differs equally from that of other provinces. Letters and sounds are often changed in such a manner as to produce an entire alteration upon the words. I found the pronunciation of the Southern Arabs

more

more foft, and better adapted to European organs, than that of the inhabitants of Egypt and Syria.

A fimilar diverfity of dialects diftinguifhes the Turkifh language. The Turks of Bafra cannot underftand thofe of Conftantinople, and are no better underftood themfelves by the Turcomans of Perfia.

Although the Arabian conquerors have introduced and eftablifhed their language in the countries which they conquered, yet their fubjects have not always left off the ufe of their mother tongue. In Syria and Paleftine, indeed, no language is to be heard but the Arabic; and yet the Syriac is not abfolutely a dead language, but is ftill fpoken in feveral villages in the Pachalick of Damafcus. In many places, in the neighbourhood of Merdin and Moful, the Chriftians ftill fpeak the Chaldean language; and the inhabitants of the villages who do not frequent towns, never hear any other than their mother tongue. The Chriftians born in the cities of Merden and Moful, although they fpeak Arabic, write in the Chaldean characters, juft as the Maronites write their Arabic in Syriac letters, and the Greeks the Turkifh in Greek letters.

Many people living under the dominion of the Arabians and Turks have loft the ufe of their mother tongue. The Greeks and Armenians

nians settled in Egypt and Syria speak Arabic; and the services of their public worship are performed in two languages at once. In Natolia, these nations speak their own languages in several different dialects. The Turkish officers sometimes extend their despotism to the language of their subjects. A Pacha of *Kayfar*, who could not endure to hear the Greek language spoken, forbade the Greeks in his Pachalic, under pain of death, to use any language but the Turkish. Since that prohibition was issued, the Christians of *Kayfar* and *Angora* have continued to speak the Turkish, and at present do not even understand their original language.

The *Kurdes*, who are nearly independent, have preserved their ancient language, of which there are in *Kurdistan* three principal dialects. I was informed that the *Sabæans*, who are commonly called Christians of St John, still speak and write their ancient language. The most learned of the few of this sect, who are settled in Basra, was a farrier; him I prevailed with to write me out the characters of his language; but he wrote them so indistinctly, that I could form no idea of his alphabet.

I was not fortunate enough to discover any *Hamjarine* inscriptions in Arabia, although I had learnt that there were such in several places written in absolutely unknown characters. I have already

already spoken, in the proper place, of an inscription, probably still more ancient, which was shown me by a Dutch renegado, and of which the characters bore a great resemblance to those of the inscriptions among the ruins of Persepolis. A *Maronite* of *Mount Libanus* related to me, that grottos and ruins were to be seen upon a hill in his country, on which were unknown inscriptions, most probably Phœnician.

The Arabic character, which was anciently in use, but is now entirely lost, was the *Kufic*. It seems to have been the alphabet of the Arabians of Mecca; for the Koran was originally written in Kufic characters. The inhabitants of Yemen have always used a different alphabet, and therefore could not read the Koran, when it was first published, after the death of Mahomet. In Yemen, I copied some inscriptions in Kufic characters, which had been engraven in the twelfth century. These characters being in some degree of a square form, are still used in inscriptions.

I had flattered myself, that I might obtain some light from medals concerning the ancient written characters of this nation; but medals are extremely rare in Arabia; when found, they are commonly sold to the goldsmiths, and immediately melted down. In Kurdistan, a great quantity of Grecian, Roman, and Persian medals,

have

have been dug up, and of them better care is taken; in places remote from great towns, they are ufed as current money.

The invention of the modern characters, which are very different from the Kufic, is afcribed to a vizier. The Arabians, Perfians, and Turks, write Arabic in fets of characters differing in feveral particulars from one another. They have alfo different modes of writing for different forms of bufinefs, each of which has its particular name.

The hand-writing of the Arabians in the common bufinefs of life is not legible. The orientals, however, value themfelves on their writing, and have carried the art of making beautiful written characters to high perfection. But the Arabians value chiefly a fpecies of elegance, which confifts in their manner of joining their letters, the want of which makes themfelves diflike the ftyle in which Arabic books are printed in Europe.

They fign their letters with a fort of cypher, to prevent the poffibility of counterfeiting their fignature; at leaft, the great and the learned do fo. Their letters folded are an inch in breadth, and the leaves are pafted together at one end. They cannot feal them; for wax is fo foft in hot countries that it cannot retain an impreffion.

CHAP.

CHAP. II.

Of the Education and Schools of the Arabians.

THE monarchs of the East do not take the same care, or lay out the same expence, for the encouragement of science as the sovereigns of Europe. In Arabia, therefore, are neither numerous academics, nor men of profound learning.

Yet the Arabian youth are not entirely neglected. In the cities, many of the lowest of the people are taught both to read and write; the same qualifications are also common among the Shiechs of the desart, and in Egypt. Persons of distinction retain preceptors in their families to instruct their children and young slaves; for they bring up such of their young slaves as appear to possess natural abilities, like children of the family.

In almost every mosque is a school, denominated *Mœddrasse*, having a foundation for the support of teachers, and the entertainment and instruction of poor scholars. In great towns are likewise other schools, to which people of middle rank send their children to receive religious instruction, and to learn reading, writing, and arithmetic. I have often seen schools of this sort in the market place; they are open like

shops

shops towards the street. The noise and appearance of passengers does not seem to divert the attention of the scholars, who sit before a small desk, and read their lessons aloud, balancing themselves constantly in their seats; to such a degree does motion appear necessary to rouse and keep up the attention of the inhabitants of hot countries. No girls attend these schools; they are privately taught by women.

Beside these small schools, there are some more considerable seminaries of education in some great towns in Arabia. These are colleges in which the sciences of astronomy, astrology, philosophy, and medicine are taught; in these the Arabians, although possessed of natural abilities, have, for want of good books and masters, made but little progress. In the dominions of the Imam, there have long been two famous academies; one at *Zebid* for *Sunnites*, and the other at *Damar* for the *Zeidites*. When I passed through these two cities, I happened to neglect making myself acquainted with the professors, or acquiring any knowledge of their system of instruction. I suppose, however, that the same studies are cultivated in these two academies as in that of *Dsjamea el Ashar* at Kahira.

The interpretation of the Koran, and the study of the ancient history of the Mahometans, are the principal employments of men of letters
among

among the Arabians. Thefe ftudies take up much time; for the ftudent muft not only acquire the ancient Arabic, but alfo make himfelf familiar with all the commentators on the Koran, the number of whom is very confiderable.

I was informed, that all men of letters undergo a public examination, before they can be promoted to any employment, civil or ecclefiaftical. Yet thofe examinations are furely conducted with partiality; for many perfons, indifferently qualified, rife to confiderable offices, while men of merit are often obliged to act as tranfcribers or fchoolmafters.

CHAP. III.

Of Arabian Poetry and Eloquence.

THE Arabians have been always accounted admirers of poetry. Their early hiftory records many inftances of the eftimation in which they held this art, even before the days of Mahomet, and of the glory which any family acquired that produced a poet.

The Arabians have no great poets among them at prefent, although they ftill cultivate poetry, and fometimes reward thofe who excel in it. The beft poets are among the Bedouins
of

of *Dsjof.* A Schiech of that country was, a few years since, imprisoned at Sana. The Schiech, observing a bird upon the roof of a house, recollected the opinion of those pious Mussulmans, who think it a meritorious action to deliver a bird from a cage. He thought that he himself had as good a right to liberty as any bird, and expressed this idea in a poem, which his guards got by heart, and which becoming generally known, at length reached the Monarch's ears, who was so pleased with it, that he set the Schiech at liberty, although he had been guilty of various acts of robbery.

The Arabians often sing the exploits of their Schiechs. Not long since, the tribe of *Khafael* having obtained a victory over the Pacha of Bagdad, made a song, in which the actions of every one of their chiefs were celebrated. But the tribe of Khafael being beaten next year by the Pacha, a poet of Bagdad made a parody of the Arabian song, in which he extolled the valour of the Pacha and his officers. In my time, the song of the Arabians still continued to be sung at Bagdad, and among the Bedouins. When *Assad,* Pacha of Damascus, who had long commanded the caravans, and was beloved by the Arabians, was assassinated by order of the Sultan, the Bedouins made an elegy on his death, and sang it openly in the towns of Syria. That piece

piece is in the form of a dialogue between some Arabians, the daughter of the Schiech of the tribe of *Harb*, and the lieutenant of the assassinated Pacha.

A Maronite informed me, that the poets of of Syria sent their compositions to the academy of *Dsjamea el Ashar*, at Kahira; and did not sing them publicly till they had received the approbation of that academy.

In a country like Arabia, where occasions of speaking in public seldom occur, eloquence is an useless accomplishment, and therefore cannot be much cultivated. The Arabians say, however, that they hear great orators in their mosques. As Europeans are not admitted to hear those sermons, I never had an opportunity to satisfy myself in respect to the truth of this account of the sacred eloquence of Arabia.

The only theatres for the exercise of profane eloquence are the coffee-houses in Arabia, Egypt, and Syria. Those coffee-houses are commonly large halls, which have their floors spread with straw mats, and are illuminated at night by a multitude of lamps. The guests are served with pipes, and a cup of coffee. As the Arabians never engage in any game, and sit still without entering into conversation with one annother, they would find their evenings extremely irksome, if readers and orators did not attend

attend in the coffee-houses to amuse them. These are commonly Mullachs, or poor scholars.

Such of them as are content with the praise of reading or repeating the works of others, select chosen passages from some favourite authors, such as, among the Arabians, *the history of Autar*, an Arabian hero who lived before Mahomet; the adventures of *Rustan Sal*, a Persian hero; or of *Beber*, king of Egypt; the history of the *Ayubites*, anciently sovereigns of Arabia; and *the life of Bahluldan*, a buffoon in the court of *Haroun El Raschid*. The least of these books contains some good morality.

Those Mullahs who aspire to the praise of invention make tales and fables, which they walk about and recite; or assuming oratorical consequence, deliver discourses upon any subjects they choose. When the orator has ended, he obtains a voluntary contribution from his hearers. This, although but a very moderate reward, encourages those poor Mullachs to learn to recite gracefully, or to compose tales and speeches with some success. At Aleppo, I heard of a man of distinction who studied for his own pleasure, yet had gone the round of all the coffee-houses in the city to pronounce moral harangues.

At Constantinople, assemblies in the coffeehouses are, for political reasons, prohibited; and the decoction of coffee is sold only in the shops.

shops. The Turks, an ignorant, grave, and silent nation, are indeed not fond of public orators, and have no relish for an amusement, so delightful to the Arabians, who have greater sensibility for the beauties of poetry and eloquence.

CHAP. IV.

Of the Astronomy of the Arabians.

THE modes of the division of time in use among the Arabians show how little progress this nation have made in astronomy. They know indeed a little of it elements; but this, it should seem, rather from tradition, than from any observations of their own.

The Arabian day consists of twenty-four hours, and lasts from sun-setting to sun-setting. Their hours are therefore of uncertain duration, and vary with the length of the natural day, or the time during which the sun is above the horizon. As they are strangers to the use of watches, none of them has any precise idea of the duraration of their hours, but, like the peasants of Europe, they distinguish the different parts of the day by vague, uncertain denominations, which only approach near the truth.

Their year consists of twelve lunar months. They begin the month with the new moon; and,

when

when the sky is so clouded that they cannot see her rise, then they make no difficulty of beginning the month a day or two later. Thus all their months go the round of the seasons; and this division of the year marks out no period for the labours of husbandry, or any of the other employments of civil life. To obviate this inconvenience, the learned reckon by other months corresponding to the course of the solar year, and consisting of the same number of days as ours.

In Arabia, as in other Mahometan countries, two great festivals are annually celebrated; that of offerings, called *Arafa* or Corban, and that of *Beiram*, immediately after Ramadan. The reckoning by lunar months occasions these festivals also to circulate through the whole year. When the fast of Ramadan falls in Summer, it is extremely distressing; for the people, however employed in labour, dare taste nothing, even in the longest days of the year, till the sun is down.

At Constantinople, the Sultan's astronomer composes every year a portable almanac, of which there are at least several copies made. But, in Egypt and Arabia, this mode of acquainting the people with the return of the festivals, and the progress of the seasons, has not been thought of; and so ignorant are they on this head, that the same festival is sometimes two days earlier, and

and fometimes as much later than the juft time, and often on different days at different places. A cloud hiding the new moon from one city, while fhe is feen by another, will be fufficient to produce thefe irregularities.

It is not for want of a paffion for aftronomy that the Arabians have made fo little progrefs in this fcience. But they want books and inftruments. I found fome of the nobles curious to fee, and to affift at aftronomical obfervations; and fome of their learned men paffed whole nights with me in examining the heavens. They have the work of *Abdarachman es Sofi* upon the conftellations, and the tables of *Ulugh Beigh*, by which fome aftronomers in the great towns are enabled to calculate eclipfes. Their inftruments are a celeftial globe of copper, beftudded with golden ftars, which they well know how to ufe; an aftrolabe of brafs, and a quadrant of wood, to take altitudes, and to determine the hour for prayer.

I was told that the Perfians, but particularly the Brachmans, were more fkilful aftronomers than the Arabians; yet, to judge from the inftruments and converfation of a Perfian aftrologer whom I met with at Surat, and of a Brachman with whom I was acquainted at Bombay, thefe two nations are equally unfkilful as the inhabitants of Arabia. In making calculations, the

the Persian used the tables of *Ulugh Beigh*, and the Brachman a book which he called *Grola Go*, and its author *Gunnis*. The Indian's instruments were a bowl of copper, having a hole in the bottom, set in water, which served him for a pendulum, with an indifferent solar circle.

It is known to the astrologers, and to all men of sense in Arabia, that eclipses are owing to the interception of the light of one heavenly body by the interposition of another. But the people still maintain the superstitious opinion, that a huge fish pursues the planet which is eclipsed. To chase away the fish, women and children get upon the roofs of the houses, and make a noise during the eclipse by beating upon brazen kettles and basons. The rise of this custom is referred to an Arabian astronomer, who persuaded the people of this fable, that they might make a noise great enough to reach the ears of the Caliph of Persia, who had refused to credit that astronomer's prediction of the eclipse.

The Arabians seem to study astronomy solely with a view to their success in the cultivation of astrology, a science highly esteemed and very lucrative in the East. When I told the first astronomer in Kahira of the contempt in which we hold astrology in Europe, he replied, that it was a divine science, the depths of which man could not fathom. He at the same time acknowledged to me me the uncertainty of his calculations; but, added he, people defire only to know what my books fay of their affairs, and that I honeftly tell them.

The Koran exprefsly forbids all Moflems to pry into futurity by any form of divination; and the moft famous commentators for this reafon reprefent the ftudy of aftrology as criminal. But, notwithftanding the decifion of thofe doctors, the Mahometans are all much attached to this fcience; the Shiites, however, more than the Sunnites. The former fect carry this fuperftition to fuch a length, as never to conclude a bargain without trying fortune, at leaft by counting the buttons on their clothes, or the beads of their rofaries. The Perfians are not all alike weak in this refpect. It is faid that *Kerim Khan*, in compliance with the popular error, undertakes nothing of confequence, without firft confulting the aftrologers; but he previoufly informs them of his defigns, and dictates the anfwers which they are to return.

CHAP.

CHAP V.

Of the Diseases and Medicine of the Arabians.

A regular and temperate life preserves the body from the attacks of disease. The Arabians, accordingly, are seldom sick, and hardly ever have recourse to physicians and medicines. When forced by extreme illness to call in a physician, they reward him poorly, and hardly pay for the value of his medicines. When the sick person dies, the physician has no reward to hope for; if he recovers, he soon forgets the services he has received. This ingratitude of their patients has taught them to use artifices often dishonest and disgraceful, in order to obtain payment from the patient beforehand.

In Arabia, therefore, we cannot expect to find great physicians. Those who there practise the art of medicine, know little more than the technical terms, such as they find them in the books of Avicenna, and some little matters about the use of simples. All the physicians whom I knew in Yemen acted at the same time as chemists, apothecaries, surgeons, and horse-doctors; and yet, by the practice of all these arts together, could hardly earn a livelihood.

The Arabians have many family noftrums, which they apply with much fuccefs. A peafant from the highlands extracted, by incifion, a lacteous juice from a fpongy tree, and by fwallowing drops of it, which he knew to be a poifon, if taken in greater quantity, gave himfelf a purge.

The Bedouin heals wounds which have been made with clear arms, by applying to them raw flefh from a camel newly killed. A man on board the Arabian veffel in which we failed from Jidda to Loheya complained of a colic, upon which his mafter put an iron in the fire, and applied it hot to him till his pains ceafed.

In Yemen the anointing of the body is believed to ftrengthen and protect it from the heat of the fun, which the inhabitants of this province, as they wear fo little clothing, are very liable to fuffer. Oil, by clofing up the pores of the fkin, is fuppofed to prevent that too copious tranfpiration which enfeebles the frame. Perhaps too thefe Arabians think a gliftering fkin a beauty. When the intenfe heat comes in, they always anoint their bodies with bad oil. At Sana, all the Jews, and many of the Mahometans have their bodies anointed, whenever they find themfelves indifpofed. The extreme unction of the Chriftians in the Eaft does not affect the health; for they are obliged to pay their patriarch fo dear a price for the pretended holy oil, that, out of frugality

frugality, the point of a filver needle only is dipped in the oil, and what adheres to it dropped upon the dying perfon.

It was formerly imagined that the Arabians would rather die than endure the adminiftration of a glyfter; but our phyfician prevailed with feveral perfons of diftinction at Cairo to take this remedy. Every one was fhocked, however, when he propofed it for a woman. Bleeding is feldom employed in Arabia; yet, a Banian bled one of us with great dexterity at Mokha. In Yemen, it is pretty frequently ufed. At Bafra, the lower people, efpecially porters, fcarify their legs, in the idea that this practice has a tendency to improve their ftrength.

Toothachs are lefs common in Arabia than in Europe, becaufe the inhabitants wafh the mouth, after eating, more carefully than we. In the towns, however, this diforder is not unknown, and is afcribed to the infectious fmell with which the air is tainted from the common fewers. At Bafra, where thefe are not carefully cleanfed, the teeth of the inhabitants are very much fpoiled; and I have feen a barber ftopped in the ftreet, by a perfon in pain, to draw out his teeth publicly. Thefe toothachs are not owing to the ufe of coffee, for they were common in Egypt before this beverage was drunk there. A Mullah told me that an Arabian had been

been cured of a tooth-ach by introducing into a hollow tooth the smoke of a certain plant, which had brought several small worms out of that tooth.

A disease very common in Yemen is the attack of the *Guinea-worm*, or the *Vena Medinensis*, as it is called by the physicians of Europe. This disease is supposed to be occasioned by the use of the putrid waters, which people are obliged to drink in several parts of Yemen; and for this reason the Arabians always pass water, with the nature of which they are unacquainted, through a linen cloth, before drinking it. When one unfortunately swallows any of the eggs of this insect, no immediate consequence follows; but after a considerable time the worm begins to shew itself through the skin. Our physician, Mr Cramer, was, within a few days of his death, attacked by five of these worms at once, although this was more than five months after we had left Arabia. In the isle of *Karek*, I saw a French officer, named *Le Page*, who, after a long and difficult journey, performed on foot, and in an Indian dress, between Pondicherry and Surat, through the heat of India, was busy extracting a worm out of his body. He supposed that he had got it by drinking bad water in the country of the *Marattas*.

This

This diforder is not dangerous, if the perfon affected can extract the worm without breaking it. With this view, it is rolled on a fmall bit of wood, as it comes out of the fkin. It is flender as a thread, and two or three feet long. It gives no pain as it makes its way out of the body, unlefs what may be occafioned by the care which muft be taken of it for fome weeks. If unluckily it is broken, it then returns into the body, and the moft difagreeable confequences enfue, palfy, a gangrene, and fometimes death.

As venomous ferpents are very common in hot, dry countries, it often happens that they bite people who have occafion to be much in the open fields. The Arabians would not, for any compenfation, teach us the fecret by which they cure their bites, and prevent the effects of the poifon. But, a Shiech at Bafra, who was celebrated for his fkill in the occult fciences, informed me, that he ufed to fcarify the wound, and then rubbed it to his mouth, and fucked the poifon without danger to himfelf, and with the happieft fuccefs. This mode of cure is not unlike that of the Hottentots, who apply bruifed flices of a fort of white onion to wounds of this fort. Over all the Eaft, the power of fympathy in curing difeafes is firmly believed. Some inftances were mentioned to me of perfons who had healed others bitten by ferpents, at a diftance, without

without seeing them, or applying any remedies to them.

Besides, the serpents of Asia are not all alike dangerous. Some are harmless and familiar, take refuge in the walls of houses, and are esteemed agreeable guests by the inhabitants. The sailors brought a serpent of this character on board our ship, after it had been inadvertently carried out, least its absence might prove unlucky to the vessel.

The leprosy seems to have been always an endemic disease in Arabia; for there is one species of leprosy which authors distinguish by the character of Arabian. Three different varieties of this disease are known here at present; of which two, named *Bohak* and *Barras*, are rather disgusting than dangerous; but the third, called *Juddam*, is very malignant, and apparently infectious. This latter exhibits the same symptoms which the English physician *Hillary* ascribes to what he calls *the leprosy of the joints*.

The Turks, from a misconception of the doctrine of predestination, use no precautions against the plague; but the Arabians, although true Mussulmans, are more careful in respect to the leprosy. The last prince of *Abu Schæhhr* used to send to the isle of *Bahhrein* all who were attacked with the leprosy, or with venereal complaints. At Basra, lepers are shut up in a house
by

by themselves; and there is a quarter in Bagdad furrounded with walls, and full of barracks, to which lepers are carried by force, if they retire not thither voluntarily; but government does not feem to provide with any care for the maintenance of thofe lepers. They come out every Friday to the market place to afk alms.

It is faid that thefe wretched creatures are much inclined to footh their mifery in the enjoyments of love. Not many years fince, a leper employed a cruel ftratagem in order to obtain a woman with whom he was in love. He wore a fine fhirt for a few days, and then caufed it to be privately fold, for a trifling price, to the object of his paffion. When he knew that the leprofy had made its appearance upon her, he informed againft her, and procured her to be fhut up with himfelf in the barracks.

At Bombay, the leprofy is not uncommon among the lower people; but it feems not to be of a dangerons nature; for there lepers are permitted to work in company with perfons not affected with the difeafe. In India, as in Arabia, the leprofy is thought to be occafioned chiefly by the unwholefome food, efpecially putrid fifh, ufed by the people. Mr Forfkal has left a defcription of the different varieties of the leprofy, which muft be valuable to phyficians.

I could learn nothing concerning the origin of the plague. It is at leaſt not owing to the putrefaction of the waters at Cairo. The Chriſtians who live on the banks of the great canal are never annoyed by it. Whatever has been ſaid concerning certain diſeaſes preſerving thoſe who are affected by them from the contagion of the plague, is founded on prejudices which have been refuted by experience, and particularly by the obſervations of *Dr Ruſſel*, a ſkilful phyſician at Aleppo.

Inoculation for the ſmall-pox has been in uſe from time immemorial among the Bedouins. Mothers perform this operation on their children, opening the ſkin of the arm with the prickle of a thorn. An Arabian of the iſle of *Lam*, ſituate on the ſouth-eaſt coaſt of Africa, informed me at Bombay, that inoculation had been known and practiſed in his country for ſeveral ages.

CHAP. VI.

Of the Occult Sciences of the Arabians.

To ſpeak of the occult ſciences of any people, is to deſcribe their ignorance, weakneſs of underſtanding, and wildneſs of imagination. Such a description would be too humiliating to human pride, did it not at the same time afford us consolation, by shewing from what endless absurdities we are saved by the study of sound philosophy, particularly of physics.

Those pretended occult sciences are in high estimation among the Arabians. None dare practise them, unless previously authorised by a master in the art, after serving a sort of apprenticeship; or, as the Arabians say, without having for some time spread the carpet for prayer before the feet of a famous master. A certain proof of their veneration for these sciences, is, that one of the first men in Mecca, and of the highest nobility in Arabia, Shiech *Mohammed el Dsjanadsjeni*, is now the most celebrated master of the science of *Ism Allah*.

This science of *Ism Allah*, or of the name of God, is the most sublime of all; for God is the lock, as Mahomet is the key; and consequently none but Mussulmans can acquire it. It enables its possessor to discover what is passing in the most distant countries, to make himself familiar with genii, and to oblige them to obey his pleasure; to dispose of the winds and seasons as he chooses; and to cure the bites of serpents, and many other diseases or infirmities. Persons who have advanced far in the study of this science, have attained, as there are instances to prove, to a facility of performing their prayers at noon, in the *Kaba* at Mecca, without going out of their own houses in Bagdad or Aden for the rest of the day. A merchant of Mecca, who had studied this science in that city, under the famous *Dsjanadsjeni*, assured me, that he had himself, when in danger of perishing at sea, fixed to the mast a billet written by the rules of art, which instantly calmed the storm. The art of discovering hidden treasure belongs also to this science, in which the *Magrebins* or Arabians of Barbary are known to excel.

The art of procuring sublime visions is not unknown to these Arabians; they use the same means which are employed by the devotees of certain societies in Europe. They shut themselves up for a long time without eating or drinking, in a dark place, and continue to repeat their prayers aloud till they faint away. After recovering from the swoon, and leaving the cave, they relate what they have seen in their trance. The common pretences are, that they have beheld God in his glory, angels, and spirits of all sorts, heaven and hell.

The second of these sciences, called *Simia*, is not of so exalted a nature; but has something human in it. It only teaches juggling tricks. Although the most sensible of the Mahometan clergy disapprove of this science, some orders of
dervises,

dervifes, however, apply to it, and practife it, as they fay, to prove the truth of their religion, and the fanctity of the founder of their order. Thefe pretended miracles are no where oftener performed than at Bafra, where I have feen a company of dervifes, of the order of *Bed-reddin*, walk all day about in the ftreets, leaping, dancing, beating the drum, and making gefticulations with fharp pointed irons, which they feemed to ftrike into their eyes.

In the fame city, I was prefent at a feftival which the dervifes of this order celebrate every year in honour of the birth of Mahomet. The fcene was in the open air, and in the court of the mofque, which was illuminated with only three lamps. Several Mullahs and dervifes began with finging fome paffages out of the Koran. They continued to fing, with the accompaniment of fome drums; and, during the mufic, the other dervifes arofe, took the fharp pointed irons, and did as if they were piercing their bodies, and even driving the irons with mallets into their flefh. Next appeared the principal actor, who, affuming an air of infpiration, directed the mufic to proceed, and to be raifed to higher animation, in order to affift his enthufiafm, or rather to ftun the ears of the fpectators. In his extacy, he threw up his turban in the air, loofened his hair; for this order of dervifes wear their hair,

hair; and pierced his body with five lances: Then mounting upon a low building, upon which a pole, sixteen feet long, and shod with a sharp iron point, had been set up, he impaled himself upon the pole, and was carried in this condition through the square.

It was an affecting sight, to see a lean man, with a long beard, and dishevelled hair, wounded all over with spikes, and then carried about spitted upon a pole. I said, as I went away, to a Mullah of my acquaintance, that the dervise performed his tricks by means of a broad belt which he carried in his long wide drawers. The Mullah replied, that he had suspected some such art, but avoided mentioning his suspicions, least he might draw upon himself the enmity of the order of *Bedr Eddin;* for that one of his brethren had experienced great persecution from those dervises, in consequence of presuming to hint his doubts of the reality of their miracles.

Understanding that the impaled dervise went also about, exhibiting in private houses for money, I offered him two ducats, if he would come and shew me what he could do. He accepted my offer, came, and began with a long harangue on the dignity of his order, and its founder, who had transmitted to his disciples the gift of working miracles. After this he prayed, and pushed the spikes with violence into his

head

head and body. I examined the places into which the points had seemed to enter, and found the skin slightly torn, but without effusion of blood. I however thought that he had suffered enough for two ducats, and dismissed him.

The science of *Kurra* teaches to compose billets, which secure the wearer from the power of enchantment, and from accidents of all sorts. Those billets are inclosed in small purses of skin, and worn on the head, the arm, or the breast. They are likewise bound upon the necks of horses and asses, to give them an appetite for their food, or to tame them when unmanageable. In the citadel of *Diarbekir*, a billet of this sort put an end to a troublesome croaking of frogs. A man of eminence in Aleppo distributes every year, gratis, billets for freeing houses from flies. The efficacy of these billets depends on the day, the hour, and the particular condition of the messenger who is sent to ask for them. Old women continue to use them, however often they fail, being simple enough to suppose always that some of the conditions requisite to the efficacy of the billets have been wanting when they have been unsuccessful. These billets are not the worse for being written by a Jew or a Christian. Being thought an astrologer, I was often asked for such. These billets are at least no worse than those for making hens lay, which

were

were publicly fold by a Jefuit, in the middle of the eighteenth century, and among enlightened nations.

The fcience of *Ramle* is properly the art of fortune-telling. Jews, as well as Muffulmans, deal in it. When a man falls fick, his friends, in order to learn whether he will recover, fend to confult a Mullah, who returns an anfwer, after examining his book, and receives for his pains a cock or a fheep.

The Sunnite clergy condemn the practice of thefe two laft fciences; yet they are tolerated, becaufe they afford a livelihood to a great number of poor fcribes. As the Arabians are in general covetous, men of wealth and diftinction too often practife thefe low arts for gaining money.

A fcience truly occult, and which every Arabian of worth muft hold in abhorrence, is what they call *Sihhr*, or pure open forcery. The end of this fcience is rather to do mifchief to another perfon than to do good to the perfon who practifes it. It is fometimes employed, however, to feduce a wife from the arms of her hufband into thofe of a ftranger. All that is requifite for this is to fix a certain billet on her door. The inhabitants of Oman are peculiarly fkilled in this execrable fcience: Yet they are certainly inferior to our European forcerers; for they

they know nothing of the art of riding through the air on a broomstick, or of nocturnal assemblies under the presidency of the devil.

I found in Arabia more votaries than I expected of an occult science of a different sort, the pursuit of the philosopher's stone. The Arabians are so passionately addicted to this science, which is the object of their highest wishes, and most eager researches, that they often ruin their fortunes by it, as the alchemists of Europe have been accustomed to do. They suppose the secret of making gold to be known in Europe, especially among the Venetians. They have books in their own language which treat of that science, and inspire them with wild hopes. It should seem, that the idea of the philosopher's stone is originally oriental, and has been brought westward, like many other foolish fables.

At Beit el Fakih, we became acquainted with two alchemists, who wrought each by the precepts of a particular book. The one, who was an amiable, and, in all other respects, a sensible man, was sure of success, as he imagined, if he could find a certain herb, which he believed to grow on the hills of Yemen. As he supposed us to be likewise alchemists, and to have come on purpose to seek that wonderful herb, he cultivated the intimacy of Mr Foskal, and was of great use to him in his botanical excursions;

but

but the poor man, who has already wafted all his own fubftance, and was then working at the expence of a rich nobleman, was not fortunate enough to find the herb he fought. There is faid to be an herb on Mount Libanus which communicates a yellow golden hue to the teeth of the goats which graze upon it. The obfervation of this fact may perhaps have given rife to the opinion of the efficacy of an herb in promoting the great work.

The other of thefe Arabian alchemifts was a fort of phyfician, fo poor that he had not wherewith to buy a glafs alembic. He believed that he fhould fucceed in making gold if he could difcover the meaning of a particular term in his book. Knowing that Mr Von Haven was a linguift, he applied to him for the explanation of a barbarous term which nobody could underftand.

SECT.

SECTION XXVIII.

AGRICULTURE OF THE ARABIANS.

CHAP. I.

Fertility of the Soil.

A traveller, who is obliged to spend the greatest part of his time in towns, and has only a tranfient view of the country, cannot well acquire juft ideas of the fertility of the lands, or the modes of cultivation. I neglected no opportunity that offered of obtaining information, concerning the ftate of agriculture in the Eaft, from fuch perfons as I underftood to be beft qualified to give it. I fhall here fet down what came to my knowledge concerning the fertility of Arabia Proper, and of thofe other countries in which the Arabians have fettlements.

The moft fertile foil I heard of is in Egypt, and in the lands lying immediately around Alexandria. By the accounts of the European merchants

chants in that city, wheat yields an hundred fold increafe; but the peafants told Mr Forſkal, that their moſt plenteous wheat harveſts afforded no greater returns than from thirty to feventy fold, and, in fome places, from fifteen to twenty fold. It is at leaſt certain, that the lands of Egypt, although watered by the Nile, afford in all other places only an increafe of tenfold. *Granger* never met with a greater produce than this laſt.

In *Mefopotamia*, in the vicinity of *Kelle*, *Bagdad*, and *Bafra*, where the lands are watered by the Euphrates and the Tigris, it is thought a fingularly good crop when the increafe is twentyfold; nobody remembers having feen thirtyfold produced.

In the plains of Aſſyria, at *Erbil*, and in the neighbourhood of *Moful*, the cultivated grounds yield only a return of ten or fifteen to one. But corn of thefe countries, which are watered folely by rain, is of a better quality, and produces more meal than what grows upon fields artificially watered. Fifteen fold is better in Aſſyria than twenty fold in Mefopotamia. In the neighbourhood of *Diarbekir*, the ordinary wheat-crop is from four to fifteen fold.

An inhabitant of *Merdan* aſſured me that he reaped fifty for one in barley; a return which he himſelf confidered as extraordinary; the ufual increafe being only from feven to fifteen. Upon more particular inquiry refpecting this fact, I learned that there were in this country two different forts of barley, the common and black barley. The latter ferves beft for the ufe of cattle, and yields fifty fold; while the increafe of the common barley never exceeds fifteen fold. There are likewife two forts of wheat, one of which yields a larger return than the other, and yet is feldomer fown, becaufe it exhaufts the ground more.

In Syria, near Aleppo, nobody could recollect more than one harveft that had yielded above twenty to one. The peafants between *Saide* and *Damafcus*, and thofe about Bethlehem, had never, in their beft years even, reaped more than from twelve to fifteen fold increafe.

In Arabia, in the environs of Mafkat, wheat yields ten to one. In the province of Yemen, agriculture feems to be farther advanced than in the other parts of the Eaft. I was affured, that, in the beft cultivated diftricts, wheat yields an increafe of fifty fold; *durra*, in the highlands, an hundred and forty; and in the Tehama, from two hundred even to four hundred. The latter product may appear incredible; but, by their mode of fowing and watering this grain, the inhabitants of the Tehama reap three fucceffive crops from the fame field, in the

fame

fame year. *Durra* is, in general, the moſt productive grain. *Granger* fays, that, on the banks of the Nile, it yields fifty to one.

Theſe particulars may afford ſome general idea of the productive powers of land in the Eaſt. The ancients, and ſome modern travellers, with a view, it ſhould ſeem, to garniſh their works with wonders, have related things abſolutely incredible of the fertility of theſe regions. Their calculations have either been intentionally enlarged beyond the truth, or the natives have impoſed upon them.

Yet it is not impoſſible to bring their accounts within the bounds of probability. It is a vague way of eſtimating the fertility of any ſoil, to ſay that the produce is in ſuch a proportion to the feed. Skilful modes of tilling and ſowing may give a great ſaving of ſeed, as I ſhall ſoon have occaſion to remark, when ſpeaking of the agriculture of the peaſants of Yemen. If, then, a piece of ground, where one half of the ſeed has been loſt through the unſkilfulneſs of the ſower, yet produces ten fold in the crop, another piece of ground, of the ſame degree of fertility, and ſown with only half the quantity of feed, will yield twenty for one, and will conſequently ſeem, upon a haſty conſideration, to be twice as fertile. This circumſtance does not appear to have been duly attended to, by either the ancients or

the

the moderns, in their accounts of the fertility of distant countries.

Neither do they state what sort of grain they allude to in their calculations of the produce of the lands. We have seen that there is a great difference between the increase of wheat and that of *durra*. The latter grain, a sort of coarse millet, known in Denmark by the name of *Sargo*, has been found in Europe to be friendly to the fertility of the lands on which it is sown; but being of little value, in comparison with our other grains, it is now very seldom sown. In the East, it appears to have been in use from time immemorial. The Arabians use it as their chief article of food. It is sown in Egypt, Mesopotamia, and Assyria. The peasants of Syria and Palestine sell their wheat, and live upon *durra*. It should seem, therefore, that what some authors have related concerning the astonishing fertility of some countries in the East, is to be understood of this durra.

CHAP.

CHAP. II.

Of the Modes of Plowing and Sowing.

THE foil not being every where alike good, and the climate varying greatly through the countries of the Eaft, the modes of cultivation here practifed are alfo confiderably diverfified. In Egypt, Affyria, Mefopotamia, and Syria, agriculture is very much neglected; and thefe provinces are fo thinly inhabited, that much valuable land is fuffered to lie wafte.

In Arabia, the government of which is lefs inaufpicious to agricultural induftry, hufbandry is in a more profperous condition. Yet the inftruments of hufbandry are, even here, coarfe and ill made. The plough ufed is of a very fimple ftructure, is drawn by oxen, and is dragged over the ground in every direction, till the foil feems to be fufficiently broken and loofened for the reception of the feed. In the neighbourhood of Bagdad, I faw affes yoked in the plough with oxen; and near Moful, two mules. In cultivating their gardens, and fuch fpots in their fields as are not acceffible to the plough, the Arabians ufe a fort of hoe, and in digging very deep, a large crow, managed by two men,

one

one of whom preffes it in the ground, and the other draws it towards himfelf with cords.

In many parts in Yemen, whole fields are cultivated like a garden. Agriculture is in fuch places, however, a very laborious tafk, for much care is requifite in watering the grounds. In the highland part of this province, the fields are often formed into terraces, and watered in the rainy feafon by canals from the hills. The inhabitants of the plain are obliged to encompafs their fields with dykes, in order that the water may remain for fome time upon the furface of the ground. I have already defcribed both thefe modes of watering the fields, in the narrative of my journies to Zebid, and in the highlands.

The inhabitants of the upper parts of Yemen colle&t the water neceffary for their fields in dams formed at the foot of the hills. Befide private dams, there are likewife very large public refervoirs, formed by carrying a wall between two hills. In the plain of *Damar*, the fields are watered out of very deep draw-wells, from which the water is drawn by ftrength of arm. It is furprifing that the Arabians adopt not the hydraulic machines which are ufed by their neighbours in Egypt, and in India.

I faw them fow in the highlands of Yemen. A peafant bearing a fackful of lentiles, dropped them here and there in the furrows, juft as we

fow

fow peas in our gardens; and, as he went on, covered the feed by pufhing in the mould with his feet from both fides. In other places, the fower followed the ploughman, and caft the feed into the furrow, which the other returning covered up with his plough. Both thefe modes of fowing are exceedingly troublefome; for the fower muft make as many turns backwards and forwards as there are furrows; but there is a faving in the quantity of the feed, no part of which can be withered by the winds, or pecked up by birds. In Arabia in general, only a fmall quantity of feed is ufed; the peafant, trufting to the regularity of the feafons, does not expofe his grain to perifh in the ground, by fowing it at an improper time. This is another proof of the fallacious nature of inferences concerning the fertility of ground, deduced from the proportion between the feed and the increafe.

In fome diftricts in Yemen, maize and durra are planted with the hand. I faw likewife, in the highlands, between *Mofhak* and *Sehan*, fome fields in which thofe grains grew in rows, like our cabbages in Europe. They were the fineft fields I ever faw in my life. The ftalks were all of the fame height, and every plant was thriving and luxuriant. In adjoining fields were fome unpromifing enough crops of the fame grain, which is a proof that the Arabian peafants

peafants are not all alike induftrious. The cornfields in the places about Beit el Fakih were alfo full of cockle weeds, and irregularly fown.

Near Mount *Mharras* I faw a peafant draw furrows with a fmall plough between ftraight rows of corn, of which the ftalks were from nine to ten inches high. His oxen were fo yoked, that they paffed between the rows without treading down any of the plants. The intention of this piece of labour was to deftroy weeds, to cover the roots of the plants with earth, and to open the foil for the reception of moifture. The weeds which ftill remained were pulled up with the hand, and given to cattle. Thus the hufbandry of *Tull* and *Dü Hamel*, although novel in Europe, is very old in Arabia.

For the prefervation of the grain, care muft be taken to drive away birds, and the deftructive animals. To this end, the peafants watch their fields by turns. In the highlands, he who watches feats himfelf on a tree; in the Tehama, on a fort of fcaffold, having a roof raifed over it.

CHAP.

CHAP. III.

Of the Harvest.

THE beginning of the harvest varies greatly through Arabia, not only by reason of the differences of the latitude of places, but chiefly in consequence of the diversities of their situations as to high and low, and the different times in the season at which it becomes convenient to water them respectively. Even within the narrow extent of the Imam of Sana's dominions, there are great differences in this respect. At Sana, their barley was cut down on the 15th of July, while at *Chamis*, nearer the mountains, the lentiles were then but a sowing. In the plain of *Beit el Fakih*, the durra was seven feet high on the first days of August; and, at the same time, the fields were ploughed and watered for a second seed in the valley of Zebid, which is only a very short day's journey from *Beit el Fakih*.

At Mafkat, wheat and barley are sown in December, and reaped about the end of March; but durra is sown in August, and reaped in the end of the month of November. The date trees are fecundated in the month of December; and, as Oman produces feveral forts of this fruit which ripen fucceffively, the inhabitants have frefh dates during the three months of February, March, and April.

In Egypt, the lands adjoining to the canals are fown in October, and the corn is ripe in the end of February. Lands which cannot be watered from the Nile are fown in November; and, in this laft cafe, the wheat is ripe in February, and the barley in March. At *Moful*, the barley may be cut in the beginning of the month of May, and the wheat within forty days after. All different grains are ripe at Bagdad twenty-four days fooner than at Moful.

The Arabians pull up their ripe corn by the roots, but cut with a fickle green corn, grafs, and whatever they intend as forage for their cattle. The indians ufe the fame inftrument in cutting their rice, and pruning their cocoa trees. Both nations have a very fimple mode of fharpening their fickles. They pour water among a quantity of fand, and rub the blade with this fand till it is fufficiently fharpened.

In threfhing their corn, the Arabians lay the fheaves down in a certain order, and then lead over them two oxen dragging a large ftone. This mode of feparating the ears from the ftraw is not unlike that of Egypt, of which I have spoken

spoken in my description of the manners of that country.

In Syria, the sheaves are spread in the open fields; and oxen drag over them a plank loaded with stones.

The Arabians being less superstitious than the Jews, make no scruple of sowing a field with a mixture of different grains, whenever they suppose that this may be done with advantage.

CHAP. IV.

Of the Domestic Animals.

In Arabia are abundance of all the domestic animals common in hot countries. The Arabians breed horses, mules, asses, camels, dromedaries, cows, buffaloes, sheep, and goats. In the fertile provinces, wild fowls are so plentiful that they are sold at a trifling price.

Of all their domestic animals, it is well known that the Arabians put the greatest value on their horses. Of these they have two great branches, the *Kadischi*, whose descent is unknown, and the *Kochlani*, of whom a written genealogy has been kept for two thousand years. The *Kadischi* are in no better estimation than our European horses,

horses, and are usually employed in bearing burthens, and in ordinary labour.

The *Kochlani* are reserved for riding solely. They are highly esteemed, and consequently are very dear. They are said to derive their origin from King Solomon's studs. However this may be, they are fit to bear the greatest fatigues, and can pass whole days without food. They are also said to show uncommon courage against an enemy. It is even asserted, that when a horse of this race finds himself wounded, and unable to bear his rider much longer, he retires from the fray, and conveys him to a place of security. If the rider falls upon the ground, his horse remains beside him, and neighs till assistance is brought. The *Kochlani* are neither large nor handsome, but amazingly swift: It is not for their figure, but for their velocity, and other good qualities, that the Arabians esteem them.

These *Kochlani* are bred chiefly by the Bedouins settled between *Basra*, *Merdin*, and Syria, in which countries the nobility never choose to ride horses of any other race. The whole race is divided into several families, each of which has its proper name: That of *Dsjulfa* seems to be the most numerous. Some of these families have a higher reputation than others, on account of their more ancient and uncontaminated

minated nobility. Although it is known, by experience, that the *Kochlani* are often inferior to the *Kadifchi*, yet the mares at leaft, of the former, are always preferred, in the hopes of a fine progeny.

The Arabians have indeed no tables of genealogy to prove the defcent of their *Kochlani;* yet they are fure of the legitimacy of the progeny; for a mare of this race is never covered unlefs in the prefence of witneffes, who muft be Arabians. This people do not indeed always ftickle at perjury; but in a cafe of fuch ferious importance, they are careful to deal confcientioufly. There is no inftance of falfe teftimony given in refpect to the defcent of a horfe. Every Arabian is perfuaded that himfelf and his whole family would be ruined, if he fhould prevaricate in giving his oath in an affair of fuch confequence.

A Chriftian, having a *Kochlani* mare whom he wifhes to have covered by a ftallion of the fame race, is obliged to employ an Arabian witnefs, who muft watch the mare twenty days, to be fure that fhe has been defiled by the embraces of no common horfe. During all this time, fhe muft not fee either horfe or afs, even at a diftance. When the mare produces her foal, the fame Arabian muft be prefent; and within the firft feven days, a notorial certificate

of

of the legitimate birth of the foal is made. If there happens to be a croffing of the two breeds, the foal, whether the father or the mother be *Kochlani*, is always efteemed *Kadifchi*.

The Arabians make no fcruple of felling their *Kochlani* ftallions like other horfes; but they are unwilling to part with their mares for money. When not in a condition to fupport them, they difpofe of them to others, on the terms of having a fhare in the foals, or of being at liberty to recover them, after a certain time.

Thefe *Kochlani* are much like the old Arabian nobility, the dignity of whofe birth is held in no eftimation unlefs in their own country. Thefe horfes are little valued by the Turks. Their country being more fertile, better watered, and lefs level, fwift horfes are lefs neceffary to them than to the Arabians. They prefer large horfes, who have a ftately appearance when fumptuoufly harneffed. It fhould feem that there are alfo *Kochlani* in *Hedsjas*, and in the country of *Dsjof*; but I doubt if they be in eftimation in the dominions of the Imam, where the horfes of men of rank appeared to me too handfome to be Kochlani. The Englifh, however, fometimes purchafe thefe horfes at the price of 800 or 1000 crowns each. An Englifh merchant

was

was offered at Bengal twice the purchafe money for one of thefe horfes; but he fent him to England, where he hoped that he would draw four times the original price.

There are two forts of affes in Arabia; the fmaller or lazy afs, as little efteemed here as in Europe; and a large and high fpirited breed, who are highly valued. Thefe latter are fold at a high price. I thought them fitter for a journey than horfes are.

I have reafon to believe, that, in Arabia, are feveral forts of camels. Thofe in the dominions of the Imam are of a moderate fize, and a light brown colour. Thofe from *Nedsjeran* are large, lubbardly, and of a dark brown colour. The dromedaries of Egypt and Arabia have only one bunch upon the back; and, by fuch as have not often feen them, can be diftinguifhed from camels only by an air of lightnefs, which makes them feem fitter for running. I never but once faw dromedaries with two bunches, and that was in a town in Natolia, to which thofe I faw had been brought from the Crimea; but they were fo large and lubbardly, that they feemed to me rather camels of a particular fpecies, than dromedaries.

Buffaloes are to be found in all the marfhy countries of the Eaft, and on the banks of the rivers.

rivers. They are even more numerous than the common horned cattle. I have seen animals of this species in Egypt, at Bombay, near the Euphrates, the Tigris, the Orontes, &c. The female buffalo yields more milk than the common cow; and the male is as fit for the yoke as our oxen. His flesh is indeed inferior to that of the ox, being hard and ill tasted. European merchants are however obliged to use it in the countries where those animals are numerous. I believe that I have often eaten the flesh of a young buffalo without distinguishing it by the taste or appearance from our beef. The Arabians have a mode of forcing the female buffalo to yield more milk than she voluntarily does, which the ancient Scythians also practised with their mares. While one milks the cow, another tickles her.

The oxen and cows of Arabia have upon the shoulder, immediately above the forelegs, a lump or bunch of fat; the bunch of the camel grows larger, or diminishes, as the animal becomes fatter or leaner. I could obtain no particular information concerning the instinct ascribed to these oxen, of forming into circular bodies, to defend themselves against beasts of prey. The story is so much the less probable, because the cattle of Arabia are distinguished by remarkably small horns.

The

The Arabians have no meadows which might afford grafs for the feeding of thefe domeftic animals. The country is too much parched for the grafs to become luxuriant enough to be ufed as hay. Straw, barley, and beans, are the articles of food upon which they nourifh their cattle. The only herb they fow exprefsly for this purpofe is a fort of bean or *phafeolus;* the Egyptians, whofe country is better watered, fow trefoil for the fame ufe. The camel eats the moft ftunted and withered roots. In Arabia, however, he lives chiefly on herbs of the gourd fpecies, which abound in the drieft countries.

SECT.

SECTION XXIX.

NATURAL HISTORY OF ARABIA.

CHAP. I.

General Reflections on the Natural History of Arabia.

ONE principal object which it became our party of travellers to keep in view, was undoubtedly the examination of the natural productions of the country through which we travelled. Every member of our company having had his particular task assigned to him, the investigation of subjects of natural history was particularly appropriated to the late Mr Forskal. His well known activity, abilities, and ardour for the cultivation of science, afforded the public room to expect from him numerous discoveries in the natural history, as well of Egypt, as of Arabia; countries which he had time to examine before his premature death. But, our hopes have been in part disappointed, by the concurrence of different unfavourable circumstances, which it may be proper to give an account of here, both in excufe for the deficiency of this article, and as an encouragement to future travellers to perfect what was fo fuccefsfully begun by our deceafed friend.

The time prefcribed for our continuance in the Eaft was fhort in the whole; and an unforfeen delay in Egypt farther abridged that portion of it which we had deftined to be fpent in Arabia. In confequence of this circumftance, we had no more time for examining the natural hiftory of Arabia than the fix months between the end of December 1762, and the beginning of June 1763, at the laft of which periods Mr Forfkal died. Hence many objects could be only curforily obferved. Befides, the frequent indifpofition of fome or other of our party obliged us often to feparate; and a reafon of this nature hindered Mr Forfkal from feeing Mount Sinai, and the productions of that part of Arabia Petræa.

The climate and foil of feveral of the countries which we vifited are lefs favourable, than is commonly fuppofed, for the increafe of vegetables and animals. The foil of Arabia is, through a great part of that country, dry and fandy, produces no plants, and is therefore unfit for the nourifhment of animals. Here the naturalift

Dress of the women in the back parts of Yemen.

turalist finds but few objects to observe; and of such a country the natural history can never be extensive. In Arabia, likewise, the heat of the sun is so intense, that the flowers no sooner blow than they are withered; and if the botanist, attentive to a number of plants at once, misses the precise moment when any one which is new to him is in flower, he can have no subsequent opportunity of examining it till the ensuing season.

This inconvenience might be avoided by observing the plants in gardens. But there is perhaps no country in the world where gardening is so much neglected as in Arabia. There is hardly a single small garden in the neighbourhood even of the greatest towns. At Beit el Fakih there is only one, which was formed by an old Dola. The Arabians, a simple frugal race, content themselves with the plainest food, without taking pains to furnish themselves with a variety of dishes. What seems to give them an aversion for the culture of gardens is the long droughts, which last sometimes for more than a year, and destroy every sprout of vegetation, together with the ravages of the grasshoppers, which complete the devastation of the fields. The Banians, being by their religion confined to a vegetable diet, plant great quantities of pulse; but these are mostly of species that are natives of
India,

India, and by confequence already known to botanifts.

Befide thefe phyfical obftacles to the inveftigation of the natural hiftory of the Eaft, there is another, arifing from the moral character of the people who inhabit thefe regions. The Arabians, an ignorant, covetous, and jealous race, cannot comprehend how the Europeans fhould be prompted by mere curiofity to expofe themfelves to fo much danger and fatigue. They afcribe to them a motive of intereft, the defire of difcovering hidden treafures, with great fkill in the fearch. The idea generally prevalent among them, of the wealth of travellers, makes a curious perfon run a great rifk of being plundered by vagabond robbers. Mr Forfkal, efcaping once with difficulty out of the clutches of a band of thefe robbers in Egypt, and being once plundered by another party, was obliged to ceafe from his fcientific excurfions. He found means, indeed, to have plants gathered for him, by an Arabian, in the neighbourhood of Kahira. But the naturalift makes his obfervations beft upon living plants, in their native fituations.

Our friend was luckier, in this refpect, in Yemen, where the fafety of a ftranger is better fecured by the laws, and the manners of the people of the conntry. The Arabians in Yemen were

fe

Prospect among the Coffee Mountains of Yemen.

so far from offering him any interruptions in his purfuits, that both men and women, of all ranks and ages, appeared to take pleafure in bringing, pointing out, and naming to him all their indigenous plants. A people living the life of fhepherds, and of hufbandmen, like the Arabians, who fpend almoft all their time in the open fields, naturally acquire a tafte for botany, and a degree of fkill in its refearches. But, in order to obtain the aid, and even the friendfhip of thefe good people, he was obliged to conform to their manners, and to content himfelf with their fcanty cheer. A life of fuch abftinence and fatigue, too fevere for a perfon brought up in European habits, undoubtedly contributed to fhorten the days of our friend.

In fpite of all thefe obftacles, Mr Forfkal's ardent induftry was fuccefsful beyond our hopes. It is inconceivable in what a fhort time he difcovered and made defcriptions of full three hundred fpecies in the animal kingdom, and of more than eight hundred in the vegetable. This number might have been yet more confiderable, had he not laid it down as a rule to himfelf, to defcribe nothing which he had not examined with the moft fcrupulous exactnefs. For this reafon had he put off, till he fhould be at more leifure, the examination of a large collection of infects and fhells. With the fame intention, he had

preferved

preserved, in spirit of wine, a great many fishes and amphibious animals. But the reader will recollect the fate of this collection, when our goods were inspected at the custom-house at Mokha, as above related.

After my return to Europe, I was intrusted with the task of publishing my friend's posthumous papers. I then discovered a new loss which natural history had suffered by his death. He had been accustomed to write down his observations on small detached pieces of paper, which could not easily be preserved together. It is true, I found 1800 of these billets, which I endeavoured to reduce into order. But I could not help inferring from the chasms here and there, that many of them were lost. Whether it be or be not so, I have, however, presented to the public all that I could recover, in two Latin works, intituled, *Descriptiones Animalium*, 4to, *Hafniæ*, 1775; and *Flora Arabica*, 4to, ib. 1775.

These two works, written in Latin, and in the manner and arrangement of *Linnæus*, are intended particularly for the use of the learned naturalist. To gratify readers of all classes, I shall here insert the most curious particular of the information contained in those works, and such as will serve to give the best ideas of the productions, common or peculiar, of the countries which we traversed.

traverſed. Although natural hiſtory was not my province, I had occaſion to obſerve tranſiently many things reſpecting it. I ſhall, therefore, intermingle my own remarks, without diſtinguiſhing them as ſuch; for the greater part of the whole is Mr Forſkal's.

CHAP. II.

Climate and Soil of Arabia.

A country, ſuch as Arabia, extending from the 30° to the 13° of northern latitude, and, by conſequence, ſituate partly between the tropics, will be naturally ſuppoſed ſubject to a very hot climate. In ſome provinces of Arabia, the heat is exceſſive. But, in this country, as in moſt others, the varying degrees of elevation, the relative ſituations of places, and the nature of the ſoil, occaſion conſiderable varieties of temperature.

Before a perſon can underſtand theſe varieties, it is neceſſary that he ſhould have a juſt idea of the phyſical circumſtances of Arabia. This country may be conſidered as a pile of mountains, encircled with a belt of flat, dry, and ſandy ground. Towards the north and the continent, this belt is formed by the deſarts of Syria,

ria, and Arabia Petræa. The plains called *Teha-ma* by the Arabians, and extending from the sea-shore to the hills, bound Arabia on those sides on which it is washed by the waters of the Red Sea, of the Eastern Ocean, and of the Persian Gulph.

In these desarts, diversified here and there only by bare rocks, and in these flat plains, there is nothing to soften the force of the sun's rays, but all vegetables are burnt up, and the soil is every where reduced to sand. The drought is so extreme, that whole years will pass without rain; and the torrents which fall from the hills are lost among the sands long before they can reach the sea. Were it not for these river-waters, which being swelled in the rainy season, are drained off to fertilize the lands, the husbandman would be unable to raise even those scanty crops which his harvests at present afford. By observations made with good thermometers, we found, that in these plains, as, for instance, at Loheya, Mokha, and Maskàt, the heats were as intense as in any other hot country whatever.

In the interior country, the temperature of the atmosphere is very different. The great ranges of lofty mountains attract vapours; and these falling down in plenteous rains cool the air, and quicken vegetation. The cold occasioned by the height of the country, produces falls of fnow; but this never lies long upon the ground. While the inhabitants of the plains fuffer by heat, thofe of the hills are obliged to wrap themfelves in pellices. We were affured that there was ice on fome of the hills, and that, at Sana, which lies among the hills in the interior country, there was fometimes froft.

The pofition of thefe mountains in the middle of a peninfula, occafions likewife another phenomenon that is equally obfervable in the peninfula formed by the Ganges, which is in the fame manner interfected by mountains. The rainy feafons, which are regular in the countries between the tropics, are, by this peculiarity of fituation, diverfified here. Weftward, in Yemen, the rainy feafon is of great fervice to the country; for it comes on in the month of June, and terminates in the middle of September; in which months the heats are moft violent, and the earth and its inhabitants in the greateft need of fuch refrefhment. In the eaftern part of thefe mountains, on the fide of Mafkat, thofe rains fall between the middle of the month of November and the middle of February. In *Hadramaut* and *Oman*, to the fouth, the rainy feafon lafts from the middle of February to the middle of April. It fhould feem, therefore, that the rains make the tour of the peninfula every

every feafon, as impelled by the prevalent winds. In the Tehama of Yemen, we heard alfo of a rain in fpring, the period of which is uncertain, but on which the fuccefs of the harvefts depends.

Thefe regular rains render the vallies lying among the mountains fertile and delightful. The Highlanders, who breathe a fine frefh air, are handfome, healthy, and brave. Another advantage which the Arabians owe to the fituation of their country, is, that it affords them at the fame time the productions of different climates. In the plains, feveral vegetables tranfplanted from India thrive well enough, and many of the animals of hot countries multiply there. The mountains produce the plants and animals of temperate climates. Arabia may thus be regarded as an affemblage of different climates, the refpective advantages of which are all to be found in the tract lying between the Red Sea and the Perfian Gulph.

The nature of the winds differs, in Arabia, with the point of the compafs from which they blow, and the tract over which they refpectively pafs. The fame wind is, in different places, dry or moift, according as it blows over the ocean, or over defarts. On the fhores of the Perfian Gulph, the fouth-eaft wind is accompanied with a degree of moifture which, when the heat is intenfe, intense, occasions violent sweatings; the north-west, passing over the great desart, is more torrid, but less disagreeable; this last wind heats metals in the shade, as if they were exposed to the sun; and its heat, suddenly added to that of the atmosphere, often suffocates men and other animals. The Arabians, when they travel, carry with them garlic and dried grapes, for the purpose of reviving such persons as may fall down fainting, from the effect of these hot blasts.

Notwithstanding its torrid qualities, this north-west wind serves to cool their liquors for the Arabians, in the middle of Summer. In order to this, they put their water into *bardaks*, or unglazed pots, made of a sort of porous earth; and then, having these pots in a place exposed to the current of this hot wind, the water is thus rendered very cool; a circumstance well-known in hot countries, and at present ascribed by naturalists to the effects of sudden evaporation.

Another wind, of a more dangerous nature, is the famous *Sam*, *Smum*, or *Samiel*, which seldom blows within Arabia, but frequently upon its frontiers. This wind prevails only on the confines of the great desart, where the agitation of the air forms a current for the vapours which are raised by the heat of the sun from that parched territory. The places the most exposed to this destructive

deſtructive wind, are the banks of the Euphrates, and ſometimes the environs of Mecca, when the north wind blows from the deſart. It is not unknown in Perſia, on the borders of thoſe arid plains; and it is ſaid to have been felt in ſome places in Spain, near the vaſt tracts of deſart ſands which deform that fine kingdom. The effects of the *Smum* are inſtant ſuffocation to every living creature that happens to be within the ſphere of its activity, and immediate putrefaction of the carcaſes of the dead. As a ſimilar rapidity of putrefaction has been obſerved to take place upon bodies deprived of life by thunder, or by the electric ſhock, it has been conjectured, that electrical matter, which is very generally diffuſed through nature, might be the cauſe of the peculiarly noxious qualities of this wind. The Arabians diſcern the approach of the Smum by an unuſual redneſs in the air; and they ſay that they feel a ſmell of ſulphur as it paſſes. However this may be, the only means by which any perſon can preſerve himſelf from ſuffering from the noxious blaſts, is, by throwing himſelf down with his face upon the earth, till this whirlwind of poiſonous exhalations has blown over; which always moves at a certain height in the atmoſphere. Inſtinct even teaches the brutes to incline their heads to the ground on theſe occaſions.

The

The other meteors of Arabia are common to it with all other hot countries. A clear sky, seldom obscured by clouds, renders storms very unfrequent in the plains. The air discharges its electric matter in globes of fire, and by the phenomena called shooting stars, which are not unfrequent, and of considerable bulk. In the most acid tracts, near the sea, the dews are singularly copious. But, notwithstanding this humidity, the air is so pure, that the inhabitants sleep in the open air; I never slept sounder than where I found my bed all wet with dew in the morning. There are, however, places where one dares not sleep in the open air for fear of being struck with a palsy. By long experience the inhabitants of those parts have learned what precautions to take, and these are always peculiarly necessary to an European unaccustomed to the climate.

Arabia enjoys the prospect of almost constant verdure. Not but that most of the trees shed their leaves, and the annual plants wither and are re-produced. But, the interval between the fall of the leaf in one year, and the re-production of new leaves for the next, is so short, that the change is hardly observable. Continual verdure is peculiar to those countries in which there are no frosts, but a rainy season instead of our winter.

From

From the singular local situation of Arabia, the inequalities in the nature of its lands may, without farther information, be inferred. These inequalities are indeed very remarkable. On one side are frightful desarts, and on the other fertile and delightful vales. The sandy belt which encircles this peninsula is almost entirely barren, and presents one unvaried picture of desolation.

This belt, denominated Tehama, as has been several times mentioned, begins at Suez, and extends round the whole peninsula, to the mouth of the Euphrates. Its breadth varies; it is, however, for the most part, about two days journey from the sea-shore to the rise of the hills; at least this is the breadth of the plain adjacent to the Red Sea. It bears every mark of having been anciently a part of the bed of the sea. Its bottom soil is a greyish clay, with a large proportion of sand, and having marine exuviæ interspersed to a great distance from the sea-shore. It contains large strata of salt, which in some places even rise up into hills. Its regular inclination towards the sea indicates that it has emerged gradually. The small eminences upon the confines of this plain are composed of calcareous stones, having a blackish appearance, and seeming as if they were burnt by the sun. The adjoining hills contain schistus and basaltes;

in this differing greatly from the ſtrata of the hills on the oppoſite coaſt of Egypt, and from thoſe of Arabia Petræa, which are chiefly made up of granite.

The ſea, no doubt, ſtill continues to recede; and the Tehama is on that ſide gradually extending its limits. The banks of coral are ſtill increaſing, and coming nearer to the ſhore, ſo as to render the navigation of the gulph every day more and more dangerous. The ſand accumulated by the billows gradually fills up the intermediate ſpace, and joins theſe beds of coral to the continent, as appears from ſome recent inſtances. Hiſtory alſo records proofs of this gradual receſſion of the waters; and mentions, as ſea-ports, ſeveral places which are at preſent inland, without noticing the preſent maritime towns, which muſt undoubtedly be of later origin than the formation of the land on which they ſtand.

Such a conqueſt over the watery element promiſes, however, little advantage to man. Theſe newly formed lands are ungrateful and barren. Nor can any better be ſanguinely hoped of the future; ſince the territory of the Tehama has remained for ſo many ages unchanged in its nature. Mr Forſkal fancied that he could diſtinguiſh a ſimilarity between the ſoil of *Hedsjas* and that of Egypt, from which he inferred, that
the

the sterility of the former was owing to the want of water. But he was certainly mistaken; for the soil of Egypt is formed of the sediment of the Nile, but that of Hedsjas of the remains of the bed of the sea. The calcareous stone of the hills of this latter province is, however, decomposed into a blackish earth, which in time becomes fit to bear some coarse vegetables.

In the Highlands of Arabia, there are as great diversities of soil as in most other cultivated countries. The most general character of the soil on these schistous hills is clay mixed with sand. But the figure of the hills is unfavourable to their fertility. They are commonly so craggy and precipitous, as to afford neither room nor soil for vegetable-productions, the good earth being continually washed away by the waters. These circumstances have likewise the effect of rendering the culture of such places extremely difficult and expensive. Terraces are necessary to be formed; of which indeed the construction is sometimes facilitated by the piles of basaltes naturally cast into regular pentagonal figures, which are broken, from time to time, from the rocks, and serve as materials for the walls.

Arabia is a country interesting in many respects; but is, in general, neither rich nor fertile.

tile. The laborious life, and indifferent fate of its inhabitants, are fufficient proofs of this truth. If it was called *Happy* by the ancients, it was only by the value and the novelty, not by the abundance of its productions, that it could merit this name.

CHAP. III.

Arabian Quadrupeds.

SPEAKING of the agriculture of the Arabians, I had occafion to mention their domeftic animals. Of thofe, fome appear to be originally natives of the country, for they are not common through the other regions of the eaft; they retain their primary inftincts in higher perfection, and are more eminently diftinguifhed by ftrength and beauty here than elfewhere. Such are the horfe, the afs, the camel, and perhaps too the ox. The camel, by its power of enduring thirft, and its containing a refervoir for water in its bowels, feems naturally deftined for an inhabitant of the defart. Its hoof is formed to tread on burning fands; and the cartilaginous texture of its mouth enables it to feed on the hard and prickly plants of thofe parched plains.

The afs, efpecially, feems to be a native of Arabia. Here are a fpecies of affes, which, in beauty, vigour, and fpirit, are no contemptible rivals to the horfe. The inhabitants fpeak likewife of a wild animal, called *Djæar*, of the fame fize and fhape as the afs, the flefh of which is excellent food.

This animal is probably a wild afs, who, in confequence of living in a ftate of independence, acquires fome varieties of form, which the Arabs, in their unfkilfulnefs in natural hiftory, miftake for the characteriftics of a different animal.

The Arabians give the name of *Bakar Uafch* to an animal which we did not fee, but of which their vague defcription can be referred only to the wild ox. They fpeak of another animal of the form of an ox, which is deftitute of horns, and feeds only by night.

On the lofty hills of Arabia Petræa, are rock-goats. The plains are ftocked with *gazelles*; and this beautiful creature is fo common, that the Arabian poets draw from it many of their allufions and fimilitudes. The hare is not a common animal here, and is to be feen only in fome mountainous parts. In the fandy tracks are numbers of thofe little animals called *Jerboa's*, Pharaoh's rats, whofe flefh the Arabians eat without any diflike. The peculiarity in

the

the ſtructure of the hinder feet of theſe animals, and their manner of leaping, which have induced our naturaliſts to give the ſpecies the name of *Mus Jaculus*, are well known.

In the foreſts, in the ſouth of Arabia, are monkies without tails, whoſe back parts are bare and red. I ſaw theſe animals in troops of ſome hundreds. Other travellers have met with them in thouſands on the hills of Aden. Theſe creatures are docile, and eaſily learn any trick which is attempted to be taught them. On this account numbers of them are exported to Egypt, where jugglers exhibit them to the people.

Of carnivorous animals, the moſt hideous and formidable is the *Hyæna*, who attacks men and beaſts with the ſame ferocity. This fierce and ſolitary animal inhabits the caverns of the deſart mountains of Arabia Petræa, and is alſo common round the ſhores of the Perſian Gulph. The hyæna marches out only at night, in that ſeaſon when the inhabitants of the country ſleep in the open air, and often carries off children from beſide their parents.

As the domeſtic animals on the ſouthern coaſt of the Perſian Gulph are chiefly fed upon fiſhes, the hyæna is ſometimes obliged to content himſelf with the ſame food. On my return into Europe, I ſaw in Denmark one of

theſe

these animals alive, in the king's collection of wild animals.

The leopard, reckoned by Mr Forſkal among the carnivorous animals, is perhaps the ſame as the panther, *(Felis pardus Linnæi)*; the more probably ſo, as he gives it the Arabic name of the panther, *Nemer*. However, the ounce or ſmall panther, named in Arabic *Fath*, is ſtill more common than the large one; neither is it regarded with any ſort of terror in Arabia, where it carries away cats and dogs, but never ventures to attack men.

Wild boars, wolves, and foxes, are to be found in Arabia; but the moſt common carnivorous animal is a ſort of wild dog, more like the fox than the houſehold-dog, and named by the Turks *Tſchakal*, by the Arabians *El Vavi*. This animal, common through all the countries of the Eaſt, is ſo well known, that I need not here add any thing concerning its figure and manners.

Mr Forſkal names ſeveral other animals of which he knew nothing, except what he gathered from the indiſtinct accounts of the natives; and ſome others of which he could only learn the Arabian names. As ſuch ſlight notices cannot enlarge the knowledge of nature, I ſhall not repeat them here. The moſt ſingular of thoſe animals, which we knew only by hearſay, hearfay, is one faid to refemble a cat, to live upon the hills, to feed on grafs, and to be a moft delicate article of food.

CHAP. IV.

Of the Birds of Arabia.

IF we had opportunities of examining but few quadrupeds, we were not more fortunate in refpect to birds. Not that Arabia is deficient in variety of fpecies; on the contrary, its productions are fufficient to nourifh a prodigious number: But a traveller haftening through a country, has it ftill lefs in his power to acquaint himfelf with the inhabitants of the air than with thofe of the earth. One cannot fee many birds, or obferve them at leifure, unlefs among people who are fond of fowling, and who, as they feek for game and fell it, bring to the curious fuch birds as they have caught or killed, and are able to give fome account of their refpective names and inftincts.

In Arabia we had no fuch advantage. The Arabians defpife the ufe of wild fowl, and regard neither the amufement nor the exercife of fowling. I thought that I could difcern two caufes of their averfion for a diverfion which

the

the favages of the north purfue with extreme fondnefs. A people who are naturally fober and frugal, and live in a climate where the ufe of animal food is injurious to health, cannot be fond of game. The precepts of the Muffulman religion muft alfo difguft the Arabians at the purfuit of wild animals, efpecially of birds. A hunter lofes his labour, and his prey becomes impure, if he has but neglected the repetition of one fhort prayer when he killed the animal; if it has not loft the juft quantity of blood required by the law; if the bird ftruggled with any remains of life after it was fhot; or if it fell upon a place which was either inhabited, or in any manner defiled. We faw no other birds, therefore, than thofe which we killed ourfelves, or thofe which we could obferve while they were at liberty.

In the fertile countries of Arabia, tame fowls are very plentiful, and all forts of poultry are bred in great abundance. The pintado is not domeftic; but thefe birds inhabit the woods in fuch numbers, that children kill them with ftones, and then collect them to be fold in the towns. The pheafant is likewife a native of Arabia, and is found in great plenty, in the forefts of Yemen, as well as the wood-pigeon, and feveral other varieties of the pigeon fpecies. In the plains of the fame province, the grey partridge

ridge, the common lark, and a fort of white crane, having the under part of the belly of a beautiful red, are alfo to be feen here.

So dry a country as Arabia cannot be fuppofed to afford a great variety of water fowls. However, in places where there was water, we found a beautiful variety of the plover, and fometimes ftorks. Sea-fowls, which live upon fifh, are numerous on the coafts of the Red fea, becaufe this gulph is very deep, and copioufly ftored with fifhes. Befide fome forts of fea-maws, we faw in an ifle of the Red fea pelicans, who had built nefts and laid eggs as large as thofe of the goofe.

The defarts of Arabia are not without oftriches, which are called by the inhabitants *Thar Edsjammel*, the camel bird. I did not underftand that the Arabians take this bird young, and tame it. One which I faw at Loheya was from Abyffinia. A beautiful lapwing, called by the Arabians *Hudhud*, is alfo common on the fhores of the Perfian Gulph. Some Arabians have been perfuaded, by a fabulous tradition, that the language of this bird may be underftood.

Eagles, falcons, fparrow-hawks, and the Egyptian vulture, *(Vultur Petenopterus Linnæi)*, are birds of prey to be met with in Arabia. The laft of thefe is very ferviceable in the country; clearing the earth of all carcafes, which corrupt very rapidly,

rapidly, and are very noifome in hot countries; He alfo deftroys the field mice, which multiply fo prodigiously in fome provinces, that, were it not for this affiftance; the peafant might ceafe from the culture of the fields as abfolutely vain. Their performance of thefe important fervices induced the ancient Egyptians to pay thofe birds divine honours; and even at prefent it is held unlawful to kill them, in all the countries which they frequent.

In feveral countries in the eaft, as alfo in Arabia, there is another bird, not lefs beneficial to the inhabitants. It is thought to be a native of *Korafan*, for it comes annually into Arabia, in purfuit of the fwarms of locufts, of which it deftroys incredible numbers. It is called *Samarman* or *Samarmog*. Mr Forfkal ranks it among the thrufhes, and calls it *Turdus Seleucus*. The fervices done by this bird, in countries expofed to the ravages of thofe infects, have given rife to feveral ridiculous and fuperftitious practices in Syria. It is thought to be attracted from *Korafan* by water, which is, for this end, brought from a diftance with great ceremony, and preferved in a ftone refervoir on the top of the tower of a mofque. When this water fails, the inhabitants of Moful are in defpair. But as this bird's inftincts prompt it not only to feed on locufts, but to kill as many of them as poffible

it

it naturally follows thefe infects in the courfe of their paffage.

We heard much talk of two fpecies of birds, which are highly valued by the Arabians, and are called *Salva* and *Sumana*. We could difcover nothing concerning the generic character of the latter; but we heard enough of the *Salva* to enable us to underftand that it is the rail, a bird of paffage which frequents a fmall diftrict in Arabia. As to quails, we received no evidence of their being birds of paffage; nor is it probable that this bird fhould traverfe defarts where no fubfiftence is to be found.

The Arabians likewife named to Mr Forfkal feveral other birds, which he never could fee, and confequently could not afcertain their genus, fuch as the *Achjal*, famous for two beautiful feathers, with which the Highlanders adorn their bonnets, and to preferve which uninjured, the bird, it feems, leaves a hole in its neft. Another, the *Thaer el Hind*, rare and remarkable for its gilded plumage, is fold very dear in Arabia. Its name feems to indicate that it is a bird of paffage, which is fuppofed to come from India.

CHAP. V.

Of Amphibious Animals and Fiſhes.

In the Arabian ſeas, we never met with the ſea-tortoiſe; the land-tortoiſe is more common; the peaſants bring the latter, by cart-loads, to the markets of ſeveral towns in the eaſt. The eaſtern Chriſtians eat theſe animals in Lent, and drink their blood with great reliſh.

We ſaw ſeveral ſorts of lizards, of which the only dangerous one was that called by the Egyptians *Gecko*. It is ſaid that the ſaliva of this creature, falling upon victuals, infects the perſons who eat them with the leproſy.

There are in Arabia ſeveral ſorts of ſerpents, the bite of which is often mortal. But the innocent are as numerous as the dangerous ſerpents. Of ſome the bite occaſions only a diſagreeable itching, which the Arabians cure by applying the leaves of the caper-tree to the wound. In general, life is endangered only by the bite of ſuch ſerpents as have a diſtinct row of teeth larger than the reſt of the teeth. The Arabians in Egypt are acquainted with this law in the ſtructure of reptiles, and play ſafely with ſerpents, after pulling out the long teeth, which

ſerve

ſerve to conduct the poiſon. In Arabia, the only ſerpent that is truly formidable is that called *Baetan*, a ſmall ſlender creature, ſpotted black and white; its bite is inſtant death, and the dead body is ſwelled by the poiſon in a very extraordinary manner.

Mr Forſkal diſcovered in the Red Sea ſeveral ſorts of Ray-fiſhes which are unknown in Europe. That ſea is in general ſtored with a great variety of fiſhes; and I was told by my friend, that in the ſhort paſſage between Suez and Jidda, he obſerved more than a hundred new ſpecies, only a part of which he could rank among the known genera. He was obliged to form four new genera, which he named *Salaria Scarus, Signanus,* and *Acanthurus*. A new torpedo which he met with, appeared ſo different from that already known, that he was induced to claſs it as a particular genus.

Among the new ſpecies are ſome belonging to genera which are found alſo in our ſeas; ſuch are ſeveral cod-fiſhes hitherto unknown; new ſpecies of mackerels, mullets, ſcari, perches. &c. Others of theſe ſpecies belong to genera peculiar to the ſeas adjacent to hot countries, ſuch as the *Chætodon* and the *Sciaena*.

In our paſſage over the Red Sea, we ſaw troops of flying fiſhes, which roſe from time to time above the ſurface of the water; but we diſcovered

covered no flying ferpent in the courfe of our voyage; although the Arabians give this name to a ferpent which fhould rather be called the leaper. This ferpent fixes himfelf by the tail to a low branch of a tree, and then giving himfelf an impetus, by means of his elaftic tail, fprings from branch to branch fucceffively, till he reaches the top.

The Arabians inhabiting the fhores of the Red Sea live almoft entirely on fifhes, as I have already had occafion to mention, and even fuftain their cattle with the fame food. Although fifhes are fo plentiful, yet a living fifh is feldom to be feen among them. For fear of violating fome precept of the Muffulman law, the fifhermen kill all their fifhes before they bring them on fhore.

CHAP VI.

Infects and Shells.

THE locufts have a great influence on the condition of the inhabitants of Arabia, and of feveral other countries in the eaft; and, therefore, I fhall fpeak of this infect at a length which others do not merit. We, however, did not find the numbers fo great as they are commonly fuppofed to be in Europe.

In

In Egypt I saw once only a cloud of locusts, which was brought by a south-wind from the desarts of Lybia; the locusts fell in prodigious quantities on the roofs of the houses, and in the streets of Kahira. I saw no more of them, till at Jidda, in November 1762, a large cloud of locusts was driven over the city by a west-wind. The cloud came from the other side of the Arabic Gulph; and, therefore, many of the insects must have been drowned in their passage. In the month of July following, we found a small quantity near mount *Sumara*, which seemed to have spent the season in Arabia. These swarms often cross the Red Sea a second time, and return to Egypt, the upper part of which adjoining to the desarts of Lybia, seems to be the cradle of these animals. I saw clouds of them in Persia, and Syria; where, in the quarter of Mosul, I found nests of these insects, which a careful police might in a great degree destroy. Small locusts, of the size of a fly, grow with amazing rapidity, and attain their natural size within a few days.

There are undoubtedly various species of this insect, which have not as yet been sufficiently discriminated. Mr Forskal calls the locust which infests Arabia *Gryllus Gregarius*, and thinks it to be different from that which is called by Linnæus *Gryllus Migratorius*, and which is a native of of the defarts of Tartary, from which it paffes through the neighbouring countries, into Poland and Germany. The *Gryllus Gregarius* merits this denomination; for the locufts of this fpecies appear to act in concert, and to live and travel in fociety. Thofe which remain after the departure of the great body are only irregular ftragglers.

The Arabians diftinguifh feveral feparate fpecies of this infect, to which they give particular names. But thefe names are not expreffive of any qualities in the nature of the animal; as they refpect only the delicacy afcribed to its flefh. They give the name *Muken* to the red locuft, which is efteemed fatter and more fucculent than any of the others; they likewife eat the light locuft; but abftain from another, called *Dubbe*, becaufe it has a tendency to produce diarrhœa.

All Arabians, whether living in their native country, or in Perfia, Syria, and Africa, are accuftomed to eat locufts. The Turks, on the contrary, have an averfion for this fort of food. If the Europeans exprefs any thing of the fame averfion, the Arabians then remind us of our fondnefs for oyfters, crabs, and lobfters. A German, who had long refided in Barbary, affured us, that the flefh of this infect tafted like

the

the small sardine of the Baltic Sea, which is dried in some towns of Holstein.

We saw locusts caught, and put into bags, or on strings, to be dried, in several parts of Arabia. In Barbary, they are boiled, and then dried upon the roofs of the houses. The Bedouins of Egypt roast them alive, and devour them with the utmost voracity. We saw no instance of unwholesomeness in this article of food; Mr Forskal was indeed told, that it had a tendency to thicken the blood, and to bring on melancholy habits. The Jews in Arabia are convinced, that the fowls, of which the Israelites ate so largely in the desart, were only clouds of locusts,—and laugh at our translators, who have supposed that they found quails where quails never were.

The swarms of these insects darken the air, and appear at a distance like clouds of smoke. The noise they make in flying is frightful and stunning, like that of a water-fall. When such a swarm falls upon a field, it is wasted, and despoiled of its verdure. The pulse and date-trees suffer greatly from the locusts; but corn, either ripe or nearly so, is too hard for their use, and they are obliged to spare it.

A small insect named *Arda*, of the bulk of a grain of barley *(Termes fatale, Linn.)* is another scourge of Arabia, and of hot countries in general.

ral. On account of some general resemblance, many travellers represent this insect as an ant, and speak of it under this name. Its instinct disposes it to travel only by night, through a sort of galleries, which it forms, as it proceeds, of fat earth. After reaching the end of its journey, it corrodes and destroys every thing, victuals, clothes, and furniture. We found an army of these in our chamber, for the first time, at Beit el Fakih. We immediately demolished the galleries which they had formed; but they, without being discouraged, or terrified at our presence, renewed their work in the night, with singular obstinacy, so that we had much ado to rid ourselves of them. They live and work together like ants.

The *arda* is also destructive to trees, the sweetness of whose leaves and fruits gratifies its taste. These insects fix upon trees of this character, and extend their galleries from the root to the top. The inhabitants of the country have no other means for preserving their gardens from utter ruin, except to surround the trees with sheep's dung, the smell of which the arda cannot endure.

There are in Arabia many ants, but most of them are harmless as our's. From among these, however, are to be excepted two species, one of which becomes troublesome by the voracity with which

which it attacks victuals, unless driven away by the odour of camphor; the other's bite is little less painful than that of the scorpion; but neither is it more deadly.

A sort of *scolopendra* likewise torments the inhabitants of this country, and affects those on whom it fixes with burning pains. This insect fixes all its feet into the flesh, so that it is impossible to rid one's self of it otherwise than by successively burning all the parts affected with a hot iron. The cuttle-fish is dangerous to swimmers and divers, of whom it lays hold with its long claws. These do not wound, but produce swelling, internal pains, and often an incipient paralysis.

Among the *Tenebriones* is one species which destroys reeds. Probably this small insect attacks likewise the stalks of corn, in which is observed a farina, which serves to diffuse the eggs of this insect through houses. This little animal is therefore one of the most troublesome insects in the country. The women of Arabia and Turkey make use of another tenebrio, which is found among the filth of gardens. As plumpness is thought a beauty in the east, the women, in order to obtain this beauty, swallow, every morning and every evening, three of those insects fried in butter. The Red Sea is full of marine insects; *Priapi, Salha, Fistulares, Medusa,* &c. Mr Forskal became more and more convinced, in the courfe of his obfervations, that the immenfe numbers of thefe animals contribute to produce the refulgence which is perceived at night in fea-water. This infect feems to be an animated phofphoric body.

We obferved a great many crabs, fome of which were fpecies peculiar to the Arabic gulph. The fhells are not lefs numerous; and fome of them of rare fpecies. The moft beautiful is a *Pinna*, the colours of which are fuperb; but this fhell is very brittle. The inhabitants avail not themfelves of this plenty of marine productions, which might afford them excellent food. Muffulmans in general eat very little fifh, and appear to have a particular averfion for crabs and fhellfifh. On the contrary, the oriental Chriftians, who are confined to long and rigid fafts, make up to themfelves for their abftinence from flefh, by the frequent ufe of fuch meats as thefe. At Suez, the Copts live almoft entirely on fhell-fifh.

I have already had occafion to fpeak, in the courfe of my travels, of the aftonifhing mafs of works formed by marine infects; namely, the immenfe banks of coral bordering, and almoft filling up the Arabic gulph. Great part of the houfes in the Tehama are of coral rock. Mr Forfkal ufed to look upon every Arabic houfe as a cabinet of natural hiftory, as rich in corals as any fuch cabinet in Europe. The reader may
therefore

therefore conceive with himſelf what a variety of madrepores and millepores are to be met with in theſe ſeas. Some are ſo curious as to tempt us conſtantly to take ſpecimens of them; but then their bulk renders it impoſſible to carry theſe away. Theſe coral rocks, riſing ſometimes ten fathoms above the ſurface of the ſea, are ſoft under the waters: And hence, being eaſily wrought, they are preferred to all other ſtones for the purpoſes of building.

CHAP. VII.

The Common and Rare Plants.

ARABIA, by its ſituation, as has been already remarked, partakes of the advantages equally of hot and of temperate climates. In the higher parts of this country, therefore, are found plants common to it with the northern parts of Europe and Aſia. The plains, on the contrary, produce vegetables which are to be met with in India and in Africa. It is, however, probable that many of theſe laſt plants had been introduced into Arabia by the Banians from their ancient country.

It is worthy of remark, that, where there are in Europe various ſpecies of any genus of plants, the

the fpecies of the fame genus to be found in Arabia are almoft all new, and have accordingly been defcribed by Mr Forfkal for the firft time. The cafe is not the fame in refpect to the plants common to Arabia with India; moft of thefe are equally to be found in both countries. The indigenous plants of Arabia have been hitherto fo little known, that Mr Forfkal was obliged to form no fewer than 30 new genera; not to fpeak of the doubtful fpecies, which he durft hardly arrange under known genera.

Of the 800 plants defcribed by my late friend, I fhall content myfelf with fpeaking of a fmall number remarkable for their novelty or utility. The firft place is, no doubt, due to thofe which are ufed for food. I have already had occafion to name fome of them in my account of the Arabian agriculture. The Arabians cultivate wheat, barley, and durra, *(Holcus Linn.)*. The latter grain, *forgo*, or great millet, feems to be a native of Arabia, for feveral wild fpecies of it are here to be found, on which the birds feed. That which is cultivated, in order to attain full maturity, requires confiderable warmth, and upon a good foil grows to a great height.

The Arabians cultivate feveral pot-herbs, of the fame nature as ours; fuch as lettuces, of which there is alfo a wild fort which is not ufed; fpinnach; the carrot *(Daucus, Linn.)*;

a

a very delicate sort of purslain with sharp leaves; a sort of raddish, of which only the leaves are eaten; water-cresses; and above all, great variety of gourds, cucumbers, pumpkins, and melons. Of pumpkins and melons, several sorts grow naturally in the woods, and serve for feeding camels. But the proper melons are planted in the fields, where a great variety of them is to be found, and in such abundance, that the Arabians of all ranks use them, for some part of the year, as their principal article of food. They afford a very agreeable liquor. When the fruit is nearly ripe, a hole is pierced into the pulp; this hole is then stopped with wax, and the melon left upon the stalk; within a few days the pulp is, in consequence of this process, converted into a delicious liquor.

The pot-herbs which are natives of India, but are now cultivated or naturalized in Arabia, are, —*Sida*, resembling our mallows; *Hibiscus*, resembling mallows also, but of which only one species is proper to be eaten, *Jussiæa*, nearly like the *Lysimachia*; *Acanthus*, a beautiful species; and *Bunias*, somewhat like our cabbages; the leaves of these plants are boiled. There are other Indian plants whose leaves the Arabians eat raw, and by way of sallad, such as *Cleome*, not unlike mustard; *Stapelia*; and *Dolichos*, a fort of bean, of which I fhall hereafter have occafion to fpeak.

There are alfo fome leguminous vegetables peculiar to the country, which require no culture. Such are *Corchorus*, and the plant like our mallows; *Sælanthus*, a new plant like the *Salix Calaf*, the leaves of which, when boiled, have a pleafing acid tafte; laftly, the celebrated *Colocafia*, (*Arcem Colocafia Linn.*), of which the Egyptians have always made great ufe, and which grows in abundance in all marfhy places in Arabia.

Nor is there in Arabia any want of vegetables diftinguifhed by the beauty of their flowers, and their fragrant fmell. The odoriferous herbs, of which we have alfo fpecies, are lavender, marjoram, the lily, and fome pinks. But, the moft fragrant, and thofe which produce the fineft flowers, are plants common to Arabia and India. Thofe valued for their perfume are *Ocymum*, the moft beautiful fpecies of the bafilic; *Inula*, a very odoriferous fort of elicampane, a native of India; *Cacalia*, from the heart of Africa; and *Dianthera*, a plant as yet but little known, of which Mr Forfkal difcovered eight fpecies. In the fandy defarts grows a plant of a new genus, named *Mofcharia*, by my friend, on account of its mufky fmell. The plants of Indian origin which afford the fineft flowers, are, *Ipomæa*, a

plant

plant like the rope weed; *Pancraticum,* called by us the sea-daffodil, a flower of the pureſt white colour; and *Hibiſcus,* a ſpecies different from the leguminous *Hibiſcus,* a flower of the brighteſt red-colour, and ſingularly large. Theſe flowers, agreeable by their form or perfume, are far from being indifferent objects to the Arabian peaſantry, who retain the ancient cuſtom of crowning themſelves with flowers on days of joy and feſtivity.

Various Arabian plants are uſed as materials for the arts, and for purpoſes of economy. An ill looking herb, like orache, and which Mr Forſkal ranked as a diſtinct genus, by the name of *Suæda,* affords abundance of an alkaline ſalt, excellent for whitening linen, and uſed by the common people, inſtead of ſoap, which is very dear in Arabia. Of a particular ſort of ruſh, the Arabians work carpets ſo fine, that the exportation of them to other countries, and even as far as to Conſtantinople, forms a conſiderable branch of trade to the people who live on the borders of the Red Sea. Two plants, natives of India, and of the interior parts of Africa, which have become very common in Arabia, namely, *Dolichos* and *Glycyne,* and reſembling French beans, produce ſuch beautiful beans, that they are ſtrung into necklaces and bracelets, which are highly eſteemed. The bean of the *Glycyne* is generally
known

known by the name of the black bean of Abyſ-
finia. The indigo-ſhrub *(Indigofera Linn.)* is
cultivated through all Arabia, blue being the favourite colour of the Arabians. Several wild
ſpecies of this plant grow very generally over
the country. We were told, that, in a ſcarcity
of this plant, the Arabians knew how to extract
indigo from a ſpecies of *Polygala*. The common
Kali (Salſola Linn.) grows in great plenty
along the Arabic Gulph, and in the iſles.
Were the Arabians capable of induſtry, they
might make ſugar for themſelves, as the cane
grows in their country in its full perfection;
they content themſelves with eating it raw, without even ſqueezing out the juice.

Through almoſt all Arabia, a ſort of *Panis
(Panicum Linn.)* or bulruſh *(Scirpus Linn.)* is
uſed for covering the roofs of the houſes. Theſe
flender coverings are ſufficient in countries where
rains are unfrequent.

One plant, although not a native of Arabia,
merits notice in this place, on account of the
diſcovery made by Mr Forſkal of an economical
ſecret among the Arabians in Egypt, in which it
is concerned. That country, in which the water
is generally bad, has, from time immemorial,
uſed for drinking a ſort of beer different in its
nature from that uſed in the north. They told us
that they could neither brew this beer, nor give

it

it an agreeable tafte, without the ufe of a grey herb, called *Schæbe*, an infufion of which was mixed with a certain quantity of meal, in order to form leaven for the fermentation both of bread and of beer. Upon feeing a fpecimen of that herb, my friend and I perceived it to be the *Lichen* of the plum-tree, a native of the ifles of the Archipelago, whence feveral fhip-ladings of it are annually brought to Alexandria.

Meadows are rare, and not rich in hot countries; in Arabia, therefore, there are are not many plants for forage. Horned cattle are not common here, and are ill-fed, and their flefh is consequently ill-tafted. Animals of a nature fuitable to the climate, fuch as camels and affes, are, as I have already mentioned, content with the drieft and hardeft fare. We have feen camels eat of a fpecies of *Euphorbia*, after it had received fome little preparation in a hole dug in the earth. This animal alfo browfes on the dry and prickly herbs and fhrubs of the defart, fuch as the *Zygophyllum*, *Hedyrarum*, *Colutea*, &c. The *Mefembryanthema*, fucculent herbs, afford another refource to the animals of the fandy plains. The Bedouins likewife prepare, of the grain of a fpecies of *Mefembryanthemum*, a fort of bread, which they eat as readily as wheat bread. The afs eats even a fpecies of *Scorfonere*, fo rough and bitter that even the camel refufes it.

All fimple nations ufe for remedies vegetables of the virtues of which they have a traditionary knowledge. The Arabians have alfo medicines of this kind, which they have ufed from time immemorial, with a degree of fuccefs of which indeed a ftranger can never be abfolutely certain. I need fay nothing of plants fo well known as aloes and euphorbia. In Arabia, the different fpecies of the latter of thefe plants are fo numerous, that Arabia may certainly be regarded as its native country. In hot countries counterpoifons are highly efteemed, on account of the numbers of venomous beafts with which fuch countries are infefted. By long experience, the inhabitants of thofe countries have learned what plants are falutary to man, and noxious to the venomous animals. The Arabians, however, appear to be ignorant of the virtues of the *Ophiorrhiza*, which is very common on their hills. But they value highly the *Ariftolochia femper virens*, which they confider not only as a remedy, but as a prefervative too, againft the bite of ferpents. In their opinion, a man who, for forty days, drinks the decoction of this herb, is in no future danger of being bitten by thofe venomous animals. Although the grounds of this opinion do not fully appear, yet it feems probable, that the jugglers, who expofe themfelves fo daringly to be bitten by ferpents, have

have some secret by which they preserve themselves from suffering by their bites. The prickly caper-tree is also esteemed an excellent antidote against poisons of all kinds.

Among the new genera of plants discovered by Mr Forskal, several are particularly curious. *Caydbeja*, called by Sir Charles Linnæus *Forskalea*, in honour of my deceased friend, grows in the driest places of the country. It has small feelers, with which it fixes itself so tenaciously upon stuffs and other smooth bodies, that it is torn in pieces before it can be removed. The *Volutella* is a very extraordinary plant; being properly a long slender thread, without root or leaves, which intwines itself about trees. It bears, however, a sort of flower, and berries, which are eaten by children. The *Polycophalos*, which resembles the thistle, has at a distance the appearance of a loose heap of balls, each of which incloses a parcel of flowers. The *Nerium obesum*, a sort of laurel-rose, is remarkable for a singular bulb, close to the earth, and of the size of a man's head, which forms all its trunk, and out of which the branches spring.

Reeds are so common about the Arabic Gulph, as to have procured the Gulph the name of *Jam Suf*, or the sea of reeds, from the ancients. One species of this vegetable is particularly worthy of notice. It grows with a vigorous vegetation, and

and in great abundance, in the bath-waters, in the diſtrict of *Ghobeybe*, where it riſes to the height of twenty-four feet. Theſe long ſolid reeds are an article of commerce. They are exported to Yemen, and there uſed in the ceilings of houſes. In the ſame diſtrict of *Ghobeybe*, nearly oppoſite to Suez, we were ſurpriſed to ſee a *Conferva* growing in the bottom of the hot baths of *Hammam Faraon*, the heat of which was at 49 degrees in Reaumur's thermometer.

CHAP. VIII.

Of Trees and Shrubs.

THE ſandy plains of Arabia are almoſt deſtitute of trees; only a few palms are ſcattered here and there. Foreſts are to be ſeen only in the Highland provinces, where the hills retain enough of earth for vegetation; but even in the Highlands are rare. The trees in thoſe foreſts are either abſolutely unknown, or at leaſt different from our European trees of the ſame genera or ſpecies. The principal of them are the following, of which I ſhall have occaſion to ſpeak ſomewhat more at length: *Sceura, Tomex, Catha, Cynanchum, Mæru, Bæka, Haledi*, and ſeveral feveral fpecies of the fig-tree unknown among us.

The Arabians cultivate feveral of our fruit trees. They have pomegranate, almond, apricot, pear, and apple-trees. Here is a fpecies of pear-tree, and a corneil-tree which are peculiar to Arabia. The Arabians likewife eat the fruit of feveral of our fhrubs, fuch as the *Afclepias* and the *Rhamnus*.

Although the Mahometans drink no wine, the Arabians however plant the vine, and have a great variety of grapes. They dry a fmall fort of grape, called *Kifchmifch*, which has no ftone, but only foft, and almoft impalpable feeds; and of thefe grapes they fell a quantity to their neighbours. They alfo make from mint a fyrup, named *Dub*, which they find a pretty lucrative article of commerce.

Several forts of lemons and oranges are found in Arabia. If an inference may be drawn from the names which the Arabians have given them, one fhould fuppofe that they have had an orange tree from Portugal, and two lemon-trees from Italy. From common oranges, cut through the middle while they are green, dried in the air, and fteeped for forty days in oil, is prepared an effence famous among old women for reftoring a frefh black colour to grey hairs.

The

The Banians have tranfported various fruit-trees from India, which are now naturalized in Arabia; fuch are the Bannana-tree *(Mufa Linn.)*; the Mangouftan, *(Mangifera Linn.)*; the *Papaya* *(Carica Papaya Linn.)*; and the *Ciffus Linn.* Arabia produces the date-tree; but their other palms, and efpecially the *Cocos*, feem to be from India.

The Indian fig-tree, *(Ticus varta)*, although now very common in Arabia, is perhaps not a native of this country. The fingular property which this tree poffeffes, of fpreading itfelf, by means of filaments fhooting from its branches, which, when they reach the ground, take root and form new trunks, is well known. Mr Forfkal faw a dozen fpecies of indigenous fig-trees in Arabia, which are not mentioned by Linnæus. Their fruit is far from delicate; feldom eatable. The bark of one fpecies is ufed in tanning leather. Of another the leaves are fo rough, that they are ufed for cleaning and polifhing iron. The reft are only fo many of the ufelefs trees of the foreft.

The tamarind, which, in Arabia, as well as in India, is equally ufeful and agreeable. It has a pulp of a vineous tafte, of which a wholefome refrefhing liquor is prepared. Its fhade fhelters houfes from the torrid heat of the fun, and its fine figure greatly adorns the fcenery of the country.

country. The inhabitants are also fond of raising over their houses the shade of the Indian fig-tree.

Arabia appears to be very rich in indigenous trees, the number of which is more than proportionate to its peculiar herbaceous plants. But great trees are not easily removed from one place to another; and those of the forests, in the back parts of the country, are seldomer seen by travellers than the other vegetables. Hence, it is no wonder that we have been hitherto so ignorant concerning the trees of Arabia. More than half the new genera classed by Mr Forskal comprehend trees only. My friend saw likewise other eighteen trees, the genera of which he had no opportunity of ascertaining; not to mention a great many others, of which he could learn only the Arabic name.

Catha is one of those new genera peculiar to Arabia. This tree, which is improveable by culture, is commonly planted among the coffee-shrubs on the hills where these grow. The Arabians are accustomed constantly to chew the buds of this tree, which they call *Kaad;* they are as much addicted to this practice, as the Indians to that of chewing betel. To their kaad they ascribe the virtues of assisting digestion, and of fortifying the constitution against infectious distempers. Yet its insipid taste gives no

indication

indication of extraordinary virtues. The only effects we felt from the ufe of thofe buds were the hinderance and the interruption of our fleep.

Elcaya and *Keura*, two trees famous for their perfume, are not known, but form two new genera. The former is common on the hills of Yemen; and the women fteep its fruit in water, which they ufe for wafhing and perfuming the head. The fecond bears fome refemblance to the palm-tree, and produces flowers of a rich and delicious fmell. Thefe flowers are fold at an high price, as the *Keura* is rather a fcarce plant. But one little knot, if preferved in a cool place, will long continue to diffufe its odours through a whole apartment.

Children eat the fruit, which is infipid enough, of a large tree called *Oncoba*, and a tall fhrub named *Mærua*. Both thefe, too, are new fpecies difcovered by Mr Forfkal. Such is alfo the *Chadara*, a large tree, and the *Antura*, a tree of a fmaller fize; neither of which has any thing remarkable to diftinguifh it, except its wood and its novelty. *Culhamia*, a large tree, alfo unknown to the botanifts, has nothing but its ufe to recommend it. *Cadaba* and *Mæfa* are fhrubs which have nothing particular about them, and might be paffed over in filence, had not Mr Forfkal taken notice of them.

Several

Several shrubs which are indigenous in Arabia are of some use to the inhabitants. The fruit of a new genus, named *Sodada*, is eaten; from the berry of another new shrub, called *Cebatha*, is extracted a very strong species of brandy, the acid taste of which is improved by a mixture of sugar. A sort of that false phaseolus, *Dolichos*, which I have mentioned in speaking of the plants, grows up to a bushy shrub, so as to form hedges in a short time, which are almost impenetrable. *Cynanchum*, a new genus, is a shrub, of which the wood called by the Arabians *March*, is used for fuel, as it has all the lightness and combustibility of tinder.

An Arabian tree, famous from the most remote antiquity, and nevertheless but little known, is that from which the balsam of Mecca is obtained. We found one of these trees in the open fields; and under its shade Mr Forskal wrote the first botanical description of the species. He at the same named it, as a new species, *Amyris;* a name which has since been adopted by other botanists. The tree has not a beautiful appearance; and, what is surprising, its qualities are not known to the inhabitants of Yemen, in which we met with it. They only burn its wood as a perfume. The wood of a sort of *Amyris*, called *Kafal*, is exported to Egypt,

Egypt, and there ufed to communicate an agreeable odour to pots boiled upon it, as fuel, which affects alfo the liquors contained in them. The Arabians, in the remoter parts of the province of *Hedsjas*, feem to be better informed; for they collect the balfam, and bring it to Mecca, whence it is diftributed through the Turkifh empire, where it is in high eftimation. Even at Mecca it is difficult to obtain any of this balfam in its original purity. America produces alfo fome trees of the genus of *Amyris*, fo that the value of the balfam of Mecca may fall in time.

We could learn nothing of the tree from which incenfe diftils; and Mr Forfkal does not mention it. I know that it is to be found in a part of Hadramaut, where it is called *Oliban*. But the Arabians hold their own incenfe in no eftimation, and make ufe only of that which comes from India. Probably Arabian incenfe was fo called among the ancients, becaufe the Arabians traded in it, and conveyed it from India to the ports of Egypt and Syria.

Senna *(Caffia Senna Linn.)* is a fhrub of which the favourite feat feems to be Upper Egypt, and that part of Arabia which lies oppofite to Upper Egypt, on the other fide of the Arabic Gulph. As there are feveral fpecies of *Caffia*, it feems probable that the fenna imported into Europe is not all the produce of the

fame

fame fhrub. The differently figured leaves indicate as much. That which we call fenna of Alexandria grows in great abundance in the territory of *Abu Arifch*. The Arabians fell it at Mecca and Jidda; whence it paffes, by the way of Suez and Kahira, to Alexandria. Senna, and other forts of caffia, are much ufed in Arabia in various difeafes. *Caffia Fiftula*, or black caffia, mixed with a little rhubarb, is the beft remedy known to the Arabian phyficians for the cure of the *Cholera Morbus*, and of diarrhœas, which are in hot countries peculiarly dangerous.

I have already had occafion to fpeak of the coffee-tree, which furnifhes the Arabians with their beft article for exportation. This fhrub, which is at prefent reared in many green-houfes in Europe, is too well known to need a defcription here. The Arabians fay that it is a native of Abyffinia; and feveral travellers affirm that they have feen it in great plenty in that country, where it produces berries not inferior in goodnefs to the coffee of Yemen. What renders this relation the more probable is, that the fruit of the wild coffee-tree is in Arabia fo bad as to be unfit for ufe. However this may be, it is at leaft certain that this fhrub thrives only on hills, and in places which are cool, and not deftitute of moifture. For this reafon, the inhabitants of the Highlands plant other trees among
their

their coffee-plants, in order to fhade them; and, in the time of the intenfe heats, water them. It fhould feem then that the Europeans are miftaken, in fuppofing that this fhrub fhould be planted in a dry foil, under a torrid fky, and in the hotteft climates. This miftake may be fufpected to be the reafon of the bad quality of the American coffee. In the account of my journey through Yemen, I have mentioned the countries where the beft coffee is to be found; and have at the fame time fpoken of the extenfive trade which the Arabians carry on in this commodity.

Their profits are lefs confiderable from the cotton-tree, of which they have two fpecies; that which grows to a fhrub; and another which bears red flowers. Almoft all the inhabitants of Arabia are clothed in cotton-cloth from India.

Arabia, as well as Egypt, produces the celebrated *Alhenna (Laufonia inermis Linn.)* the leaves of which, pulverifed and wrought into a pafte, form a cofmetic which is in high repute through the eaft. The women of thofe countries, with this drug, ftain their hands and feet, or at leaft the nails of thefe, of a red colour; which is yellowifh, or deeper, according to the manner in which the powder is applied. They think their charms improved by this painting; and, indeed, it may, by contraft, render the black and yellow of their complexion lefs difagreeable than they

would

would otherwife be. This fhrub, in its fize and character, has a refemblance to our privets.

The fenfitive plant, of the genus *Mimofa*, is well known. In Arabia are feveral fpecies of this genus, all either trees or fhrubs, which ferve the inhabitants both for ufe and pleafure. One of thefe trees droops its branches whenever any perfon approaches it, feeming as if it faluted thofe who retire under its fhade. This mute hofpitality has fo endeared this tree to the Arabians, that the injuring or cutting of it down is ftrictly prohibited. Another of thefe *(Mimofa Selam)* produces fplendid flowers, of a beautiful red colour, with which the Arabians crown their heads on their days of feftivity. The flowers of another *(Mimofa Lebbex)* are no lefs remarkable for a fine filky tuft, formed by their piftils. The leaves of another *(Mimofa Orfæta)* preferve camel's milk from becoming four, fo that it retains all its fweetnefs for feveral days. The fmoke of the timber of this fame tree expels a worm, which fixes itfelf in the flefh of the human neck, and produces epileptic fits. This fpecies of the mimofa is difperfed through Afia, Africa, and America; it is well known that the fenfitive plant was brought into Europe from the latter of thefe continents.

At Beit el Fakih, Mr Forfkal found fome fine trees, which were the ornament of the place; but

but he could not learn either their name or their country. He fuspects them to have been brought from India by the Bramins. But, as their characteriftics were different from thofe of any other known fpecies, he has claffed them in two new genera, under the names of *Hyperanthera* and *Binectarium*. Thofe trees were large, of a majeftic form, and covered with beautiful flowers. The *Ciffus*, perhaps another native of India, is at prefent common in Arabia, where it has been naturalized, as well as the *Tomex*, a great tree, the properties of which we are unacquainted with. The *Ciffus* is valued as one of the beft counterpoifons; and is on this account held in high eftimation; it is the *Ciffus Illa Linn.* A fpecies of *Glycyrrhiza*, or liquorice-fhrub, is common in Arabia and India.

Arabia does not produce many poifonous vegetables; yet here is found a very dangerous fhrub of a new genus, called by Mr Forfkal *Adenia*. The buds of this fhrub are one of the moft violent poifons, if dried, and given in drink as a powder; they have the fudden effect to fwell the body in an extraordinary manner. A fort of caper-tree *(Capparis fpinofa Linn.)* is the only remedy againft the effects of this poifon. This latter fhrub is fo common in Arabia, that the antidote is always to be found befide the poifon.

Mr Forſkal likewiſe enumerates other eighteen trees which he ſaw, and which are indigenous in Arabia; but their genera he could not determine. Of the moſt part he learned the Arabic names, and of a few, ſome of the properties. In Yemen he ſaw two trees, one of which was like the lemon, the other like the apple-tree; but the inhabitants themſelves know neither their names nor qualities. *Noemam*, a tree from the coffee mountains, is often confounded with the caſſia-tree. *Bæka* and *Anas* are trees very common in the Highlands, the juice of which is cauſtic and poiſonous. *Schamama* bears a fruit which taſtes and ſmells like a lemon. *Gharib Elbæke* is a tree on the hills in the territory of *Abu Ariſch*, from which diſtils an agreeable juice, which affords pleaſant morſels to the birds. *Segleg*, another tree of Abu Ariſch, bears leaves from which there is a juice expreſſed which paſſes for an excellent remedy in caſes of weakneſs of ſight. *Sym el Horat*, or the poiſon of fiſhes, is the fruit of an unknown tree in Arabia Felix; from which great quantities of it are exported by the ports of the Red Sea. It is uſed in fiſhing. Fiſhes are fond of it, and ſwallow it eagerly; after which they float in a ſtate of ſeeming intoxication on the ſurface of the water. This ſeems to be a ſort of *nux vomica;* which

which is alſo obtained from the weſtern coaſts of India.

We neglected to inform ourſelves, in Arabia, concerning the production of manna; and what we learned from a monk, in a convent near Suez, was a monaſtic legend, not worth repetition. The tree from which manna is obtained in Meſopotamia, by the ſhaking of its branches, is an oak, as I have been credibly informed by ſeveral different perſons. This manna is white and ſaccharine. But, at Baſra, I had a ſpecimen ſhewn me of the manna *Tarand-jubin*, which is gathered in Perſia from a prickly ſhrub; it, as well as the former, is in round grains; but theſe are yellowiſh. As Arabia-Petræa abounds in prickly ſhrubs, poſſibly this manna may be found alſo there; although in thoſe deſart places it cannot be very plentiful. Both theſe ſorts of manna are uſed as ſugar, in ſeveral diſhes of meat, eſpecially paſtry. They are nouriſhing, and, when newly gathered, have no purgative qualities.

The cedar grows not in Arabia, but ſeems to be a tree peculiar to Mount Libanus. The Arabians have little wood fit for building; their trees are moſtly of a light, porous texture. *Sceura*, a new genus deſcribed by Mr Forſkal, a tree that grows on the ſea-ſhore, is ſo ſoft an wood, that no uſe can be made of it.

CHAP.

CHAP. IX.

The Minerals of Arabia.

IN the account of my journey, and in speaking of the soil of Arabia, I have already had some occasion to mention the nature of those stones of which the hills are here composed. I have likewise spoken of the masses of basaltes between *Hadie* and *Kachma*, from the upper parts of which pentagonal fragments are from time to time detached, and darted down into the vallies.

Beside calcareous, vitrifiable, and sand-stones, we saw also a ferruginous spar, mixed with brown or white selenite, almost transparent. We found likewise, in the neighbourhood of Loheya, a blueish gypsum, a grey schistus, and spheric marcassites, in beds of grit-stone; from which stones are hewn for building. Arabia affords, however, stones of greater value. The onyx is common in Yemen; and we saw even quantities of these stones on the road between *Taæs* and *Mount Sumara*. In a hill near the town of *Damar* is found the stone *Ayek Jemani*, which is in the highest estimation among the Arabians. It is of a dark red, or rather a light-brown colour, and seems to be a fort of carnelian. The Arabians fet it in rings or bracelets, and afcribe to it the virtue of ftopping the bleeding of wounds when inftantly applied. Among the *ftones of Mokha*, which are, properly fpeaking, Indian carnelians, brought from Surat to Arabia and Europe, pieces are often found which bear a perfect refemblance to this *Ayek Jemani*.

I could learn nothing of the precious ftones, properly fo called, which are fuppofed to be found in Arabia. It does not feem even probable that emeralds were ever found here. The hill which has been denominated the hill of emeralds is in Egypt, on the oppofite fide of the Arabic Gulph, and forms a part of that large chain of mountains which are compofed chiefly of granite.

We faw two little hills, confifting almoft entirely of foffile falt; one near *Loheya*, and the other in the neighbourhood of Hodeida. Thofe maffes of falt are piled up in large tranfparent ftrata, and inclofed in a cruft of calcareous ftone. The Arabians formerly dug up this falt, but the galleries of the mines have funk down, and it is now neglected. We were told, however, that foreign veffels fometimes come to lade with this falt, from the hill near the ifle of *Kameran*, in the neighbourhood of Hodeida.

Arabia

Arabia does not appear to be rich in metals. The old Greek and Latin writers go even so far as to assert that it is absolutely destitute of iron. This is not true; for grains of iron are to be seen among the sands which are washed down by the rains. Magnets are commonly to be met with in the province of *Kusma;* and at *Saade* are iron-mines, which are wrought at present. It must, however, be confessed that the iron of Yemen is coarse and brittle; disadvantages in it which cannot be remedied. Besides, the scarcity of wood makes this iron dearer than that which is brought from distant countries. For this reason, iron is a commodity which strangers can always dispose of to advantage in the ports of the Red Sea.

In Oman are many very rich lead mines. As this metal is more easily fusible, the inhabitants of this province export great plenty of it. This trade is carried on from the harbour of *Maskat*.

As the ancients honoured one part of Arabia with the title of Happy, it should seem that they must have ascribed to it all possible advantages. The Greeks and Latins accordingly make ample mention of the immense quantity of gold which this country produced. In remote times possibly, when the Arabians were the factors of the trade to India, much of this precious metal might pass through Arabia into Europe; but that

that gold was probably the produce of the mines of India. At prefent, at leaft, there is no gold-mine in Arabia. The rivulets bring down no grains of this metal from the hills; nor does the fand fhew any marks of fo rich an intermixture. A philofopher of Loheya ftrove to perfuade us, that he himfelf, and no body elfe, was acquainted with fome mines in the country; but he was a babbler to whofe ftories we could not give the flighteft credit.

All the gold now circulating in Arabia is from Abyffinia or Europe, and is received in payment either for coffee, or for India goods, which are fold at Jidda or Mokha. The Imam of Sana, when he wifhed, fome time fince, to ftrike a little gold coin, was obliged to melt down foreign money for the purpofe. The gold which paffes from Europe into Arabia, confifts almoft altogether of Venetian fequins. On this account fome Arabians afked, if the Venetians were the only nation in Europe who had gold mines. Others fancied that the Venetians were in poffeffion of the philofopher's ftone.

Thefe prejudices and popular rumours ferve to keep up the old partiality of the Arabians for the purfuit of the art of tranfmuting other fubftances into gold. An Arabian no fooner meets with any obfcure book upon this fubject, by fome pretended adept, than he fets himfelf to
chemical

chemical proceſſes, which he purſues as far as the circumſtances of his country will permit. I have already given the ſtory of two alchemiſts of Beit el Fakih who had ruined themſelves by reſearches into the art of making gold. This taſte is very general in Arabia; moſt of thoſe alchemical enthuſiaſts think themſelves ſure of ſuccefs, if they could but find out the herb which gilds the teeth, and gives a yellow colour to the fleſh of the ſheep that eat it. Even the oil of this plant muſt be of a golden colour. It is called *Haſchiſchet ed dab*. I was aſſured that it is common in the vales of Mount Libanus, and is alſo to be found on the high hills of Yemen.

SECTION XXX.

VOYAGE FROM MOKHA TO BOMBAY.

CHAP. I.

Departure from Mokha.

THE veffel belonging to Mr Scott, with whom we were to take our paffage for Bombay, having been detained for a confiderable time at Mokha, we could not leave the city till 23d of Auguft 1763. Although Meffrs Cramer and Baurenfeind were at that time very ill, they, however, determined not to lofe the opportunity of leaving Arabia. As to myfelf, my health was fo far re-eftablifhed, that I could fafely venture upon the voyage to India.

The famous ftreight of Babel-Mandel, where the Arabian Gulph joins the ocean, and where we arrived on the fecond day of our voyage, may be about ten German miles in breadth. It is interfperfed with fmall ifles, of which that neareft Africa is called *Perim*, and forms with the African continent a channel, through which fhips ufually pafs, notwithftanding the rapid current which prevails in it. In the fea, between Arabia and India, there is generally a rapid current driving to the eaft, with fo much violence, that it is impoffible to reckon the rate at which a fhip runs in paffing here. In this fea we met likewife with north winds fo cold that we were obliged to put on warmer clothes.

In this firft part of our voyage, Mr Cramer's health feemed to recover daily; but Mr Baurenfeind grew worfe and worfe. He funk into a a deep lethargy, and died on the 29th of Auguft. The defigns of this artift, of which I have publifhed a part, fufficiently befpeak his praife.

Next day after Mr Baurenfeind, died alfo our fervant, *Berggreen*, a Swede, who had made feveral campaigns in the fervice of a Colonel of Huffars. This man, who was naturally robuft, and had been inured to fatigue, had at firft laughed at the idea of the hardfhips of a voyage to Arabia; but he funk under them at laft, as well as Mr Cramer, as I fhall hereafter relate.

This melancholy fate of my fellow-travellers leads me to recollect the fimilar end of two learned travellers into the eaft, which deferves to be made known. The one was Mr Donati, who was at the head of a fociety of learned Italians, fent by the King of Sardinia to travel in Afia. Soon after their arrival in Egypt, this fociety quarrelled among themfelves. Mr Donati's companions returned to Italy, and he proceeded alone on the journey, attended only by a young interpreter from Kahira, and an Italian fervant. He went by Damafcus to Bafra, in order to find an opportunity of paffing on to India. But, being naturally impatient, and weary of waiting for an European veffel, he embarked on board a fmall open fkiff, in which he purpofed to proceed to Mangalore, on the coaft of Malabar. The fatigue was too much for him; and he died on board this veffel, three days before it reached India. Before his death, he gave money to his fervants to carry them home; but this the Italian lofing all at play, in defpair, turned Muffulman at Mafkat.

Mr Donati was well qualified to make the moft of fuch a journey as that he had undertaken. His knowledge was very extenfive; and he poffeffed all the requifite firmnefs and activity of fpirit. He was farther poffeffed of a ftill more neceffary quality, courage, which danger could not fubdue, and of which he gave frequent proofs in Egypt, when attacked by the
Arabians,

Arabians, who, at laſt, learned to reſpect his intrepidity.

This philoſopher had taken, although in vain, all poſſible precautions to make his papers and the curioſities which he had collected in Egypt and Syria reach the Sardinian Court. He had intruſted to the Arabs with whom he ſailed all his effects, begging them, before his death, to convey the whole to the viceroy of Goa, who would not fail to forward them to the Court of Turin. I met with one of thoſe men in India, who told me that they had faithfully diſcharged their commiſſion, and that the whole of Mr Donati's effects were in the hands of the Portugueſe viceroy. In 1772, however, nothing had been obtained from him; and I know not if any part of the deceaſed traveller's effects has been yet received in Italy. It was in 1763 that the Arabs, on board whoſe veſſel Mr Donati died, were on the coaſt of Malabar.

The other learned traveller to whom I above alluded, was a French phyſician named *Simon*, well ſkilled in natural hiſtory, and a conſiderable proficient in aſtronomy. He arrived long before us in Syria, and was well received by his countrymen at Aleppo. Not finding leiſure enough while he was among thoſe Europeans, to proſecute his reſearches, he went to Diarbekir, in the hope of being there left at liberty for his inquiries. In that city he lodged with the capuchins, the only Europeans in the place; but, difgufted by the mummeries and ridiculous obfervances of thofe monks, he, in a fit of defpair, refolved to become Muffulman.

Although the Turks make much of an European phyfician, Mr Simon faw himfelf neglected as foon as he had made profeffion of Mahometifm; juft as if he had loft his fkill in his profeffion, with the change of his religion. Becoming weary of Diarbekir, he retired to Bagdad, and there lived by the fale of drugs, and the practice of medicine. Still retaining, however, his tafte for natural hiftory, he continued to botanize in the adjacent country with great activity. A Perfian khan in the neighbourhood, whom he had refufed to vifit, had him carried off, when he was out upon one of his botanical excurfions, and compelled him by the baftinadoe to prefcribe for him. Mr Simon not fucceeding in the cure of the khan, was again baftinadoed, and imprifoned. The fucceffor of the deceafed khan being likewife fick, and learning that the prifoner was an European phyfician, took him out from confinement, entrufted his health to his care, and was fortunately cured by Mr Simon's fkill. But this fuccefs proved only a fource of new misfortunes to the ill-fated philofopher. His new mafter refufed him permiffion

to

to return to Bagdad, and carried him with him, in all his campaigns, in the late civil war in Perfia. In one of thofe expeditions, an enemy furprifed the khan, and Mr Simon was flain on that occafion, with his mafter, and their whole party.

The paffage between Arabia and India was formerly thought very dangerous. Ships were carried on by fo rapid a current, that they could neither keep their reckoning, nor diftinguifh the coaft during the rainy feafon : Several were confequently loft on the low coafts of Malabar. Thefe misfortunes have ceafed to take place, fince an obfervation was made, which has been thought new, although Arrian fpeaks of it as being known to the ancients, in the Indian ocean, at a certain diftance from land, a great many water ferpents, from 12 to 13 inches in length, are to be feen rifing above the furface of the water. When thefe ferpents are feen, they are an indication that the coaft is exactly two degrees diftant.

We faw fome of thefe ferpents, for the firft time, on the evening of the 9th of September; on the 11th we landed in the harbour of Bombay; and on the 13th entered the city.

CHAP.

CHAP. II.

Of the Ifle and the City of Bombay.

The ifle of Bombay is two German miles in length, by rather more than half a mile in breadth. A narrow channel divides it from another fmall ifle of little value, called by the Englifh *Old Woman's Ifland*. Bombay produces nothing but cocoa's and rice; and on the fhore a confiderable quantity of falt is collected. The inhabitants are obliged to bring their provifions from the continent, or from *Salfet*, a large and fertile ifland not far from Bombay, and belonging to the Marattas. Since I left India, the Englifh have made an attempt upon Salfet, which is indeed very much in their power, and the public papers fay that they have been fuccefsful. I know not whether they may be able to maintain themfelves in it againft the Marattas, whofe armies are very numerous.

The fea-breezes, and the frequent rains, cool the atmofphere, and render the climate of this ifland temperate. Its air was formerly unhealthy and dangerous, but has become pure fince the Englifh drained the marfhes, in the city and its environs. Still, however, many Europeans die

fuddenly

fuddenly here; but they are new-comers, who fhorten their days by a mode of life unfuitable to the climate; eating great quantities of beef and pork, which the Indian Legiflator had wifely forbidden, and drinking copioufly of the ftrong wines of Portugal in the hotteft feafon. They likewife perfift obftinately in wearing the European drefs, which by its ligatures impedes the free circulation of the blood, and by confining the limbs, renders the heat more intolerable. The Orientals again live to a great age, and are little fubject to difeafes, becaufe they keep the body at eafe in wide flowing robes, abftain from animal food and ftrong liquors, and eat their principal meal in the evening after funfet.

The city of Bombay, fituate in the northern part of the ifland, is a quarter of a German mile in length; but narrow. It is defended by an indifferent citadel towards the fea, and at the middle of the city. On the land fide, its fortifications are very good. During the war the Eaft India Company expended no lefs than 900,000 French livres a-year, in the conftruction of new works for its defence; and, although thefe works are no longer carried on with the fame activity, yet the fortifications of Bombay are ftill continued, fo that it muft be in a fhort time the moft confiderable fortrefs in India. Befide the town, there are in the ifland fome fmall forts fufficient to protect it from any irruption of the Indians.

In this city are feveral handfome buildings; among which are the Director's palace, and a large and elegant church near it. The houfes are not flat roofed here, as through the reft of the eaft, but are covered with tiles in the European fafhion. The Englifh have glafs windows. The other inhabitants of the ifland have their windows of fmall pieces of tranfparent fhells framed in wood, which renders the apartments very dark. In the eaft it is the fafhion to live during the dry feafon in chambers open on one fide. The houfes of Bombay are in general neither fplendid nor commodious in any great degree.

The harbour is fpacious, and fheltered from all winds. A valuable work, which has been conftructed at the Company's expence, is, two bafons, hewn out in the rock, in which two fhips may be at once careened. A third is now preparing. This work, which has been very expenfive, likewife brings in a confiderable annual return. Strangers pay very dear for liberty to careen in thefe bafons. While I was there I faw a fhip of war belonging to the Imam of Sana, which he had fent to Bombay folely on purpofe that it might be refitted.

CHAP.

CHAP. III.

Of the Inhabitants of Bombay.

THE toleration which the English grant to all religions has rendered this island very populous. During these hundred years, for which it has been in the possession of the Company, the number of its inhabitants has greatly increased; so that they are now reckoned at 140,000 souls, although within these twenty years they did not amount to 70,000.

Of these the Europeans are naturally the least numerous class; and this the rather as they do not marry, and their numbers consequently do not multiply. The other inhabitants are Portuguese, or Indian Catholics; *Hindoos*, the original possessors of the country; *Persians* from *Kerman;* Mahometans of different sects; and in the last place some Oriental Christians. My journey to Surat will afford me occasion to speak more at length of the Hindoos and Persians, who chiefly inhabit the invirons of this city; adding the observations I also made on these people at Surat.

The English, as I have mentioned, have an handsome church at Bombay, but only one Englifh clergyman to perform the fervices of religion in it; and, if he fhould die, the congregation would be abfolutely deprived of a paftor; for the Company have no chaplains in their fhips, and entertain no clergy in their fettlements on the coaft. Wherefore, when a child is to be baptized, which is not often, as the Englifh rarely marry in India, a Danifh miffionary is fent for, to adminifter the facrament of baptifm.

The Catholics, a fcanty remainder of the Portuguefe, and a great number of Indians, their converts, are much more numerous than the Proteftants. They have abundance of priefts, as well Europeans as Indians, who attend their ftudies at Goa. To fuperintend this herd, the Pope named fome years ago a bifhop of Bombay, but the governor of the ifland fent him away, declaring that they needed not Catholic priefts of fo high a rank. The Catholic churches are decent buildings, and are fumptuoufly ornamented within. The Jews had once a college and a church in the middle of this ifland. Their college is at prefent the country-houfe of the Englifh governour. And the old church has been converted into a fuite of affembly-rooms.

All religions, as I have already remarked, are here indulged in the free exercife of their public worfhip, not only in their churches, but openly,

in

in feftivals and proceffions, and none takes offence at another. Yet Government allows not the Catholic priefts to give a loofe to their zeal for making profelytes. When any perfon choofes to become Catholic, the reafons muft be laid before Government, and if they are judged valid, he is then allowed to profefs his converfion. The priefts complain of the difficulty of obtaining this permiffion. They, however, have confiderable fuccefs in converfion among the flaves, who, being ftruck with the pomp of the Romifh worfhip, and proud of wearing the image of a faint upon their breafts, choofe rather to frequent the Catholic churches than any others, and perfuade their countrymen, as they fucceffively arrive, to follow their example. I had purchafed a young Catholic negro at Bombay, who was alfo born of Chriftian parents, and intended to bring him with me into Europe; but, fearing afterwards that the Muffulmans in Perfia and Turkey might give me trouble, and pretend that I was carrying away a Mahometan boy in order to make him a Chriftian, I gave him away before my departure from India.

CHAP. IV.

Of the Government and Power of the Englifh on the Coaft of Malabar.

THE Englifh Eaft India Company govern their fettlements in a mode of adminiftration different from that of the Portuguefe and Dutch. Thefe laft nations intruft the difpofal of all places to the power of a fingle governor; the Portuguefe to the viceroy of Goa; the Dutch to the governor-general of Batavia. The conquefts of the Englifh are, on the contrary, all divided into four independent governments, each of which receives its orders immediately from the Court of Directors at London. The feats of thefe four governments are, *Bombay* for the coaft of *Malabar*, *Madras* for the *Coromandel* coaft, *Calcutta* for *Bengal*, and *Bencoolen* for the ifland of *Sumatra*.

Although independent of one another, the feveral Englifh governors are however obliged to lend one another mutual aid in extraordinary exigencies. On a late occafion, news being received at Bombay of an infurrection, the council of Bombay, without waiting for orders from the Court of Directors in London, fent troops and

and artillery to Calcutta. Thefe different eftablifhments are all governed in the fame manner. All proceffes between fubjects of the Company are determined by the law of England.

The council or regency of Bombay confift of a governor, with the title of prefident, and twelve counfellors, who are all merchants, except the commander of the troops, who held lately the rank of major. The Company have of late made fome changes upon this arrangement. The prefident muft be a military man; the commander of the troops is a brigadier, and has a voice in the council; and the director of the naval affairs has a place among the twelve counfellors who were formerly all merchants. The other fervants of the Company are factors and writers of different ranks. Thefe rife from lower to higher places in the order of feniority,—even to the very firft offices, that only excepted of prefident; who is nominated by the Court of Directors in London. The fervants of the Company are fometimes transferred from one department to another. Mr Spencer, a very intelligent man, who was a counfellor at Bombay when I was there, was foon after transferred to the place of firft prefident at Calcutta.

The prefident of the council of Bombay is obliged to refide in the ifland; as are alfo thofe counfellors who hold the offices of treafurer and
infpector

inspector of the Company's stores. The other counsellors are sent out to manage the concerns of the Company's trade in the establishments dependent on the government of Bombay. In my time, the directors of the trade at *Surat, Tellicherry, Anjengo,* and *Basra,* were members of the council. In three of these places, the Company have forts in which they keep up garrisons of sufficient strength. Since I left that country, the English have conquered *Baradsch,* a great town, north from Surat, which was subject to a Nabob of its own, and was formerly the seat of a Dutch factory. A counsellor from Bombay now resides as director in this city.

Factors are sent to the inferior settlements; such as, in the province of *Scindi,* the great city of *Tatta,* the seat of the sovereign of the country; *Lar Bunder;* and *Schah Bunder.* The Company have likewise factors at *Abu Schæhr, Cambay, Onor, Calicut,* and even in the fort of *Victoria*. This fort stands on a great river, which holds its course through the interior country, even to as great distance as *Puna,* the seat of the chief of the Mahrattas. The English acquired this place, with some adjacent villages, from the Mahrattas, in exchange for *Geri,* a fortress once belonging to the famous *Angria,* of which they had taken possession. The Company expected, that, by means of this river, they might extend

their

their trade through the country of the Mahrattas. This project having, however, failed, they avail themselves of the fort, and purchase butcher-meats from the Mahometans in the neighbourhood, as the Hindoos about Bombay will not sell their cattle for slaughter.

It is for the benefit of the Company to send its servants successively to different places, before they are advanced to the first employments. Factors thus gain a knowledge of the affairs of all the different settlements subject to the government of which they are afterwards to be counsellors. The Company, however, allows but very moderate salaries to its factors and directors. But they are permitted to trade on their own account in India only from *Delegoa* near the Cape of Good Hope, to China, and northward, as far as Jidda and Basra. By means of this extensive trade chiefly, do the directors acquire that wealth which is the astonishment and envy of their countrymen in Europe.

These advantages for the acquisition of wealth in trade, are reserved for the English exclusively. The Company admit strangers into none but the military department of their service. In it they must enter the lowest rank; but advancement is pretty rapid; for their mode of life cuts off the officers very fast. At Bombay, I saw officers from various nations; chiefly however
Germans

Germans and Swifs. The troops are well paid; but I could not think the fervice agreeable; for the writers, who are more directly in the career of advancement, look upon the foldier with that contempt which monied men commonly think themfelves entitled to fhew for perfons who are in their pay.

In the government of which Bombay is the centre, the Company maintain feventeen companies of regular troops, confifting each of about an hundred and twenty men, with three companies of artillery. The foldiers are moftly Europeans, except fome *Topafes*, or Catholic Indians, dreffed in the European fafhion. At Bombay there is alfo a body of three thoufand *Sepoys*, or Indian foldiers, Pagan and Mahometan, who wear their own original drefs, and are commanded by their own officers. Each company of this corps has an inferior European officer to teach the *Sepoys* their exercife; for, when commanded by Europeans, they form good troops. At Surat, the Company have in their pay a fmall corps of Arabs from the Perfian Gulph, who are in fuch high reputation in India for their courage, that every Rajah defires to have fome of them in his fervice.

The artillery of Bombay is in very good condition, owing to the care of a Swede, whom the Englifh fent out in 1752, and who brought with

with him a company of gunners whom he had
raifed in Germany. Bombay was thus furnifhed with a good number of able workmen, chiefly mafons and carpenters. Thofe Germans
likewife engaged many of their countrymen to
leave the Dutch, and enter into the Englifh
fervice.

The whole coaft from Bombay to Bafra is
inhabited by people addicted to piracy, fuch as
the *Malays,* the *Sangeries,* the *Kulis,* the *Arabs,*
with other petty nations. It might be eafy for the
Englifh to exterminate thefe pirates; as they
fhewed in 1765, by poffeffing themfelves of the
territory of the Malayans; which however they
foon after ceded to the Indians for a round fum
of money. But it is the Company's intereft to
leave thofe plunderers to fcour the feas, and
hinder other nations from failing in the fame
latitudes. The Englifh are therefore content
with protecting their own trade; for which purpofe they maintain in the government of Bombay eight or ten fmall fhips of war, with a number of armed barks. The Indians dare not
travel from one port to another, otherwife than in
caravans, and under the protection of an Englifh
veffel, for which they are obliged to pay very
dear.

The Company find it not neceffary to pay
their court in a particular manner to any nation

in

in thefe latitudes, except the Mahrattas, who are mafters of the coaft and of the ifles about Bombay, and by confequence in fome meafure mafters of the fubfiftence of this fettlement. The marine force of the Mahrattas is not formidable; but they can bring 80,000 cavalry into the field. This refidue of the old Indians, retired among the hills, ftill retain power which renders them formidable to the Moguls. The great Aurengzebe, to keep peace with the Mahrattas, granted them a fourth of the cuftoms paid by feveral provinces; a revenue which they have found means to enlarge fince the rife of the laft troubles in Indoftan. They ventured to attack the Englifh, in a time of peace, and in 1765 took a man of war pertaining to that nation. The Company, inftead of revenging this infult, thought it more prudent to fettle the affair amicably. The fovereign of the Mahrattas, who is a Bramin, as are alfo his principal officers, refides at *Puna*, a great town in the interior country. He farms out his provinces to the Bramins, who again employ under-farmers of their own Caft. According to accounts, the government of this nation is good, although arbitrary. Juftice is impartially adminiftered; agriculture and manufactures flourifh; and the country is very populous. The Mahrattas, although they thus practife juftice among themfelves, are, however,
guilty

guilty of great barbarities in their frequent incursions into the neighbouring provinces under the government of Mahometans. They pillage and lay waste all before them in the most cruel manner.

CHAP. V.

Of the Trade of Bombay.

THE permission which the Company's servants enjoy of trading on their own account, appears to many persons to be injurious to the interests of the Company. It must be confessed that this private trade is liable to abuses, and may on certain occasions prove hurtful to that of the Company. Yet, judging upon the whole, I am induced to think it advantageous alike to the masters and to the servants. A liberty of trading on their own account inspires factors with spirit and activity, and affords them means of acquiring fuller imformation concerning various branches of commerce. Thus is the trade in general benefited, and business extended.

A recent instance will shew both the good and the bad side of this account. In the first part of my work, I have mentioned the privilege the English enjoy at Jidda, of paying lower duties than

than any other nation. Since the extenfion of their conquefts in India, they have engroffed almoft the whole trade of the Red Sea; fo that, few fhips from other nations now reforting to Jidda, the cuftoms of that city have confiderably declined. The Turks and Arabs, not daring to raife thofe duties, in violation of the tenor of their treaties with the Englifh, contrived to make the purchafer of goods imported by fhips from Bombay pay a fecond duty. This falling ultimately upon the Englifh merchant, the Company complained, but could obtain no redrefs. They then threatened to forfake the harbour of Jidda, and to fend their fhips ftraight to Suez. The Turks and Arabs, confidering the navigation of the Arabian Gulph as the moft dangerous in the world, paid no attention to thofe menaces.

At laft, Mr Holford, an able feaman, determined to accomplifh them. To this end, it was neceffary to obtain the confent of the regency of Cairo, and affurance of good treatment at Suez. Ali Bey, who was then mafter of Egypt, giving himfelf no concern about the interefts of the Pacha of Jidda, or of the Sherriffe of Mecca, offered the Englifh the moft advantageous conditions; hoping to derive great profits from the India trade running in this new channel. Since Mr Holford, in 1773, made a fuccefsful voyage up the Arabic Gulph, and conducted the firft

Englifh

English ship streight to Suez, several vessels have every year sailed from India for this port. In 1776, five of those English ships entered the harbour of Suez. The passage has been found so short and convenient, that the regency of Bombay now send their couriers by the way of Suez to England. In this way, they receive answers to their dispatches within the same length of time which was formerly consumed in the conveyance of their packets to London.

But, this change in the conduct of this trade, is not yet of long standing. By the diminution of the expences of freight which it produced, the English reduced the prices of India goods so considerably, through all the Levant, that the Company no longer found sale for those stuffs which they had been accustomed to send from London to the Levant. They have, therefore, prohibited their factors from trading, on their own account, from India streight to Suez. But, as this trade has been once opened, the Company might send their own ships to Egypt. The only consideration to hinder them, is, that of the instability of the government of Cairo, and the frequent disturbances which render Egypt unsafe for the merchant.

All the English ships for India sail to one of the four principal settlements. Those which sail for Bombay are commonly five months
in

in their paffage. In one inftance, the voyage is known to have been performed in three months and eighteen days. Few of thofe fhips, of which there arrive commonly four in the year, return to Europe immediately after difcharging their cargoes. They, for the moft part, make firft fome voyage to a different fettlement, as far often as China, by which they gain confiderable freights, when the governor favours them fo far as to grant them his permiffion. Each of thefe fhips was formerly to take out 40,000 crowns; but, fince the Company have acquired fuch an extent of territory in India, they have no neceffity to fend ready money from London to their fettlements.

The principal article with which the fhips from India are freighted, is cloth of all forts, which is fold moftly at Bafra, and in Perfia. The others are cochineal, ivory, iron, copper, guns, arms, &c. The crew of thefe fhips carry out likewife, each man a parcel of goods, on his own account. A great part of the cargoes of thefe fhips is publicly fold, foon after they are unladen. The Indian merchants gather in to the fale; and the goods are difpofed of by auction, to the higheft bidder. The remainder are carried to the dependent fettlements.

The fhips return to Europe, laden with pepper from Malabar, faltpetre from Scindi, and

stuffs

stuffs from Surat. The crews carry home parcels of perfumes, gums, and spiceries of different sorts, the produce of India.

CHAP. VI.

Antiquities of the Isle Elephanta.

THIS small isle, situate near Bombay, belongs to the Mahrattas, and is inhabited by an hundred poor Indian families. Its proper name is *Gali Pouri.* The Europeans call it Elephanta, from the statue of an elephant, formed of black stone, which stands in this island, in the open plain, near the shore. This island being of small importance, the Mahrattas take no care of it; and the English are at liberty to visit it without passports, which are requisite, when they go to the isle of *Salset*.

Several travellers mention the isle of Elephanta, and the Indian temple in it; but this only in a transient manner, and without seeming to have known all the importance of those remains of remote antiquity. To me the temple appeared so remarkable, that I visited the island three different times, in order to draw, and describe its curiosities.

It is an hundred and twenty feet long, and the fame in breadth, without including the meafurement of the chapels and the adjacent chambers. Its height within is nearly fifteen feet, although the floor has been greatly raifed by the acceffion of duft, and of the fediment of the water which falls into it in the rainy feafon. The whole of this vaft ftructure, fituate in a hill of confiderable height, is cut out in the folid rock. The pillars fupporting the roof are alfo parts of the rock which have been left ftanding by the architect. They are of an uncommon order; but have an agreeable enough effect.

The walls of this temple are ornamented with figures in *bas-relief*, fo prominent, that they are joined to the rock only by the back. Many of thefe figures are of a coloffal fize; being fome 10, fome 12, and fome even 14 feet high. Neither in defign, nor in execution, indeed, can thefe *bas-reliefs* be compared with the works of the Grecian fculptors. But they are greatly fuperior in elegance to the remains of the ancient Egyptian fculpture. They are alfo finer than the *bas-reliefs* from the ruins of Perfepolis. No doubt, then, but the arts were cultivated by the ancient Indians with better fuccefs than is commonly fuppofed.

Probably thefe figures mark events relative to the mythology and fabulous hiftory of the Indians,

dians, for they feem to be reprefentative of Gods and Heroes. But, to be able to underftand them, we fhould know more than we at prefent do of the manners and religion of this ancient nation. The modern Indians are fo ignorant, that I could obtain from them no information concerning thofe antiquities. One man, who pretended to explain the character of one of the largeft ftatues, affured me that it was *Kaun,* one of their ancient fabulous princes, famous for his cruelties committed upon his fifter's children. This ftatue, which is in other refpects well formed, has eight arms; an emblem of power, which the Indians give to their allegorical figures.

I have given defigns of thefe allegorical figures, (in the larger works), which will make them better underftood than dry defcription can. There are, however, fome particulars about them, which prove the ftability of the manners of the Indians, and afford points for the comparifon of ancient with modern cuftoms. None of thefe figures has a beard; and all of them very fcanty whifkers. At prefent, the young Indians wear all whifkers; and fuch as are advanced in life leave commonly the whole beard to grow. The lips of thefe figures are always thick; and their ears are lengthened out by large pendents; ornaments which they almoft all wear. Several

of

them wear a fmall cord, in the fafhion of a fcarf; a mode now prevalent among the Bramins.

One woman has but a fingle breaft; from which it fhould feem, that the ftory of the Amazons was not unknown to the old Indians. Several figures, as well mafculine as feminine, have one arm leaning on the head of a male, or a female dwarf; from which it fhould feem that thefe monfters of the human fpecies have always been an object of luxury and magnificence among the taftelefs great. Several of thefe figures have hair on the head, which feems not to be of its native growth, but is perfectly like a wig; fo that this covering for the head appears to be of very ancient invention. The female bofom is always perfectly round; from which it feems that the Indian fafhion of wearing thin wooden cafes upon the breafts is alfo very ancient. One woman too appears bearing her child in the fame attitude which is ftill in ufe among the Indians, and which forms thofe children to ftand firmly upon their feet and legs.

The head-drefs of thefe female figures is commonly an high-crowned bonnet. I have, however, obferved alfo a turban. Some are bareheaded, and have their hair at leaft well combed, if it is not rather a periwig they wear. Several are naked. The drefs of others is more

nearly

nearly like that of the moderns. Some of the women wear a cap. In many places the handkerchief, ftill ufed through all India, is obfervable in the hands of the inferior figures.

In feveral parts of thefe *bas-reliefs* appears the famous *Cobra de Capello*, a fort of ferpent, which the human figures treat with great familiarity. Thefe ferpents are ftill very common in the ifle of Elephanta, the inhabitants of which are not afraid of them, but fay that they are friendly to man, and do no harm, unlefs when intentionally provoked. Certain it is, however, that their bite is mortal.

On each fide of this temple is a chapel, nine feet high, confequently lower than the principal building. The walls of thefe chapels are alfo covered with *bas-relief* figures, on a fmaller fcale than thofe upon the walls of the temple. Behind the chapels are three chambers, the walls of which difplay no fculptures; their ufes I could not conjecture.

The fmalleft of the chapels, having no fculptured figure, but that of the God *Gonnis*, is ftill in a ftate of neat prefervation, which muft be owing to the cares of the prefent inhabitants, whom I faw repair thither to perform their devotions. Before the entrance into this chapel, I found a pile of fhapelefs ftones, newly bedaubed with red paint. I fhould fuppofe that the modern Indians no longer adore their ancient Gods, but have adopted new objects of worship, whom they reprefent by ftones painted red, for want of more artificial ftatues. In many places through India, indeed, may be feen fimilar piles of red ftones, which are held in high veneration among a people who have now almoft entirely loft all knowledge of the fine arts.

The reft of the temple being perfectly neglected, is now the haunt of ferpents and beafts of prey. One dares not enter it without firft making feveral difcharges of fire arms, to expel thofe creatures. Even after ufing this precaution, a Dutchman was once in great danger from fwarms of wafps of a peculiar fpecies, which he had roufed from their nefts with his gun. In the hot feafon, horned cattle refort to the lower chambers of the temple, to drink of the water which is depofited there during the rains.

As little is there any hope of obtaining any information from the prefent inhabitants of the ifland, concerning the period when this temple was built. Thofe good folks relate with fimplicity, that a number of ftrangers came one night into the ifland, and reared this edifice before the return of day-light. Men feem fond of the marvellous in India, as elfewhere.

On a hill, at a fmall diftance, there is faid to be another temple. But, to it, there is no open road :

road; and, as the grafs was at that time very tall, my guides would not accompany me thither, for fear of ferpents and wild animals.

Befides, this is not the only old temple remaining in India. I have already mentioned thofe in the ifle of Salfet, three of which ftanding at *Kanari*, *Ponifer*, and *Monpefer*, have been defcribed by M. Anquetil. I have already mentioned, that accefs into this ifland cannot be obtained without a paffport from the Mahratta governor at *Tana*, or perhaps from the fovereign. Such a paffport I durft not afk for the purpofe of gratifying my curiofity as to the temples; as the Mahrattas had lately feized a veffel, and were not, even then, in a good underftanding with the Englifh.

Freyer has defcribed the temple of *Dunganes*, and *Thevenot* that of *Iloura*, both hewn out in the folid rock, like that of Elephanta. Near Fort Victoria is another very large temple, hewn out alfo in folid rock, and divided into twenty-five feparate chambers. One perfectly like this is to be found in the vicinity of the town of *Teridfchanapalli*.

Thefe monuments of the ancient fplendour of the Indians deferve, upon feveral accounts, the attention of our men of learning. We go to fee pyramids nowife worthy of comparifon with thefe pagodas. It would require more labour

and

and ſkill to cut out ſuch ſpacious apartments in rocks, and to ornament them with ſuch large and beautiful pieces of ſculpture, than to raiſe thoſe huge piles of ſoft, calcareous ſtones, which the builder found ready at his hand. The pyramids appear to have been reared by the toil of barbarous ſlavery; the temples of India are the works of a magnificent and enlightened people.

The Indians are, beſides, the moſt ancient of the nations whoſe hiſtory is known, and have beſt retained their ancient uſages and opinions. We know that the inhabitants of other countries in the eaſt, the Greeks, and perhaps too the Egyptians, drew the firſt elements of their knowledge from India. It may farther be preſumed, that the examination of Indian antiquities would throw new light on thoſe opinions and modes of worſhip which were by degrees diffuſed through other parts of the eaſt, and ſpread, at laſt, into Europe. Theſe diſcoveries, again, would throw new light on the antiquities of other nations.

Theſe hopes are the more plauſible, as the Indians have ſtill books which were written in the moſt remote times, and of which the language is at preſent underſtood. The books might explain the monuments; and the monuments again might ſerve as a commentary upon thoſe books, and the hiſtory of the nation.

It

It were to be wiſhed, that ſome enlightened ſcholars would undertake a voyage into India for the purpoſe of inveſtigating its antiquities. But, ſuch an undertaking is more than can be expected from any private perſon, and might be worthy of the patronage of a prince or a nation. The Portugueſe, who were for two centuries maſters of Salſet, muſt have been well acquainted with theſe temples, for they converted that of *Kanari* into a church. But, inſtead of ſeeking to make thoſe monuments known to other nations, they ſought to conceal them, and covered the fineſt of the *bas-reliefs* with plaſter. The Engliſh, although they have been ſettled at Bombay for theſe hundred years now, have ſtill neglected theſe reſearches. It is to be hoped that they will at length think of meriting the gratitude of the public, by bringing thoſe hidden curioſities to light, which lie in the extenſive conqueſts on the continent, now poſſeſſed by that nation.

SECTION XXXI.

VOYAGE TO SURAT.

CHAP. I.

Occafion of this Voyage, and Departure from Bombay.

THE reader will recollect that Mr Cramer and I were both fick when we arrived at Bombay in September 1763. Our intention was to return into Europe through Turkey, and to take our paffage on board a fhip of the Company's which was to fail for Bafra the beginning of the next year ; but, the ftate of our health would not allow us to take that opportunity. Mr Cramer, finking at length under his complaints, died at Bombay, on the 10th of February 1764, in fpite of the cares of a fkilful Englifh phyfician.

Being now the fole furvivor of all our party, I thought it my duty to attend to my own prefervation, and to provide for the fafe conveyance of our papers to Europe, as I feared that thefe would be loft, if I alfo fhould die by the way.

Forefeeing

Foreseeing that I should have to undergo the same fatigues in passing through Turkey, which I had already encountered in Arabia, and which the weak state of my health was unfit to bear, I resolved to set out straight for London, by the first ship which should sail for Europe. In the mean time, to gratify my curiosity with a sight of Surat, I took the opportunity of going on board an English ship bound on a voyage to that port.

We sailed from Bombay on the 24th of March 1764, and were obliged to stop at *Mahim*, a small town in the northern part of the isle, where a member of the Council of Bombay constantly resides. An incident which took place at this time may serve as an instance of the military spirit and skill of the Portuguese. Proud of their ancient conquests, they scorn to make peace with any of the Indian nations, all of whom they regard as rebels. Being thus in terms of continual hostility with their neighbours, they dare not sail these seas without an escort. A small fleet of merchant ships bound from Goa to *Diu*, under the protection of two frigates, was seen, one evening, off Bombay. In the night we heard a brisk firing of guns, and imagined that the Portuguese were engaged with the Mahrattas. But, in the morning, it appeared that their exploits had ended merely in the

destruction

deftruction of a quantity of bamboos, from 30 to 40 feet high, which the fifhermen had fet up in a fand bank for the purpofes of their fifhing. Thofe valiant Portuguefe had taken the bamboos for the mafts of an hoftile fleet. To crown their glory, the admiral found himfelf compelled by the governor of Bombay to pay damages to the fifhermen.

On the 26th of March we arrived in the road of Surat, at the diftance of three German miles from the city. We went on fhore at *Domus*, a village diftinguifhed by the refidence of fome, and by a vaft Indian fig-tree, which is held in high veneration. Of this tree (the *Ficus vafta* of Linnæus,) I have already fpoken in giving the natural hiftory of Arabia. To the defcription above given of it, I may here add, that it grows to a great age; the new fhoots from the branches of the primary ftem continuing to nourifh the top of the tree, even after the parent ftock is entirely decayed.

At *Domus* we took a *Kakkri*, the carriage common in the country, which is neither more nor lefs than a covered cart, drawn by two oxen, which are driven by a peafant feated on the pole. I had here an inftance of the great drynefs of this country, for the movement of our light carriage raifed a cloud of duft about us.

I

I never suffered so much from the dust, even in caravans of some hundreds of camels, horses, and mules.

CHAP. II.

Of the City of Surat, and its Environs.

THIS city stands in a large and fertile plain, on the banks of a considerable river, named *Tappi*. On the land side, it is encompassed with two brick walls, which divide it into the inner and the outer town. The citadel stands within the inner, on the shore of the *Tappi*, and is divided by trenches from the town. One may walk round the outer wall in two hours and a half; the space which it incloses is chiefly occupied by gardens, having but a very few houses.

The larger houses are flat-roofed here, as through the rest of the east, with courts before them. The houses of the common people are high-roofed. Although Surat has been long under the dominion of the Mahometan Moguls, yet here is no handsome mosque with towers, as among the Turks and Arabians. The squares of this city are large, and the streets spacious, but not paved; so that the dust is insufferable. Each street has gates of its own, with which it is shut up in times of turbulence; and these are as frequent here as at Cairo.

At Surat provisions are plenteous and cheap; the air, too, is wholesome, notwithstanding the warmth of the climate. I here observed Farenheit's thermometer at 98° in the month of March, while the wind blew from the north. In the month of May the thermometer stood at 93° degrees at Bombay, which lies two degrees farther to the south.

One thing unfavourable for Surat, is, that ships cannot enter the harbour, because the *Tappi* is full of sand-banks. This river is too low in the dry season; and in the rains swells too suddenly, to such a height as to overflow all the neighbourhood. Were the river confined by dikes, the stream which, during the rains, often rises eight and twenty feet above its ordinary level, would carry away all the sand, and thus clearing the channel, would afford ships access to the very walls. But, the despotic governments of Asia neglect every thing that might contribute to the general good of their subjects.

General toleration and entire liberty are enjoyed in this city by all religious professions; and its inhabitants are accordingly very numerous. The Europeans residing here estimate the population of the city at a million of souls.

But

But this calculation is evidently above the truth, —by two thirds, I have reafon to believe.

One thing fingular in Surat is, that here is no hofpital for human beings, but an extenfive eftablifhment of this nature for fick or maimed animals. When the Europeans turn out an old horfe, or any other domeftic animal, to perifh as ufelefs, the Indians voluntarily affume the care of it, and place it in this houfe, which is full of of infirm, decrepid cows, fheep, rabbits, hens, pigeons, &c. I faw in it a great tortoife, which was blind and helplefs, and, as I was told, 125 years of age. The charitable Indians keep a phyfician of purpofe for thefe animals.

The environs of Surat are not without gardens, which are the property either of Europeans, or of natives of the country. The fineft of thofe belonging to Europeans is the property of the Dutch Eaft India Company. Its afpect is rich and charming.

To get an idea of the character of an Indian garden, I went to fee one which was formed by a late Nabob, at the expence of 500,000 rupees. This garden is of confiderable extent, but has not the leaft appearance of regularity in the defign, and has in it nothing in the fafhion of our gardens, but a few ponds and fountains: the reft is a confufed medley of buildings and fmall orchards. Among the buildings is one of great dimenfions,

dimenſions, having baths and ſaloons, and ornamented with the magnificence of India, which
bears no reſemblance to ours. The other buildings are *harams* for the Nabob's wives, entirely
ſeparate from each other, ſo that each lady can
hold her little court apart. Every haram has
ſome one good apartment; but all the reſt of it
conſiſts of very narrow chambers for the ſlaves.
What ſtruck me particularly in this garden,
was the paſſage from one ſuite of rooms to another, by paths ſo narrow, ſo winding, and ſo
blocked up by doors, as to afford a ſtrong inſtance of the diſtruſt with which the unfortunate great in deſpotic countries regard all about
them; ſo that they are never free from anxiety,
and are obliged to ſtand continually on their
guard againſt ſurpriſe.

I ſhould have wiſhed to draw a plan of Surat.
But I ſoon found that the Europeans in India
would not leave me ſo much at liberty, in this
reſpect, as the Turks and Arabians had done.
The climate of hot countries, and the nature of
the government of ſettlements ſo diſtant from
the mother country, ſeem to alter the national
character of the people of Europe. The Engliſh
governor of Surat would not allow a Frenchman to live in a high apartment from which he
had a view of the citadel. At Mokha, I was
told of an Arabian merchant who had languiſh-
ed

ed some years in the prisons of Batavia, for having had the curiosity to measure the dimensions of a cannon.

CHAP. III.

Of the Inhabitants of Surat, and some Peculiar Customs.

A GREAT commercial city must be peopled by men of different nations. The principal inhabitants of Surat are Mahometans, and mostly strangers, although employed in the service of the government. They are equally zealous in the observance of their law as the Turks and Arabians. Although of the sect of the Sunnites, they tolerate the Shiites, and even permit them to celebrate the festival of *Haſſein*. They make no scruple of drinking wine publicly, or of lending money upon interest.

All people of distinction in Surat, and through the rest of India, speak and write the Persian language. Hence has this language been received at the courts, and the knowledge of it is very useful for the dispatch of business. In trade, corrupt Portuguese is the language used; and this is in India what the Lingua Franca is in the Levant.

The

The Muſſulmans of Surat bring about them a great many *Fakirs* of their own religion, who are the moſt inſolent beggars in the world. Thoſe Fakirs will often ſit down before a houſe, and continue there till the owner pay the ſum they aſk, or make a compoſition with them. As the police interferes not to check theſe inſolent mendicants, people muſt be content with getting quit of them at any price.

At Surat, I had occaſion to witneſs the Muſſulman proceſſion at the feſtival of Bairam. The counſellor from Bombay, who reſides in the citadel of Surat, and repreſents a Nabob, is obliged to announce this ceremony by a diſcharge of cannons, and to aſſiſt at it in perſon. It is a ſtrange ſight, to ſee an Engliſh merchant in the European dreſs, attended by a party of Britiſh ſoldiers, and with the train of an Indian prince, conduct and regulate a religious feſtival of the Mahometans. The Engliſh director made the Indians ſenſible of his importance upon this occaſion, by refuſing to diſcharge his cannons in the night; a favour requeſted of him by the Nabob of the city, in order to give the people timely warning of the approach of the feſtival.

In this proceſſion there was nothing remarkable, except the numbers of *kakkris*, *palanquins*, and horſes, a few cannons, a great deal of martial muſic, and the Nabob's ſoldiers. The governor

vernor rode upon an elephant, on the back of which he fat on a fort of throne, raifed upon four pillars. This elephant was, like moft of the horfes and oxen which drew the *kakkris*, painted red.

Kakkris, the carriages moft common through India, are of a very fimple conftruction, run upon two wheels, and are drawn by oxen: the driver fits on a large pole, confifting of feveral bamboos. It is not in any ornaments about thefe vehicles, but in the cattle which draw them, that the object of pride and expence to the Indian lies; a pair of white oxen for one of thefe carriages will coft 600 rupees. Thefe oxen have the points of their horns ornamented with filver; their pace is quick, but lefs fo than that of horfes.

The citizens of Surat difplay their magnificence likewife in their palanquins. A palanquin is known to be a fort of couch fufpended from a bamboo, and borne by four men. The traveller reclines in this vehicle, and is fhaded from the fun by a curtain. A palanquin, completely ornamented with filver, covered with rich ftuffs, and fufpended upon a handfome bamboo, properly bent, will coft above 200 pounds Sterling. The bamboo only of the governor of Bombay's palanquin, exclufive of the other ornaments, coft 125 pound pounds Sterling. The bearers of the palanquins are Indian fervants, who wear no clothes, except a fmall linen cloth about their loins, with clofe flat bonnets on their heads, as liveries, and are commonly employed in keeping the rooms clean within the houfes. The European ladies are at firft fhocked at the indecency of being carried by naked men, but foon learn to accuftom themfelves to it. The palanquins of the Mahometan ladies are incommodious wooden boxes, entirely clofe, and fixed upon a ftraight pole.

The Hindoos, the aboriginal inhabitants of the country, of whom I fhall foon fpeak more at length, compofe the moft confiderable part of the population of Surat. They are almoft all of the caft of the Banians; and hence their fkill and dexterity in matters of calculation and economy often raife them to places of confiderable truft, in the collection of the taxes and cuftoms for the Mahometans. Thefe Banians, being born to trade, have engroffed the commerce of India to fuch a degree, that all foreign nations are obliged to employ them as brokers; in which employment they give better fatisfaction than the Jews in Turkey. Europeans have never found reafon to repent the intrufting even of their whole fortune to the Banians, who continue to give aftonifhing proofs of their probity

and

and fidelity. Some of them are very rich; but they live all in a ſtyle of moderate ſimplicity, wearing for dreſs only a plain robe of white cotton.

At Surat are numbers of *Perſees* or Perſians, who are ſkilful merchants, induſtrious artiſans, and good ſervants. In the ſame city are alſo Armenians, Georgians, and Jews; but of none of theſe any conſiderable number. The Indian Catholics, commonly called Portugueſe, from their ſpeaking the India dialect of the Portugueſe language, are numerous here. At Surat, the day is reckoned from ſunſet to ſunſet, and is divided, not into 24 hours, but into 60 *garris*. Here are no clocks; the progreſs of the day is meaſured by different means. In a conſpicuous ſituation, a man ſtands to put a cup of copper, pierced with a hole in the bottom, from time to time under water; every time the cup ſinks, a *garri* is counted, and the man announces its lapſe by ſtriking the number which it makes upon a plate of metal that ſounds like a clock. Each *garri* conſiſts of 24 of our minutes. In the houſes of the great, too, where clocks and watches are not wanting, this old faſhion of meaſuring time is ſtill kept up.

CHAP. IV.

Of the Government of Surat, and the Revolutions it has undergone.

Surat, and the great diftrict of which it is the capital, belonged for a long time to the great Mogul, who, to keep fo diftant a province the more effectually in obedience, put it under the government of two Nabobs independent on one another. The one refided in the city, and was properly the governor of the province. The other had the command of the citadel, and enjoyed the title of admiral, with a fmall revenue appropriated to the maintenar ͬ a fmall fleet for the defence of the coaft againft pirates.

After Shah Nadir's expedition into Indoftan, the diftant Nabobs of this vaft empire aimed all at independence, and left the Mogul nothing but a fhadow of authority, afking him only for form's fake to confirm them in their places. *Teg Beg Khan*, Nabob of Surat, a rich and powerful man, followed this example, and procured his brother to be declared Nabob of the citadel. The two brothers then looked upon the whole province as their patrimony, and acquired immenfe wealth.

Teg

Teg Beg Khan dying in 1746, without children, left his fortune to his relations, by which several of them were raifed to a condition which enabled them to afpire to the government of the city. His brother died on the following year; and his widow, a woman extremely rich and ambitious, ftrove to make her fon-in-law Nabob at once of the town and of the citadel.

The conteft of the different competitors for the fupreme authority produced a civil war in the town of Surat, like that which arifes from time to time among the Begs of Cairo, and of which we in Europe can form no idea. Each of the rivals raifed as many troops as he poffibly could; with thefe he cantoned and intrenched himfelf in his houfes and gardens, and from time to time endeavoured to furprize or drive away his opponents. During thefe hoftile operations, which were not attended with great flaughter, the inhabitants were content with fhutting the gates neareft to the fcene of action, and continued to go about their ordinary affairs, without fear of being pillaged. Nay, they were fure of receiving compenfation whenever any cafual injury was done to any perfon through means of the difturbances. Hence trade fuffered no interruption.

Some of the rival candidates imprudently called in the Mahrattas; and they, without doing

any

any thing for any party, made the victors pay for their affiftance, although they had apparently favoured the vanquifhed. Since that time, the Mahrattas have enjoyed a third part of the amount of the cuftoms of Surat; and one of their officers conftantly attends to receive this tribute.

The Englifh and Dutch had always kept their factories in a ftate of defence, and on the occafion of the difturbances, they increafed their military preparations. The nobles of the country then had recourfe to thofe powerful traders. Each of the two European nations took part with one of the competitors, furnifhed him with ammunition, intrenched themfelves in their factories, and fought againft each other, although not openly at war. The Nabob, protected by the Englifh, was at laft expelled from the city. But, in 1758, he returned; and his mother-in-law, the rich widow above-mentioned, made fo good an ufe of her treafures, that the Nabob for whom he had been expelled was obliged to yield to him the government of the city.

When the Englifh faw the city in the hands of their creature, they began to think ferioufly of gaining poffeffion of the citadel. The council of Bombay, in 1759, fent Mr Spencer, one of their number, a man of abilities, and beloved by the Indians, to Surat, with a confiderable force.

force. The Nabob opened the gates of the city to the Englifh, and allowed them to lay fiege to the citadel undifturbed. It was taken in a few days. To avoid giving offence to the Indians, the Englifh declared, that they made the conqueft in the name of the great Mogul, and waved his flag from the walls of the citadel.

This expedition thus accomplifhed, Mr Spencer fent a long reprefentation to the Court of Delhi, in which he ftated the reafons which had induced the merchants of Surat to put themfelves under the protection of the Englifh, and to expel the ufurper Nabob from the citadel. He afferted that thofe petty tyrants had fuffered the fleet neceffary for the protection of trade to fall into a ftate of decay, and that none but the Englifh could reftore it. He offered, at the fame time, that if the Mogul would grant to the Company the poft of Admiral, with the revenues annexed to it, they would maintain a fleet which fhould give full fecurity to trade. Thefe facts were attefted, and the propofals feconded by the principal inhabitants of Surat, who figned the memorial. The great Mogul, who in his prefent weaknefs durft not fend a governor to the province, but confidered it as loft, readily granted the Company's requeft; and a member of the council of Bombay now difcharges the office of Nabob and Admiral at Surat. Upon this

this title, the Company enjoy a third of the revenue from the cuftoms of this city, with other funds of income ftill more confiderable; which enables them to keep on foot a body of troops, with fome fmall fhips of war.

The Englifh are, at prefent, the actual fovereigns of Surat. They keep the Nabob of the city in a ftate of abfolute dependence; allowing him only an income on which he may live fuitably to his dignity. The Indians are in part content with their new mafters. The merchants are no longer in danger of the avaritious extortions of the Nabobs; yet they complain of the felfifh fpirit of thofe mafters. The Indians dare not fail without a paffport from the admiral. When the Englifh wifh to fend goods to any port, the Indians are denied paffports to that port till the feafon of the monfoon is over; whereas the Englifh are favoured, fo that they have all the time neceffary to pre-occupy the market. Of this I have feen inftances; which, if frequently repeated, muft undoubtedly ruin the trade of the natives.

CHAP.

CHAP. V.

Trade of Surat.

The great trade carried on at Surat renders this city the store-house of the most precious productions of Indostan. Hither is brought from the interior parts of the empire an immense quantity of goods, which the merchants carry in their ships to the Arabic Gulph, the Persian Gulph, the coast of Malabar, the coast of Coromandel, and even to China. The provinces near this city are full of manufactures of all sorts.

Ship-building is a branch of the business carried on here. In this art, indeed, the Indians are servile imitators of the Europeans, but they have in great plenty, and at a low price, that excellent wood called *Tœk*, which is not liable to be attacked by worms, and is so lasting, that at Surat there are to be seen ships 90 years old which are still in a condition to sail the sea.

Of foreign nations, the Dutch have next after the English, the most considerable establishment at Surat. They have here a director, several merchants, a number of writers and servants, and a few soldiers. Their trade has, however,

however, declined, till it has become trifling. The affairs of this nation in India feem to be rather in diforder, fince the Englifh obtained poffeffion of the citadel. The Nabob of the city has obliged the Dutch to pay him 90,000 rupees, and fend away the cannons of their factory.

The affairs of the French are yet in a worfe ftate. Since the lofs of Pondicherry, their director has been fo neglected, that he can hardly find credit for the means of a fcanty fubfiftence. This nation are here in no eftimation, but what is paid to their capuchin friars, who are generally beloved and refpected at Surat. Thefe good regular clergy have done effential fervice to the public, by keeping a regifter of all events that have happened in Indoftan, from 1676 to the prefent time.

Such nearly is alfo the condition of the Portuguefe in India. In my time, they had a Jefuit of Hamburgh for their director. I have been told, however, that, fince I left Surat, they have raifed their trade, by fending thither a director of their own nation who was born at Goa.

There fometimes arrive at Surat fhips belonging to nations who have no permanent eftablifhments in that city. A Danifh veffel put in here while the citadel was befieged, and was favoured with the protection of the Englifh, to whom the captain did good fervice upon the accafion.

casion. In consequence of the favour which he thus obtained, he accomplished his business in a manner very much to his advantage. A Swede, who came hither some years after, was less fortunate, although the Nabob had, for the payment of a moderate duty, allowed him freedom of trade. Selling his iron and copper at a lower rate than the English, he soon disposed of his whole cargo advantageously as he thought. But, when he was preparing to depart, the Nabob demanded from him an extraordinary duty of 100,000 rupees, and put him under arrest, till it was paid. The Swede not daring to apply to the English, with whom he suspected his mischance to originate, directed his ship to sail for China, and remained under arrest. At last he compounded with the Nabob, who for 20,000 rupees, set him at liberty. Such treatment must deter other nations from trying their fortune at Surat.

In all appearance, the English must shortly engross the whole trade of this city. Being at once sovereigns and rich merchants, they have every means in their power by which foreign nations can be excluded, or the Indians restrained from this source of opulence.

CHAP. VI.

Manners of the Hindoos.

THE Hindoos are the primary inhabitants of the vaſt empire of Indoſtan. Having lived a- mong theſe people at Bombay and Surat, I ſhall here bring together ſome obſervations which I made upon the Hindoos in thoſe two cities, and alſo upon the *Perſees*, a ſtranger colony ſettled in this part of India.

This people, perhaps the earlieſt civilized na- tion in the world, are mild, laborious, and na- turally virtuous in their diſpoſitions. All who have opportunities of obſerving the lives of the Hindoos, admire their patience, probity, and be- nevolence; but they are at the ſame time the moſt unſocial people in the world. By their manners and religious principles, the Hindoos detach themſelves not only from other nations, whom they conſider as impure races; but even the different caſts or tribes of themſelves have little mutual intercourſe. No Hindoo will eat with a ſtranger; nor any Hindoo of a ſuperior caſt with another of a caſt that is inferior. A poor ſervant, if a *Bramin*, would think himſelf dif-
honoured

honoured by fitting down at table with a *Rajaput* or *Banian*, although his mafter.

It is generally known, that the Indians are diftributed into a number of tribes or cafts. As far as I could learn, there are four principal cafts; the *Bramins*, or priefts; the *Rajaputs*, or men of the fword; the *Banians*, or merchants; and that of the artifans and labourers. Thefe four general cafts are fubdivided into more than 80 others, each of which has its own ceremonies, and patron deities, as I have been affured by feveral perfons.

Thofe permanent divifions have led fome travellers into the miftake that the fon was always obliged to embrace his father's profeffion. The fon may not quit his native caft, but may choofe among the employments which are practifed by that caft. There are Bramins who hold fovereign authority; as, for inftance, the prince of the Mahrattas. Thefe fame Bramins become magiftrates under the government of Rajaput princes, and farmers of the revenue under the Mahometans. I have been acquainted with Bramins who were merchants, and with Rajaputs and Banians who were artifans.

This liberty is the more neceffary, as it is impoffible for a Hindoo to be received from an inferior into a fuperior caft. I was told of a fingular inftance of fuch a promotion; but even it

I will not warrant as true. A Rajaput fovereign defiring to be admitted into the caft of the Bramins, the priefts, after a long refufal, at length granted his requeft, on the condition of his fetting up in the temple the ftatue of a cow, of fuch a fize, that a man might enter it behind, and go out by its mouth. The fovereign, after paffing feveral times through this golden cow, was fuppofed to be regenerated, and received into the caft of the Bramins.

This cuftom hinders ftrangers from being naturalized among the Hindoos, or embracing their religion; and there is no people lefs inclined to make profelytes. But, it is their rigorous obfervation of their ancient laws of feparation which has reduced thefe people to their prefent humiliated ftate. If, at the time of the conqueft, the Hindoos had fuffered the Tartars to incorporate with the vanquifhed nation; the conquerors muft have adopted the manners and the religion of their new fubjects. Their conduct in China gives probability to this idea. But the Hindoos expreffing fo great an averfion for their new mafters, made them prefer Mahometifm, and forced them to bring in from time to time foreign Mahometans, to govern the conquered people. Since that period, the Hindoos have been an abject herd of flaves, fubject to the vexatious oppreffion of a defpot who re-

turns

turns the contempt which they have expressed for him.

The power of the Mahometans indeed becomes daily less: and there are at present some Hindoo princes who may restore their nation to its ancient splendour. The Mahrattas have successfully begun a project which has this aspect. It is the exorbitant power of the English that at present retards the progressive improvement of the Hindoos. But, when this colossal statue, whose feet are of clay, and which has been raised by conquering merchants, shall be broken in pieces, an event which may fall out sooner than is supposed, then shall Indostan become again a flourishing country.

In almost all the circumstances of their mode of life, the Hindoos distinguish themselves from the rest of mankind. Their usual diet consists of rice, milk, and fruits. The law, however, which forbids them to eat animal food, seems to have been rather suggested by the climate, than by religious consideration. The Rajaputs eat mutton, as well as the flesh of some other animals; but all the casts alike respect the cow, and abstain from eating beef. None of the casts are so much straitened in respect to food as the Bramins; they deny themselves the use of most leguminous vegetables which are eaten by the other Hindoos; nor will they eat of any dish that

that has not been dreffed by a man of their own caft, or drink water which a Bramin has not drawn. They obferve frequent fafts, infomuch that I was told by a Bramin, that it was almoft impoffible for any perfon to confine himfelf to a ftrict obedience to the precepts of their religion in refpect to regimen.

Thefe priefts alfo impofe upon the people a multiplicity of minute obfervances in their eating, which are all founded on the chimerical notion of the poffibility of contracting pollution by communication in this way. The Hindoos in common are averfe to ufe the fame difh with a ftranger, or with a man of a different caft. They will rather ufe broad leaves for plates, and drink out of the hollow of the hand.

All the parts of the Hindoo drefs differ in form from thofe ufed among the Turks and Arabians. Merchants, however, wear a turban, the cap, and a long robe of white cotton cloth. Their flippers are fitted with metal clafps. The lower people go naked, wearing only a piece of linen round the loins, and a turban on the head. Under rain the peafants put on a hood, which is formed of the leaves of the palm-tree. This cuftom of India has been already mentioned by Herodotus.

The drefs of the ordinary women confifts of a large linen cloth, ftriped red, which they

wrap

wrap about the loins, and another ſtill larger, which they fold round the body and bring over the head. They wear all two wooden caſes upon their breaſts; which hinders the neck from being ever drawn down among the Hindoo as among the Mahometan women. Theſe good Hindoo females are very induſtrious. At Bombay, I ſaw women earn a livelihood by the hardeſt labour, who yet wore rings in their noſe, and in their ears, on their fingers, on their arms, and on their feet. But theſe were ornaments of luxury which deſcend from generation to generation.

The Hindoos ſtill retain the practice of burning their dead. But the European and Mahometan governments prohibit, and the Mahrattas ſeldom allow the living wife to burn herſelf on the funeral pile of her deceaſed huſband. A Bramin told me, that his family had been highly diſtinguiſhed, by his grandmother having, in honour of her virtue, obtained permiſſion to burn herſelf with her huſband.

CHAP.

CHAP. VII.

Of the Religion of the Hindoos.

AN European wifhing to acquire a knowledge of the religion of thefe people, cannot gain much information from the Bramins, who never ftudy any of our languages. I was acquainted with fome Banians who fpoke Englifh, and from them I received fome knowledge on this head.

They all unanimoufly affured me, that the moft fenfible and enlightened Hindoos acknowledged and worfhipped only one Supreme Being. But the Bramins have found out inferior deities, accommodated to the weak conceptions of the people, who could not comprehend abftract ideas, if they were not reprefented by images. They agreed too, that the Bramins had, for their own purpofes, clogged, by degrees, the original fimplicity of their religion, with abfurd fables, and ridiculous pieces of fuperftition. I mentioned their paffionate veneration for the cow, and their various reprefentations of her. As to this, they replied, that in thofe images they revered only the divine goodnefs, which had given

given man an animal fo gentle, and of fuch indifpenfible utility.

I could learn nothing certain concerning their inferior deities, whom they feem to revere rather as faints and patrons. A Banian compared their three principal deities, *Brama*, *Viftnou*, and and *Medeo*, to the Chriftian Trinity.

The Hindoos believe all in the doctrines of the metempfycofis, and of the purification of fouls by their paffage through feveral different bodies. This doctrine is not however the only caufe of their abftinence from every thing that has life in it. In hot countries, the flefh of animals in general, and of the ox in particular, is thought very unwholefome food. The Rajaputs eat flefh, and the Mahrattas furnifh the Europeans whom they take prifoners in war, with animal food, without fcruple. It might be fuppofed that the fingular charity of the Indians for animals takes its origin from this opinion.

The precept of purification with water is rigidly obferved through all India. At Surat, I faw every morning crowds of women and young girls going out to bathe in the Tappi. They gave their clothes to fome Bramins who fat on the banks, and, after wafhing, changed their wet clothes for thofe dry dreffes, with fuch dexterity, that not the fmalleft part of the body could be feen. The Bramins then made a red mark on the brow of each, and, after a fhort prayer, they returned all to town.

This daily fanctification feems to be the chief employment of the Bramins. They are alfo called in, on the occafion of the birth of a child; they tie round his arm a fmall cord, which he wears through life as a mark of his extraction. They affift alfo at nuptials; but only by fixing the hour which is favourable for the contract, not by pronouncing any nuptial benediction.

The Hindoo feftivals are fufficiently numerous, and are partly civil, partly religious. They celebrate the return of the new year with illuminations, and rejoicings of all forts. The feftival of the cocoa-nut feems to have originated with the moft remote antiquity. At another feftival, in commemoration of a certain hero, they bedaub one another with red paint, to reprefent the hero returning from battle, covered over with blood.

They have likewife two orders of Fakirs or mendicant pilgrims, the *Bargais* and the *Guffeins*, who travel about armed, and in troops of fome thoufands. Thefe two orders are fworn enemies; and whenever they meet, bloody combats enfue. During my ftay at Surat, a little army of thefe Fakirs encamped near the city. The government did not like their vifit; and would

would permit them to enter only in fmall numbers.

The ftories of the ridiculous penitence of the Fakirs are well known. Their fanaticifm has not yet become cold; and there died lately at Surat one of thefe madmen, who had lived fhut up in a cage for twenty years, with his arms conftantly raifed above his head.

CHAP. VIII.

Of the Perfees.

At Bombay, at Surat, and in the vicinity of thefe cities, is a colony of ancient Perfians, who took refuge in India, when their country was conquered by the Mahometan Arabs, eleven centuries fince. They are called Perfees. Being beloved by the Hindoos, they multiply exceedingly; whereas their countrymen in the province of Keman are vifibly diminifhing under the yoke of the Moflem Perfians.

They are a gentle, quiet, and induftrious race. They live in great harmony among themfelves, make common contributions for the aid of their poor, and fuffer none of their number to afk alms from people of a different religion. They are equally ready to employ their money
and

and credit to fcreen a brother of their fraternity from the abufes of juftice. When a Perfee behaves ill, he is expelled from their communion. They apply to trade, and exercife all forts of profeffions.

The Perfees have as little knowledge of circumcifion as the Hindoos. Among them, a man marries only cne wife, nor ever takes a fecond, unlefs when the firft happens to be barren. They give their children in marriage at fix years of age; but the young couple continue to feparate, in the houfes of their parents, till they attain the age of puberty. Their drefs is the fame as that of the Hindoos, except that they wear under each ear a tuft of hair, like the modern Perfians. They are much addicted to aftrology, although very little fkilled in aftronomy.

They retain the fingular cuftom of expofing their dead to be eaten by birds of prey, inftead of interring or burning them. I faw on a hill at Bombay a round tower, covered with planks of wood, on which the Perfees lay out their dead bodies. When the flefh is devoured, they remove the bones into two chambers at the bottom of the tower.

The Perfees, followers of the religion of *Zerduft* or *Zoroafter*, adore one God only, Eternal and Almighty. They pay, however, a certain worfhip to the fun, the moon, the ftars, and to

fire,

fire, as vifible images of the invifible divinity. Their veneration for the element of fire induces them to keep a facred fire conftantly burning, which they feed with odoriferous wood, both in the temples, and in the houfes of private perfons, who are in eafy circumftances. In one of their temples at Bombay, I faw a fire which had burnt unextinguifhed for two centuries. They never *blow* out a light; left their breath fhould foil the purity of the fire.

The religion of the Perfees enjoins purifications as ftrictly as that of the Hindoos. The difciples of Zerduft are not, however, obliged to abftain from animal food. They have accuftomed themfelves to refrain from the flefh of the ox, becaufe their anceftors promifed the Indian prince who received them into his dominions never to kill horned cattle. This promife they continue to obferve under the dominion of Chriftians and Mahometans. The horfe is by them confidered as the moft impure of all animals, and regarded with extreme averfion.

Their feftivals, denominated *Ghumbars*, which return frequently, and laft upon each occafion five days, are all commemorations of fome part of the work of Creation. They celebrate them not with fplendour, or with any particular ceremonies; but only drefs better during thofe five days,

days, perform fome acts of devotion in their houfes, and vifit their friends.

Not having had opportunity to make any continued train of obfervations on the manners and religion of the Perfees, I muft refer the reader to the memoirs fubjoined by *Mr Anquetil du Perron* to his tranflation of the *Zendavefta*, or facred book of *Zoroafter*. It is well known that this learned Frenchman went to India of purpofe to ftudy the language and religion of the Perfees.

The diverfity of opinions and manners among the inhabitants of India is inconvenient for Europeans, who cannot have countrymen of their own for fervants; which is the cafe with almoft all foreign merchants. An European, who has none but natives of the country in his fervice, if he fhould wifh to eat a hare and bacon, would find it no eafy matter to procure thefe difhes. The Hindoo would not bring them to him, for he dares not touch a dead body; nor the Perfee, becaufe the hare is an unclean animal; nor yet the Muffulman, for he dares not touch fuch difhes.

NOTES

NOTES TO VOL. II.

NOTE A. p. 5.

I KNOW not if we fhould find a complete detail of the hiftory of Arabia of fuch importance as may at firft be imagined. Their local circumftances feem to have given a degree of permanency to the character of the inhabitants of this country; in confequence of which, the hiftory of one or two centuries may be fairly efteemed equal to the hiftory of the whole period of their national exiftence. Yet, as it feems probable that many of the circumjacent countries have received their firft fupplies of population from Arabia; it were, on this account, indeed, a defireable object to trace the

progrefs

progress of their colonies, and the circumstances which excited among them the spirit of colonization. The Sabæans were probably a powerful nation in Arabia; and history relates, that Melek-Yafrik, one of their Monarchs, conducted the colony which first occupied the north-western division of Africa.

NOTE B. p. 7.

SOME valuable information concerning the Arabians in the eastern parts of Africa may be seen in Bruce's travels; a book which I am happy to agree with the most respectable Reviewers, in considering as one of the most valuable presents that any traveller has for a long while made to the British Public.

NOTE C. p. 8.

To Ludolff, Lobo, and especially to Bruce, I must refer the reader for the history of Abyssinia.

NOTE D. p. 10.

BAILLI, late Mayor of Paris, in his History of Astronomy.

NOTE E. p. 11.

PERHAPS the reader of Colonel Vallancey's writings may be perfuaded that thefe infcriptions found at Perfepolis, and in the interior parts of Arabia, are in the Ogham character of the old Irifh.

NOTE F. p. 12.

THESE remarks are ingenious. But, from the tenor of Sacred Hiftory, it fhould feem that the origin of the Jews is not lefs ancient than that of the Arabians. They are both from the fame ftock, and are collateral branches.

NOTE G. p. 13.

EVERY reader will here think of the Hiftorical Difquifition concerning India, with which the firft Hiftorian of the prefent age has lately favoured the world, in addition to his other works. The different channels through which the trade between Europe and Afia was fuccefsfively carried on, are there ably traced; and the effects pointed out which its fluctuations produced upon the intermediate countries.

NOTE H. p. 13.

There is very little probability, indeed, that any confiderable number of the Arabians were ever converted to Chriftianity. They have always been chiefly idolaters, or Mahometans.

NOTE I. p. 14.

Perhaps the Caliphs might have been more fuccefsful in fubjugating their fellow-countrymen, if Syria, India, Egypt, and Spain had not prefented more inviting fcenes of conqueft and of empire.

NOTE J. p. 20.

The Mahometan religion was introduced among the Moors nearly about the middle of the feventh century. The Moors, defcendents of thofe Sabæans, who had anciently fettled in that part of Africa, were fubdued and incorporated with the victorious Moflems. Ever fince that period, paftoral tribes of wandering Arabs have occupied Mount Atlas, and a confiderable extent of the north-weft divifion of *Africa*.

NOTE

NOTE K. p. 39.

For an account of the rites and ceremonies of the pilgrimage to Mecca, I muſt refer the reader to *Recueil des Rits Ceremonies du Pelerinage de la Mecque; par M. Galland.—A Amſterdam,* 1754.—A moſt curious little work, which Galland has tranſlated from the Arabic, and which I once intended to tranſlate from the French, and inſert here.

NOTE L. p. 89.

See the Elder Pliny's account of Arabia in Book VI. of his Natural Hiſtory.

NOTE M. p. 92.

It is folly to ſuppoſe that any literary art can make progreſs among the Mahometans, while deſpotiſm, indolence, and ſuperſtition, the great enemies of literary improvement, continue to maintain their ground among them.

NOTE M. p. 107.

One cannot read ſuch an account as this, without reflecting with pleaſure, that the ſuperior

rior activity and science of the Europeans have enabled them to engross the commerce of the universe.

NOTE N. p. 116.

MASKAT enjoys advantages of situation, which, under an enlightened government, might render its native inhabitants among the most enterprising and the richest merchants in the world.

NOTE O. p. 140.

HANWAY, and the travellers in Persia, may be consulted for the history of Nadir-Shah.

NOTE P. p. 203.

IT should seem, from what is here related, that the Arabians, notwithstanding the simplicity of their modes of life, are little less fantastic in their point of honour than our duellists of Europe.

NOTE Q. p. 205.

THE comparison is indeed fair and natural; and, after all the contests which have been agitated concerning the primary modes of government,

ment, the patriarchal has undoubtedly been the next after the paternal. By the *paternal* I mean the government of a Father over his Children; by the *patriarchal*, that of a Head over a Family of relations.

NOTE R. p. 230.

The use of this *Busa* or *Bouza*, is one proof, among innumerable others, that mankind have been, in all ages, and in all states of society, passionately fond of fermented liquors. To what nastiness has not this taste occasionally prompted them?—Witness their use of *Kava* and *Koumiss*.

FINIS.

www.ingramcontent.com/pod-product-compliance
Lightning Source LLC
Chambersburg PA
CBHW031956300426
44117CB00008B/781